Date Due

MAY 1 0 1996		
DEC 0 5 1996		
MAY 8 07		
MAY 1 0 2001		
AUG 0 8 2005		
10-18-06 DEC 0 3 2010		

BRODART, CO.   Cat. No. 23-233-003   Printed in U.S.A.

Children
and
Disasters

Issues in Clinical Child Psychology

Series Editors: **Michael C. Roberts,** *University of Kansas, Lawrence, Kansas*
Lizette Peterson, *University of Missouri-Columbia, Missouri*

CHILDREN AND DISASTERS
Edited by Conway F. Saylor

A Continuation Plan is available for this series. A continuation order will bring delivery of each new volume immediately upon publication. Volumes are billed only upon actual shipment. For further information please contact the publisher.

Children
and
Disasters

Edited by
CONWAY F. SAYLOR
The Citadel
Charleston, South Carolina

PLENUM PRESS • NEW YORK AND LONDON

Library of Congress Cataloging-in-Publication Data

Children and disasters / edited by Conway F. Saylor.
      p.   cm. -- (Issues in clinical child psychology)
   Includes bibliographical references and index.
   ISBN 0-306-44431-3
   1. Child disaster victims--Mental health. 2. Post-traumatic
stress disorder in children. 3. Crisis intervention (Psychiatry)
4. Disasters--Psychological aspects.   I. Saylor, Conway F.
II. Series.
   [DNLM: 1. Disasters. 2. Crisis Intervention--in infancy &
childhood. 3. Stress, Psychological--in infancy & childhood.
4. Stress, Psychological--therapy. 5. Stress Disorders--Post
-Traumatic--prevention & control.   WS 350.2 C5364 1993]
RJ507.D57C48 1993
155.9'35'083--dc20
DNLM/DLC
for Library of Congress   93-13208
                                                         CIP

ISBN 0-306-44431-3

© 1993 Plenum Press, New York
A Division of Plenum Publishing Corporation
233 Spring Street, New York, N.Y. 10013

Printed in the United States of America

To Bart, Sara, Paul, and Maggie Jo
and
to the family, friends, and former strangers
whose support enabled us to recover after our own disaster

Contributors

Ronald W. Belter, Ph.D., Department of Psychiatry and Behavioral Sciences, Medical University of South Carolina, Charleston, South Carolina

Bruce E. Compas, Ph.D., Department of Psychology, University of Vermont, Burlington, Vermont

Timothy K. Daugherty, Ph.D., Department of Psychology, The Citadel, Charleston, South Carolina

Joanne E. Epping, B.A., B.S., Department of Psychology, University of Vermont, Burlington, Vermont

A. J Finch, Jr., Ph.D., A.B.P.P., Department of Psychology, The Citadel, Charleston, South Carolina

Howard M. Gillis, Ph.D., Division of Behavioral and Developmental Pediatrics, University of California, San Francisco Medical Center, San Francisco, California

Linda J. Gudas, Ph.D., Department of Psychiatry, The Children's Hospital, Harvard Medical School, Boston, Massachusetts

Cathy Dodds Joyner, M.Ed., Charleston–Dorchester Community Mental Health Center—Division of Children, Adolescents and Families, Charleston, South Carolina

Jane M. Keppel-Benson, Ph.D., Department of Psychology, Virginia Polytechnic Institute and State University, Blacksburg, Virginia

Avigdor Klingman, Ph.D., Chair, Department of Counseling, School of Education, University of Haifa, Haifa, Israel

Janice M. Kowalski, Ph.D., Department of Psychiatry, Evanston Hospital and Northwestern University and Medical School, Evanston, Illinois

Thomas H. Ollendick, Ph.D., Department of Psychology, Virginia Polytechnic Institute and State University, Blacksburg, Virginia

Ronald H. Rozensky, Ph.D., Department of Psychiatry, Evanston Hospital and Northwestern University and Medical School, Evanston, Illinois

Conway F. Saylor, Ph.D., Department of Psychology, The Citadel, Charleston, South Carolina

Eitan D. Schwarz, M.D., Department of Psychiatry, Evanston Hospital and Northwestern University and Medical School, Evanston, Illinois

Mitsuko P. Shannon, M.D., Department of Psychiatry and Behavioral Sciences, Medical University of South Carolina, Charleston, South Carolina

Ira H. Sloan, M.D., Department of Psychiatry, Evanston Hospital and Northwestern University and Medical School, Evanston, Illinois

Cynthia Cupit Swenson, Ph.D., Charleston–Dorchester Community Mental Health Center—Division of Children, Adolescents and Families, Charleston, South Carolina

William Yule, Ph.D., University of London Institute of Psychiatry, London, United Kingdom

Foreword

This book is one most people would rather not think about—until they need it! Natural disaster, technological catastrophe, and calamity caused by aberrant human behavior are things most of us would rather not have to think about. By definition they are overwhelming, generally beyond preventive control, and highly disruptive. Often they leave death, massive destruction, mind-numbing exhaustion, and utter helplessness in their wake. Dr. Saylor's moving preface sums up the reality well: One cannot truly grasp the psychological impact of a disaster unless one lives through it.

A hurricane, earthquake, flood, industrial plant explosion, nuclear accident, airplane crash, or armed hostage taking is a story for the nightly news until it happens in your neighborhood or affects someone you love. Many disasters leave adults feeling helpless, depressed, looking for answers that do not exist, or experiencing symptoms of posttraumatic stress. Given their cognitive, emotional, and social immaturity, children would seem to be at even greater risk. Magical thinking, the loss of family and caregivers, immature coping systems, and other characteristics of children all seem destined to yield ever greater distress for child survivors of disasters. Until now, there were only isolated scholarly papers peppered about the literature for emergency planners and mental health professionals to draw on in assisting such children.

As its centennial gift to the nation, in 1993 the American Psychological Association developed a disaster intervention program in coordination with the American Red Cross. How fitting it is that this book should follow closely on the heels of that event. The effort to integrate theory, research, and practice in a single volume is highly successful. Saylor and her colleagues have provided a valuable resource for disaster planners, crisis interveners, clinicians, and social science investigators. This book truly

complements psychology's efforts to facilitate the protection and rehabilitation of children who will be victims in future disasters.

Nietzsche told us, "That which does not kill us, makes us stronger."
Some would say that is making the best of a bad situation. Unsatisfied with
mere survival, Saylor and her colleagues show us the way to prepare for
and foster the recovery of our children in ways Nietzsche could not have
imagined.

GERALD P. KOOCHER, Ph.D.

Harvard Medical School

Series Preface

The untoward events of *any* year call for this book on disasters and children. Events of 1992 in particular emphasized the need we saw for a compendium of research-based and intervention-oriented presentations on the psychological aspects of children who have experienced disasters, whether natural or human-caused. Thus, we find it appropriate that the first volume in this book series, *Issues in Clinical Child Psychology*, clearly and directly fulfills the specific needs of mental health professionals working with children in practice and research under extraordinary circumstances.

Indeed, this book series was established to provide necessary professional resources on traditional as well as newly emerging issues within the psychological, behavioral, and developmental perspectives on childhood problems. The books in the series will present a variety of viewpoints, representing the divergent approaches to children's healthy development. The series will feature authored and edited books focused on the conceptualization and assessment of, intervention in, and prevention of problems within clinical child and pediatric psychology. A wide range of topics will be included, from developmental psychopathology and child psychiatry to explorations of the communities, schools, and family systems within which children grow, from behavioral pediatrics and child health to considerations of psychology's role in the evolving public policy that affects children. The series' central theme will be challenges to and contributors of behavioral science to the developing child.

We are pleased to present this first volume in the series, *Children and Disasters*, edited by Conway F. Saylor, with chapters by carefully selected contributors, each presenting an important aspect of the prevention and treatment of children's mental health problems following crises. Dr. Saylor has prepared a highly useful and valuable composite of what is currently known in this field. Its worth will particularly be demonstrated in future years, within the inevitable panoply of calamities affecting children and families in the world.

MICHAEL C. ROBERTS
LIZETTE PETERSON

Preface

This is the book I needed in September of 1989. As my family, my neighbors, my friends and colleagues, and I faced the staggering task of rebuilding after hurricane Hugo, I wished I knew what psychology had to offer by way of wisdom and data. As a clinical child psychologist, I knew of relevant research in the areas of posttraumatic stress disorder (PTSD), stress and coping, and trauma in children. However, the disaster situation seemed distinct from other areas in its widespread impact on children and their families. It seemed important that someone generate a comprehensive volume that would combine relevant theory and basic research, critical reviews of the studies and procedures available to date, and practical observations for the professional thrust into the disaster environment either by choice or by happenstance.

Like many of my fellow authors, I underestimated the extent to which my personal experiences with a disaster and its aftermath would motivate and shape the character of my work. It is striking to me that this is one of the hallmarks of the disaster area: Those who touch it professionally are inevitably moved by it personally, and many who have been personally touched by it go on to make contributions to developments in the field. This phenomenon makes sense in the context of the definition we have chosen here for disaster: a traumatic event out of the realm of ordinary experience that is relatively sudden in onset and adversely affects a large group of individuals, in this case, children. Fortunately, it is out of the realm of "ordinary experience" for most of us to enter a scene in which children have been gunned down on their school playground, have witnessed the destruction of their homes and communities by natural disasters, have hidden in fear of death from military assaults, and/or have discovered the adults on the scene to be as powerless as themselves in the face of sudden and terrible danger. We are necessarily jarred loose from our cool objectivity, at least temporarily, as we find ourselves drawn to understand and assist children who are victims of disaster.

Although the disaster environment does have the special qualities of being rare and personally compelling, there is a solid foundation of basic and applied research to orient and guide the professional entering this area of clinical intervention and/or research. It is both possible and necessary for those becoming involved with children and the systems that surround them (families, schools, and communities) to be familiar with the disaster literature, including theory as well as the observations and data already accumulated. This work is too important and complex to be approached without the proper orientation.

Perhaps you have picked up this book because you are suddenly in the midst of a disaster involving children: A tornado struck your town, a train derailed in your community, or a school selected for senseless violence was close to your home. Suddenly, you are being called on to become an "instant expert." I designed this volume with you in mind. I encourage you to immerse yourself in Chapters 1–4, which orient you to the crucial basic knowledge of stress, coping, PTSD, and grief in developmental and systems contexts. Take the time to discover what has already been observed about children in similar crises by examining the extensive reviews in Chapters 5–8. Finally, take to heart the thoughtful and practical observations made on assessment and intervention in Chapters 3, 9, 10, and 11. Most of these authors have been where you are now and have tried to capture, in succinct form, the key issues you may face.

Ideally, you have picked this book up before you have been called on to assist with intervention and/or research with child disaster victims. The field is recognizing that extensive training and networking of professionals before a disaster ever occurs are the most effective way to approach the mammoth task of disaster work. Training initiatives currently under way with the American Red Cross, the American Psychological Association, and state psychological associations reflect this awareness and hold great promise for our enhanced capability for proper disaster response. Unfortunately, the specific and unique needs of children are typically under-represented in such initiatives, so it falls on the professional to seek out and incorporate this body of knowledge into his or her work.

I am grateful to several individuals whose support and commitment made *Children and Disasters* happen. Mariclaire Cloutier, my Plenum editor, is an extraordinary person whose genuine compassion for these children, coupled with her expertise in volume development, was the driving force in its inception and completion. Michael Roberts proved to be a mentor, friend, and colleague of the highest caliber in my early years of breaking into the field, in my recovery and research after hurricane

Hugo, and now in the production of this book. I am honored and appreciative to be associated with these editors, both personally and professionally.

During the years in which I completed my own disaster studies and edited this volume, I was partially supported in my research with "trauma" victims of a different sort—premature infants and their families—by the Early Intervention Research Institute and Follow-up Institute of Utah State University (U.S. Department of Education Contracts 300-85-0173 and HS90010001). My colleagues in Utah, especially Glen Casto, have made valued contributions of personal support and research consultation throughout this period. I am indebted to Nancy Miller, Fran Trotman, and Mary Cave for clerical support at various points in this project. I also thank Sherri Stokes, who went above and beyond the call of duty in her editing assistance, truly adopting the book as a "labor of love." Finally, I acknowledge the never-failing calm and wisdom of Al Finch, who has encouraged me through this and just about every other crisis of birth, life, and transition in my professional career.

It is the support of family, friends, and colleagues that keeps us moving through the day-to-day adventures as well as the major life events. It is these same individuals who make the difference between mastery and defeat for the disaster victim. If this volume contributes to the reader's being a more effective professional in the disaster environment, a more insightful colleague, or a more compassionate friend or relative, all our efforts will have been worthwhile.

CONWAY FLEMING SAYLOR

Contents

**Chapter 3. Issues in the Assessment of Posttraumatic Stress
Disorder in Children** 45

A. J Finch, Jr., and Timothy K. Daugherty

**Chapter 4. Concepts of Death and Loss in Childhood and
Adolescence: A Developmental Perspective** 67

Linda J. Gudas

Introduction

Children and Disasters
Clinical and Research Issues

CONWAY F. SAYLOR

It is difficult to conceive of any image as compelling as a child who has become the victim of a manmade or natural disaster. How is a child to make sense of, or ever recover from, an experience so devastating and widespread that even otherwise reliable adults seem overwhelmed and powerless? The horrible aftermath of hurricanes, earthquakes, and tornadoes, as well as the sudden, senseless losses in shootings or plane crashes, grab prominent media coverage with alarming frequency. Adults are profoundly moved by their exposure to such events, even with the knowledge and resources many have for understanding and coping. How much greater, and more complex, are the needs of children challenged to understand and respond to such events? In spite of this great need, the psychological literature on children and disasters has, until recently, been small in volume, diverse in quality, and difficult to access.

This book is designed to draw together data, theory, and observation that address children's psychological response to disaster. Like the work in the disaster field, this book is characterized by tremendous diversity in scope, nature, and quality. On one hand, some of the richest material available comes in the form of observations made in the trenches by professionals who have been called on to function as "instant experts" (Rozensky, Kowalski, Schwartz, & Sloan, 1990) at the scene of a disaster.

CONWAY F. SAYLOR • Department of Psychology, The Citadel, Charleston, South Carolina 29409.

Children and Disasters, edited by Conway F. Saylor. Plenum Press, New York, 1993.

1

This clinical and anecdotal material is woven through many of the chapters, but is especially prominent in the intervention chapters, which were all written by colleagues who have worked with children following disasters. At the same time, attempts have now been made to empirically and systematically document the immediate and long-term effects of various types of disasters on children. These studies are summarized and critically reviewed in a manner which should allow the reader to expediently access the available knowledge about the impact of any given type of disaster on children. Finally, there are basic areas of knowledge which are so fundamental to work with children in the disaster environment that they must be understood and incorporated into future work. While some of this work has its roots in early psychological literature (concepts of grief and mourning for example), other parts represent the "cutting edge" of research and conceptualization in areas such as stress and coping.

DEFINING DISASTER

While the definition of a "disaster" varies with the source and purpose, there is general consensus that a disaster is an event that has the following properties: involves the destruction of property, injury, and/or loss of life; has an identifiable beginning and end; adversely affects a relatively large group of people; is "public" and shared by members of more than one family; is out of the realm of ordinary experience; and, psychologically, is traumatic enough to induce distress in almost anyone, regardless of premorbid function or earlier experiences. The focus of this book is disasters which include children and adolescents among their victims, either in the majority, as in a schoolyard shooting, or in the minority, as in the typical plane crash. Obviously, children are not affected in a vacuum. All discussion of children and disasters is in the context of their families, peer groups, school groups, and communities.

Federal agencies consider a "catastrophic disaster" or "near-catastrophic disaster" to be one that may kill, injure, and/or displace tens of thousands of people, as well as disrupt business and services formerly serving those people (American Red Cross, 1991). In disasters of this scope, the Federal Emergency Management Agency (FEMA), the American Red Cross, other relief agencies, and even the military might become involved in disaster response. Disasters happening on a much smaller scale, e.g., hostage situations, tornadoes, and lightning strikes, may not receive this kind of attention, but are equally catastrophic psychologically for the victims.

Child "disaster victims" may be persons directly exposed to the trauma, e.g., injured by a bullet or crouched in a corner when the roof blows off, or indirectly exposed by observation of family members, class-mates, and neighbors suffering the direct assault. Increased media cover-age of major disasters raises the possibility of children even more removed from the situation being upset by a trauma. However, the primary focus of study in this volume is children and adolescents whose lives are person-ally touched when disaster claims their neighbors and loved ones, and/or they themselves. As is discussed in several of the chapters, the degree of exposure and the extent of loss may be key factors in the psychological impact of a disaster on a child and his/her family.

Some disasters are cruel acts of nature, such as earthquakes, hurri-canes, tornadoes, or lightning strikes. Other disasters are traceable to man's own cruelty, such as shootings and hostage situations. Human error can underlie technology-related disasters, ranging from plane crashes and boat sinkings to major chemical spills and nuclear reactor leaks. In many disasters, technology and/or human failure and natural forces combine to create the disaster, such as when dams break and flooding follows. Interestingly, there is some disagreement about whether natural or man-made disasters take the higher toll psychologically. In this volume several authors present competing opinions and data regarding the differential impact of each kind of disaster.

Though they may have elements in common, no two disasters present the same logistical and psychological challenges to their victims, child or adult. For example, hurricane Hugo (1989) and hurricane Andrew (1992) looked quite similar when the numbers were added up and the photo-graphs of damaged homes were examined. However, the varied cultural, socioeconomic, geographic, historical, political, and even meteorological factors gave a unique character to each. While learning from observations made in previous, similar disasters, it is as crucial to approach each "disaster environment" with the same openness as one might approach a new individual client or family. Careful assessment of both objective factors (e.g., What exactly happened here?; To whom?; For how long?; Was there any warning?) and victims' subjective impressions (e.g. Were they afraid they might die?; Did they feel their actions could have changed what happened?; Is there someone to blame?) are crucial to the defining and understanding of each disaster.

There are a number of areas which have relevance to disaster work with children but were beyond the scope of this volume and its disaster definition. Children who are abused, lose loved ones to accidents, survive individual house fires, and/or personally witness a murder or other violent acts experience many of the same emotions as the children featured here and are prime candidates for posttraumatic stress disorder (PTSD). How-ever, because of the individual or within-family scope of these events, they are not targeted for focus here. There are many excellent volumes reviewing issues of child abuse and Posttraumatic Stress Disorder from multiple perspectives, in detail. Work with adult disaster victims, while relevant and in many cases similar to child disaster work, is primarily noted here only if it sets the context for the work with children. Studies which include adolescent disaster victims are mentioned throughout, but, as is the case in many areas of psychological study, the unique needs and characteristics of adolescents have not been addressed in proper depth in the literature as a whole or in this volume.

Finally, there is one area selected for inclusion which some contend is outside of our disaster definition: children and wars. Although it is arguable that wars are predictable and/or chronic conditions without discrete beginning and end points in some parts of the world, the research on wars and children is an important complement to the other literature reviewed here. To date, the studies of war's impact on children have been scattered and relatively sparse. In consideration of wars representing the ultimate "man-made disaster," and of this research being one of the few which is truly international in scope, war's impact on children was selected as a major focus in this volume (see Chapter 8).

ISSUES IN DISASTER RESEARCH

Although this volume attempts to succinctly and critically summarize the best research studies available, there is a marked diversity in the quality and design of the studies in the disaster area. Most authors conclude their disaster research with a plea to future investigators to do the job much better than they themselves have been able to. Indeed, many of the studies cited represent a heroic effort, both on the part of the investigators and on the part of the disaster victims who consented to be studied at the time when their world seemed to have turned upside down.

The fact remains that disaster studies will always have unique obstacles and challenges that may compromise their scientific integrity relative to other types of research. There is no opportunity for random assignment to experimental groups. There is seldom systematically collected baseline or predisaster data to compare with postdisaster observations. The research is often conducted with few resources in areas that have limited access to everything from livable space to working telephones, copiers, and computers. Fortunately, disasters occur infrequently. Unfortunately, low incidence events are difficult to study in the systematic fashion that tends to advance our knowledge in other areas. Additionally, disasters tend to occur in places and at times that are virtually unpredictable. Federal funding currently earmarked for rapid access by potential disaster investigators represents a step in the direction of enhancing the quality of disaster research. Still, there is much to be overcome.

The methodological problems that are a consideration in any area of psychological study are often magnified in disaster research with children. Although subject selection and access are always a concern, the problem is acute in the disaster environment, and the investigator may have to permeate the "trauma membrane," a protective system around the child victims (discussed in Chapter 7). The selection of appropriate assessment instruments, always a challenge to clinical child researchers, is particularly difficult for "normal" children touched by a trauma far beyond "normal" experience. Finch and Daugherty (Chapter 3) discuss the numerous approaches to data collection in disaster studies, all with advantages and disadvantages, and none with uniform acceptance as the "best" approach to the assessment of children who may experience posttraumatic stress.

Ethical concerns are similarly magnified in times of crisis, and even long after the trauma of disaster. It is questionable whether a parent in the midst of his or her own greatest personal trauma can intelligently decide about "informed consent." In fact, some question whether families in this situation should be "bothered" at all with potential research participation. Although some data suggest that disaster victims or persons with other life challenges may receive comfort from the opportunity to help others by contributing to our knowledge base, one can never know on a case-by-case basis whether a potential subject is one who will be helped, unaffected, or stressed by the experience of research participation. Debriefing, follow-up, and access to supportive services become particularly important in these situations. Research protocols need to be carefully selected to impose minimal stress on already overwhelmed participants, and to only include components with a high probability of yield. Finally, confidentiality may be difficult to properly maintain, particularly when a sample of disaster victims is small and now recognized in the community. One should not begin to approach a population of child disaster victims unless he or she has the clinical and research training to treat these issues with sensitivity and integrity, as well as the resources to "finish the job" by disseminating intelligent findings in a way that they will indeed be useful to future disaster victims.

ISSUES IN DISASTER INTERVENTION

Clinical concerns fall along many of the same lines as the research issues discussed above. Once the "trauma membrane" begins to form, it is unclear how "outsiders" may best help child disaster victims and their families. The intervention chapters in this volume emphasize the enormous importance of trust and collaboration in clinical work with this population, and they make practical suggestions on how to earn and honor that trust. Issues of turf protection and privacy may be prominent in individuals or systems who have already been violated by the disaster experience itself. In an effort to regain a sense of mastery and control, the adults who have been responsible for these children may resist well-intentioned offers of assistance. Although clinicians may see some urgency in implementing intervention services, children and families may be quite distinct in the timing of their grief work, and in turn the pace at which they become ready to involve others in facilitating that work.

Those "inside" the traumatized systems may have their own liabilities as interventionists. Although teachers and administrators in a school may be the best interventionists following a disaster which impacts on their students, they themselves may need support as well (see Chapter 10 and Jones, 1991). In catastrophic disasters, local mental health workers may be asked to function as interventionists for others when they themselves have been victims and are in the midst of their own reactions. As Joyner and Swenson (Chapter 11) discuss, even those caretakers who were not initially victims will begin to feel the stress of functioning in an environment where the need is so great. Gillis (Chapter 9) recognizes the impact that close work with child disaster victims may have on the therapist, and he cautions against transference and emotional involvement that may be counter-therapeutic. Potential interventionists need to carefully assess their own capacity with the ongoing help of supervision by peers and experts not as close to the situation. Most large-scale disaster-relief programs now recognize the need to "take care of the caretakers." Even so, when the crisis is in its acute stages, there may be a pull to disregard this caution.

Although it may sound simple, a point that is often overlooked by clinicians and the public alike is that primary survival needs must be met before psychological needs can be addressed. Few would doubt the wisdom of treating an injured child's bullet wound before addressing his/ her psychological trauma. However, in our experience, a flurry of activity aimed at meeting the psychological needs of disaster victims often precedes the provision of basic needs such as food and shelter. After hurricane Andrew, local counselors and members of the Miami press frequently called us to inquire into the psychological impact of this event on the children. Although their concern was important, it occurred at a time when thousands of children and their families had no water, food, shelter, diapers, medicine, and/or electricity. Other than acute crisis intervention, intensive intervention with child disaster victims may need to wait until families have been able to adjust to their new situation. As described by

Joyner and Swenson (Chapter 11), those hoping to serve the psychological needs of this population may need to begin by getting out of traditional roles and settings to provide practical assistance such as cleanup, food preparation, home repairs, and child care.

Ethical issues are of paramount importance, but they may become tricky in disaster intervention. As mentioned with regard to research, confidentiality may be difficult to maintain as the usual systems and procedures are bypassed or unavailable in the disaster environment. It is the interventionist's responsibility to clearly define his or her role and limitations to the targeted children and their families. The interventionist should also be careful in assessing the limits of his/her expertise. Someone who has been a brilliant psychotherapist and/or treated serious psychological disorders in a standard outpatient practice may or may not know how to adapt therapeutic models, procedures, and timing of therapy to the disaster environment. The importance of peer supervision, contact with others who have worked with disaster victims, and additional study cannot be overemphasized. Ideally, predoctoral and postdoctoral educational forums will offer opportunities for more and more professionals to train for this kind of work long before they are called on to engage in it.

There are also glaring cultural issues which are a particular concern in disaster intervention. As desperate as an interventionist might be for guidance, it could be tempting to apply the procedures reported with one disaster population to another without careful adaptation to the present disaster's unique population characteristics. As an extreme example, lessons learned in the San Francisco Bay area earthquake studies may have little relevance to earthquake victims in a remote third-world country. Lessons taught about separation of religion and psychological intervention may need to be reconsidered as one approaches disaster victims whose strong beliefs color their interpretation of what has happened. In general, the literature on children and disasters is lacking in studies that examine variables of ethnicity, religious orientation, gender, and socioeconomic status relative to intervention and outcome. Again, the burden may be on the interventionist to seek consultation and supervision from persons more familiar with and trusted by the target populations.

Certain important elements of disaster intervention have received minimal attention in this volume or elsewhere. After a disaster, children who have survived the initial trauma may be subjected to intensive media exposure. The potential impact of media coverage on child trauma victims has been discussed (e.g., by Libow, 1990), but to date, it has been underresearched. A second major issue is the interaction between parent adjustment and child adjustment in families touched by disaster. Although research is cited throughout this volume which documents the relationships between child and parent distress, little has been researched or written about the implications of this phenomenon for intervention approaches or priorities.

The developmental status of children at the time of a disaster is alluded to throughout the literature. However, in point of fact, there has been inadequate attention paid to the interaction between psychosocial or cognitive development and reaction to either a disaster or a postdisaster intervention. Little is known about the long-term impact of a disaster that strikes at a critical developmental stage of a youngster's life. What are the special implications, for example, when a young adolescent is disfigured in a disaster at a time when peer approval and appearance are such major factors? What might be the implications for a preschooler at a crucial point in the separation process when a disaster gives him/her indelible reasons to fear being apart from parents?

Throughout this volume, an effort is made to present findings in a developmental context so that the potential interventionist can learn to approach children with this perspective. A second perspective which is essential to child disaster victim work is the "systems" model, very broadly defined. Although much attention has been paid to family therapy in traditional mental health settings, multiple systems are even more significant factors in disaster work. The systems to be considered in assessment of potential resources/assets (or potential problem sources) include, but are not limited to, the child's peers, family, extended family, teachers, religious leaders, and neighbors. Members of the child's social support systems may be vehicles for delivering intervention to the child in a costeffective or nonintrusive way. At the same time, a system can impose obstacles to the intervention process. For example, a school system may be unwilling to consider preventive intervention after a disaster has touched members of its student body, or families may covertly or overtly deny the child permission to fully feel his/her grief. In any case, it is essential that intervention with children after a disaster consider and involve the members of the relevant systems.

FUTURE DIRECTIONS

The literature in this volume represents the very early stages of a clinical research area that is of critical importance at an international level. In spite of continuing advances on the technical side of disaster work— communications, transportation, and meteorological forecasting, for example—there are relatively few "hard data" to direct the delivery of effective psychological intervention to children and families after a disaster. The kinds of studies required to answer questions about long-term outcomes, individual differences, cultural factors, and intervention cost-effectiveness are the kind that require collaborative effort with substantial funding. Flexibility and creativity must be built into the systems through which research funding is allocated. Additionally, networking and disaster preparation efforts must be fully supported on a steady basis rather than waiting for a major, visible disaster to gather momentum.

A promising movement for mental health disaster intervention in general is the recent effort by the American Psychological Association (APA), the American Red Cross, and the state psychological associations to collaborate on training and networking initiatives (California Psychological Association, 1991). It will be important for these initiatives to receive input from specialists in clinical child psychology so that relief workers in these networks will be knowledgeable about the needs of children, the most vulnerable disaster victims. The APA's clinical section on children (Division 12, Section 1) has commissioned a task force to gather relevant data on this subject and make recommendations for enhanced capability to meet the need for effective outreach to children after a disaster. Similarly, the American Academy of Pediatrics section on psychosocial issues has a working task force on children and disasters. The more these types of professional organizations can network, and the more interchange and collaboration can happen between federal agencies and these professional groups, the more optimistic one can be about forward progress in this area.

In the meantime, this book provides a starting point to explore the complex and compelling issues surrounding children and disasters.

REFERENCES

American Red Cross. (1991, Nov.). *Disaster services regulations and procedures: Disaster mental health services.*

California Psychological Association. (1991, Oct.). *Interim project report: A call for action.* Unpublished report.

Jones, C. A. (1991). Who takes care of the caretakers? *Advances in Behaviour, Research, and Therapy, 13,* 181–183.

Libow, J. (1990, Nov.). *Child trauma victims and the media: Clinical considerations.* Presented at the Association for the Advancement of Behavior Therapy Meeting, San Francisco.

Rozensky, R. H., Kowalski, J. M., Schwarz, E. D., & Sloan, I. H. (1990, August). Multiple shootings in an elementary school: Sequelae, intervention, and follow-up. In M. Roberts (chair), *Children's responses to natural and human-made disasters.* Symposium presented at the annual meeting of the American Psychological Association, Boston.

1

Stress and Coping in Children and Families
Implications for Children Coping with Disaster

BRUCE E. COMPAS and JOANNE E. EPPING

Natural disasters such as hurricanes, tornadoes, earthquakes, and volcanic eruptions strike with a suddenness and intensity that is sobering to all who experience or observe such events. Disasters that are the consequence of human technology, error, or greed are often unexpected, traumatic in magnitude, and equally compelling as natural disasters. Regardless of the source of the traumatic event, we are left to consider the pain, anguish, suffering, loss, and death that has struck the victims in these situations.

The first and most compelling question that arises for many individuals when they receive news of a disaster is: What about the children? For example, the cyclone that struck Bangladesh in the spring of 1991 offered a series of stark images of scores of children who had been killed and countless others who were left terrified, alone, and confused. Although compassion was warranted for all who had experienced this devastating event, the greater vulnerability of children generated an even stronger response for many observers. Children often appear to lack the resources and skills needed to manage the physical and psychological stress that is associated with disaster.

BRUCE E. COMPAS and JOANNE E. EPPING • Department of Psychology, University of Vermont, Burlington, Vermont 05405.
Children and Disasters, edited by Conway F. Saylor. Plenum Press, New York, 1993.

Our purpose is to consider the options and resources that children have for coping with disasters. First, we briefly review the literature on the psychological effects of disasters to establish the stressful nature of these events. Second, we consider the issues in the conceptualization and measurement of coping in children. Third, we review the literature on children's coping with stress, emphasizing developmental changes and stabilities in coping and the effects of family characteristics on children's coping. Finally, we consider the implications of this literature for enhancing our understanding of children's coping with disaster.

THE PSYCHOLOGICAL IMPACT OF DISASTER

A disaster is defined as an event with a relatively sudden and identifiable onset that is caused by external or environmental factors and is associated with adverse effects on a group of individuals (Rubonis & Bickman, 1991). Disasters differ from other types of stressful events in that they are broader in scope than other stressors that occur on an individual basis. Disasters can be distinguished on the basis of several features including their cause, speed of onset, severity, scope of impact, duration, and number of human casualties.

What is the psychological toll of exposure to natural or human-made disasters? Are the psychological consequences short-lived or long-lasting? Do disasters produce common effects on all who are exposed to them, or are there individual differences in psychological reactions to disaster? These questions have been the focus of a large body of psychological, psychiatric, and sociological research on adult disaster victims and a growing literature on children and disasters. A recent meta-analysis of the effects of disasters on adults indicates that such events lead to a moderate increase in psychological distress and to symptoms of psychopathology in disaster victims (Rubonis & Bickman, 1991). Findings from 52 studies have indicated that disasters (e.g., floods, earthquakes, fires, tornadoes, nuclear accidents, and plane crashes) were associated with a 17% increase in the prevalence of psychopathology as compared to control groups or predisaster levels of psychopathology. The size of the effect varied as a function of several factors including the type of psychopathology, the methodology of the study, the victim's characteristics, and the disaster's characteristics. Rubonis and Bickman (1991) concluded that greater psychopathology was associated with female victims, a large number of casualties, and natural as opposed to human cause of the disaster.

For our present focus, it is unfortunate that the Rubonis and Bickman (1991) review included only one study in which the sample was exclusively children. We were unable to identify a similar comprehensive review of the impact of disasters on child and adolescent psychopathology. However, evidence from a number of studies indicates the presence of at least short-term psychological distress in a portion of children exposed to disaster (e.g., Dollinger, 1986; Dollinger, O'Donnell, & Staley, 1984; McFarlane, 1987; Seroka, Knapp, Knight, Siemon, & Starbuck, 1986). Childhood problems associated with disasters have included conduct problems, sleeplessness, fears, and sad or depressed affect.

It appears that natural and human-caused disasters take a substantial psychological toll on children. It is also evident, however, that not all children who are exposed to disasters display maladaptive responses. The substantial variability in distress and psychopathology in both child and adult victims of disaster suggests that an important priority for research is an identification of the sources of individual differences in reactions to disaster. The more general literature on psychosocial stress points to cognitive appraisals of the disaster, coping efforts, and the responses of other family members, especially parental psychological distress, as primary candidates for future investigation.

DEFINING THE CONCEPT OF COPING

Few concepts in the behavioral sciences have proved as difficult to define and operationalize as the constructs of stress and coping. A variety of different conceptual models are available that describe and explain the nature of stressful events, their impact on individuals, and the processes of coping and adjustment. Further, a wide range of instruments is available to measure aspects of stress and coping, although the majority of these measures are not theoretically based. We have drawn on the seminal work of Lazarus and Folkman (1984), who defined coping as "constantly changing cognitive and behavioral efforts to master specific internal and/or external demands that are appraised as taxing or exceeding the resources of the person" (p. 141). Two issues seem especially pertinent in conceptualizing children's coping with disasters: (1) delineation of subtypes of coping and (2) trait, stage, and process conceptualization of coping.

Subtypes of Coping

Several conceptual models have been used to guide research on how children and adolescents cope with stress (for reviews, see Compas, 1987; Compas, Malcarne, & Banez, 1992), including the cognitive appraisal model of Lazarus and Folkman (1984), the two-dimensional model of primary and secondary control (Rothbaum, Weisz, & Snyder, 1982; Weisz, Rothbaum, & Blackburn, 1984), Murphy and Moriarity's ego-psychology model (1976), and the monitoring–blunting model (Miller, 1980). In spite of the apparent diversity of these models, all of these approaches emphasize a basic distinction between two fundamental types of coping, a distinction that centers on the intention or function of coping efforts. The first type of coping refers to efforts to change or master some aspect of the person, the environment, or the relation between these two elements that is perceived as stressful. For example, a child whose home and belongings have been damaged by a natural disaster may expend effort to reclaim or rebuild possessions that were damaged in the catastrophe. This type of coping has been labeled *problem-focused coping* (Lazarus & Folkman, 1984), *primary control coping* (Band & Weisz, 1988), *Coping I* (Murphy & Moriarity, 1976), *approach coping* (Altshuler & Ruble, 1989), *problem-solving* (Wertlieb, Weigel, & Feldstein, 1987), *active coping* (Peterson, 1989), and *monitoring* (Miller, 1980). The second type of coping refers to efforts to manage or regulate the negative emotions associated with the stressful episode. For example, the same child who has experienced a disaster may seek reassurance from his/her parents or use other methods to assuage the fears and anxieties that have resulted from the event. This type of coping has been labeled *emotion-focused coping* (Lazarus & Folkman, 1984), *secondary-control coping* (Band & Weisz, 1988), *Coping II* (Murphy & Moriarity, 1976), *emotion manipulation, tension reduction, avoidance* (Altshuler & Ruble, 1989), *emotion management* (Wertlieb *et al.*, 1987), *avoidant coping* (Peterson, 1989), and *blunting* (Miller, 1980).

These broad categories of coping can be further delineated based on the different functions of problem- and emotion-focused coping. For example, we have examined subtypes of problem- and emotion-focused coping in our research on the ways that parents and children cope with the crisis of the diagnosis of cancer in a mother or father (e.g., Ey, 1992; Worsham, Ey, & Compas, 1992). From the time of diagnosis, each family member responds to a series of individual structured interviews every four months over a period of one year that include questions concerning the ways that he or she is coping with the cancer experience at that point in time. In our analyses of these interview responses, problem-focused coping is further delineated as (1) planful problem-solving or (2) confrontive coping. Emotion-focused coping is classified as (1) denial or avoidance; (2) distraction or minimization; (3) wishful thinking; (4) self-control of feelings; (5) seeking meaning; (6) self-blame; and (7) expressing and sharing feelings. These data provide the opportunity to examine developmental differences in the use of these subtypes of coping in a sample of children, adolescents, and adults who are coping with a common family health crisis. In addition, analyses of finer grained distinctions among subtypes of coping of this type are considered an important next step in understanding the effectiveness of various coping efforts.

In light of the unexpected and uncontrollable nature of disasters, examination of subtypes of emotion-focused coping may be especially important to pursue in studies of children who have been exposed to such events. Because disasters may offer children few opportunities to exert control over their surroundings, children may need to rely on efforts to manage their emotions associated with these events. Not all types of emotion-focused coping may be equally beneficial in coping with traumatic events, however. For example, it will be important to determine if distraction/minimization and seeking meaning are more effective in managing emotions in the face of traumatic events than are denial/avoidance and self-blame.

Trait, Stage, and Process Conceptualizations of Coping

Coping efforts are influenced by both characteristics of the person and characteristics of the situation with which she or he is coping. Different models of coping however, give relatively greater emphasis to personal as opposed to situational factors, leading some to be more trait-oriented and others to be more stage- or process-oriented. That is, conceptualizations of coping differ in the degree of cross-situational and temporal consistency or variability that is expected in an individual's coping. Further, those models that examine possible changes in the coping process over time differ in the degree to which change is viewed as following an invariant sequence of stages. The relevance of this issue to understanding children's coping with disasters is twofold. First, children may be expected to cope in similar or varied ways with qualitatively different types of disasters. Second, children can be expected to cope in consistent or varied ways with the same disaster over the course of time.

There has been very little study of the sequential patterns of children's coping across time with disasters. Some parallels may be drawn from data which portray stages of coping with predictable and controlled stressors, such as medical procedures. In one study which assessed children's responses to the appraisal stage of coping (e.g., learning one is going to have a medical procedure) and the encounter stage of coping (e.g., coming in contact with the stressful procedure), Peterson, Harbeck, Chaney, Farmer, and Thomas (1990) found that active coping in appraisal, where in role-play children asked questions and looked at the medical instruments, was strongly related to proactive encounter coping or coping which involved preprogrammed techniques, such as distraction or sensory focus.

In contrast, children who avoided information in role playing during appraisal were more likely to report reactive encounter coping, which involved catastrophizing, doing nothing, or behaving aggressively.

Peterson et al. (1990) argued that there were two dimensions to the children's encounter coping. One dimension involved the proactive (volitional, planned) versus reactive (out-of-control) quality. The other involved the extent to which children approached the stimulus. Thus, children might cope by blocking out the stimulus (using imaginative distraction) or by approaching the stimulus (redefining the procedure as "torture" and behaving heroically). The degree to which responding was proactive was unrelated to whether it involved approaching or blocking the stimulus. It is important to note that active appraisal coping such as asking questions and vigilantly looking at the equipment was often followed by what appeared to be rather passive encounter coping, when, in fact, the child was really engaged in proactive encounter coping, which is psychologically very active (imagining being somewhere else or fantasizing that the physician is an enemy agent). The continuity between stages of coping appeared to be in the extent to which the child was able to planfully gather and utilize information about the event, not the degree of overt activity involved.

Studies of coping in college students and adults have provided a solid body of information on the cross-situational and temporal stability of coping. The results of several studies provide support for a process model as opposed to a trait model of coping. For example, temporal aspects of coping were examined by Folkman and Lazarus (1985) in a study of undergraduates' efforts at coping with an examination at three points in time: before the exam (Time 1), after the exam but before the grades were returned (Time 2), and after grades were returned (Time 3). This prospective design allowed an analysis of the degree to which the students' reports of coping remained consistent or changed over the three stages of the exam process. Support was found for a process-oriented model of coping, as significant changes occurred in coping over time. Problem-focused coping, seeking social support, emphasizing the positive, and self-isolation decreased from Time 1 to Time 2, whereas distancing increased. Wishful thinking and distancing decreased from Time 2 to Time 3.

Compas, Forsythe, and Wagner (1988), also using a college student sample, examined both temporal and cross-situational change and consistency in coping with stress in the domains of academic achievement and interpersonal relationships. Students reported on an ongoing stressor or hassle in each domain once a week for four weeks. Patterns of coping were characterized by moderate consistency in response to the same stressor over time and low consistency across the interpersonal and academic stressors. There was very little consistency in the use of seven subtypes of coping (e.g., distraction, situation redefinition, direct action) across the two different stressors, with most correlations below .20, failing to reach significance. The correlations for the use of the subtypes of coping in response to the same stressor over time were higher; most of these reached significance, falling between .30 and .50. Further, the temporal stability of coping was predicted by the individuals' initial levels of negative affect. Those individuals who reported higher levels of initial anxious, depressive, and angry emotions were more stable in their coping over the following three weeks. This pattern suggests that coping is influenced by both person and situation factors, with person factors exerting relatively greater influence when the situation remains stable. These findings suggest that it will be important to study coping with disasters at different points in time as the demands of the stressor and the resources available to children may change. Further, it will be useful to examine how children cope with different stressful aspects of a single disaster, as events of great magnitude are likely to present children with multiple different stressors with which they must contend.

There are precious few data on the coping patterns of children or adolescents across situations or over time in the same context. Most studies have sampled child and adolescent coping in a single context at a given point in time. The assessment of situational and temporal consistency and variability has been further clouded by the use of measures that ask the participants to report on how they cope "in general." The use of such instruments prohibits the analysis of situational or temporal processes by asking the respondents to aggregate their own coping efforts and report on an ill-defined central tendency in their own thoughts and actions. The few studies that have addressed consistency and variability in coping in younger populations have suggested that children may be more consistent in their coping across different situations than are adults. For example, both Wills (1986) and Compas, Malcarne, and Fondacaro (1988) have reported significant correlations that were moderate in magnitude for young adolescents' use of coping strategies across different situations. These findings lead to the hypothesis that coping becomes more differentiated with development. It is expected that this increased differentiation would be reflected in greater variability in response to the demands of different stressful situations. This hypothesis, however, has not yet been directly tested.

If coping does change over the course of a stressful episode, do the changes follow a pattern or sequence that is consistent across individuals who are exposed to similar stressors? That is, does coping occur in a sequence of stages? Stage theories of coping have been applied frequently to the study of coping with disasters and loss (e.g., Lystad, 1985; Wortman & Silver, 1989). For example, Cohen and Ahern (1980) described several unique features that they hypothesized to be associated with the pre-impact, impact, and postimpact phases of disasters. Similarly, Titchener and Ross (1974) discussed five phases of psychological response to disasters and other stressors. These stages include a preimpact phase, in which the person becomes aware of the impending stress; an impact phase, which results in the collapse of coping responses; a third phase of disorientation and blunting of awareness; a fourth phase involving regressive behavior; and finally, a reconstitution phase. In spite of the clinical appeal of these models, research on adults has not supported stage models of coping and adjustment to traumatic and loss-related events (Wortman & Silver, 1989), and stage models of children's responses to disasters have not been empirically tested. Although coping responses appear to change over the course of a disaster, there are substantial individual differences in the emotional reactions to and the coping efforts directed toward such events.

In summary, research supports the conceptualization of coping as a process that is responsive to the varying demands of different situations and changes in the same stressful encounter as it unfolds over time. The adoption of a process-oriented model of coping has two important implications for research on adjustment to disasters. First, the assessment of coping needs to be sensitive to situational and temporal changes. It will be at best insufficient and at worst misleading to ask disaster victims how they cope in general. Second, optimally adaptive coping may differ across types of disasters and at different points in the course of a disaster episode.

DEVELOPMENT OF COPING DURING CHILDHOOD AND ADOLESCENCE

The tremendous variability in the developmental level of children who are exposed to disasters represents a substantial challenge for mental health professionals who try to understand the psychological impact of disasters and who endeavor to develop and deliver effective services to disaster victims. Children and adolescents, who vary in their level of cognitive, social, emotional, and biological development, present professionals with a much wider variation than is encountered by those working with adults. As a consequence, it is imperative that mental health professionals concerned with child and adolescent victims of disaster take a developmental approach in their research and practice.

The general literature on child and adolescent coping has identified some important developmental patterns. Specifically, six fairly recent studies of how children and adolescents cope with a wide range of stressors have examined developmental changes and stabilities in problem- and emotion-focused coping (Altshuler & Ruble, 1989; Band, 1990; Band & Weisz, 1988; Compas, Malcarne, & Fondacaro, 1988; Curry & Russ, 1985; Wertlieb et al., 1987). All six of these studies have found at least some evidence of a positive relation between reports of emotion-focused coping and age or some other marker of developmental level (e.g., cognitive developmental level). Evidence for this developmental change has been found in samples of school-aged children ranging from 5½ to 10½ years old (Altshuler & Ruble, 1989; Curry & Russ, 1985; Wertlieb et al., 1987), children and adolescents aged 6–17 (Band, 1990; Band & Weisz, 1988), and older children and young adolescents aged 10–14 (Compas, Malcarne, & Fondacaro, 1988). This developmental increase in emotion-focused coping has been founded on reports of coping with medical and dental stressors (Altshuler & Ruble, 1989; Band & Weisz, 1988; Curry & Russ, 1985) and interpersonal stressors (Compas, Malcarne, & Fondacaro, 1988).

In contrast to this consistent finding of developmental increases in emotion-focused coping, no consistent developmental changes have been found in problem-focused coping, with three studies finding no change with age (Altshuler & Ruble, 1989; Compas, Malcarne, & Fondacaro, 1988; Wertlieb et al., 1987) and two studies finding a decrease in problem-focused coping with age (Band & Weisz, 1988; Curry & Russ, 1985). The two findings of decreases in problem-focused coping were both noted in reference to medical/dental stressors (Band & Weisz, 1988; Curry & Russ, 1985), whereas no changes in problem-focused coping were found in relation to a wider range of stressors (Altshuler & Ruble, 1989; Compas, Malcarne, & Fondacaro, 1988; Wertlieb et al., 1987).

In the broader literature on the development of children's problem-solving skills, which can be considered germane to the study of coping (cf. Compas, 1987), there is evidence that there are increases with age in certain types of abilities. For example, Spivack and Shure (1982) found that the capacity to generate multiple solutions to interpersonal problems emerges around age 4 or 5, whereas the ability to use means–ends thinking (i.e., identifying the sequence of steps needed to solve a problem) does not appear until around ages 8–10. Interventions designed to improve children's problem-solving skills have been successful in increasing both of these skills (Spivack & Shure, 1982). More recently, Compas, Banez, Malcarne, and Worsham (1991) reported on coping with interpersonal stress in a sample of 6- to 12-year-old children. The use of problem-focused coping increased with age, $r = .45$, $p < .01$, whereas emotion-focused coping was unrelated to age, $r = .02$.

Worsham *et al.* (1992) also investigated developmental differences in reports of problem- and emotion-focused coping in coping with the diagnosis and treatment of cancer in mother or father in a sample of children (aged 6–10), adolescents (aged 11–18), and young adults (aged 19–35). This investigation offered an opportunity to examine developmental changes in coping with a health-related stressor across a much wider range of developmental levels than most previous studies. As part of the study, we asked each family member to report on how he or she had coped with the cancer and her or his own intentions in using each coping strategy. That is, the participants indicated whether they were trying to change something about the stressful situation (problem-focused), to manage their feelings (emotion-focused), or to accomplish both of these objectives with a single coping act (both problem- and emotion-focused). Emotion-focused coping increased with age across these three groups, F $(2,126) = 4.00$, $p < .02$. Specifically, children reported significantly fewer ($p < .05$) emotion-focused coping strategies than did adolescents or young adults; adolescents and young adults did not differ from each other in their reports of emotion-focused coping. Reports of problem-focused coping did not differ across the groups, although all age groups reported using very little strictly problem-focused coping. Reports of the use of strategies that were intended to achieve both problem- and emotion-focused intentions also increased with age, F $(2,126) = 4.96$, $p < .008$. By allowing the respondents to describe the coping strategies that they had used to try to address both problem- and emotion-focused objectives, we obtained a somewhat different picture of the development of problem-solving skills. The use of complex strategies that serve multiple intentions appears to increase with developmental age in a manner similar to the age-related increase in emotion-focused coping (Compas & Worsham, 1991; Worsham *et al.*, 1992).

In summary, studies of coping in children and adolescents suggest that problem-focused and emotion-focused coping skills emerge at different points in development. Problem-focused skills appear to be acquired earlier, and there is some evidence that the acquisition of problem-solving skills is apparent by the preschool years. One reason for the earlier development of these skills may be that they are more readily acquired through the modeling of adult behaviors, as many of these coping strategies involve overt behavior and are observable even by young children. Emotion-focused coping skills appear to develop in later childhood and early adolescence. This may be the result of several factors, including younger children having less access to their internal emotional states, their failure to recognize that their emotions can be brought under self-regulation, and the emotion-focused coping efforts of others being less observable and therefore less easily learned through modeling processes.

FAMILY PROCESSES IN COPING
DURING CHILDHOOD AND ADOLESCENCE

Theoretical and empirical treatments of the coping process have a history of examining how *individuals* manage stress in their lives. However, researchers and clinicians concerned with stress and coping processes have long been aware that the ways that children and adolescents cope with disasters cannot be understood solely in individual terms (e.g., Benedek, 1985; Lystad, 1984). Coping with general life stress as well as coping with catastrophic events occurs in a social context. Contextual factors serve both as resources that aid and facilitate effective coping and as impediments or blocks to adequate adjustment. Although children and teens function in a variety of proximal contexts (family, school, and peer group) and more distal settings (neighborhoods, cities, and societies), the family stands out as preeminent in understanding coping processes in response to disasters.

Family characteristics and processes may be related to coping in a variety of ways. First, family members can serve as resources for children and adolescents who are coping with a disaster through the provision of social support and information. Second, at the opposite end of the continuum of the provision of social support, family members can be impediments to the coping process by interrupting or constraining the coping efforts of a child or teen or by turning to the child or adolescent for help in coping for themselves in ways that exceed the child's developmental capacity. Further, disasters may impede the family's ability to aid children in coping if there is separation or loss of family members as a result of the event. Third, family members, especially parents, can serve as models for coping strategies that may be employed by a child. Fourth, families generate rules and enact regulatory processes that influence the coping strategies used by the individual family members. Finally, families operate as systems in which the coping efforts of individual family members may affect and be affected by the coping efforts of other family members in addressing a common problem.

Social support from family members has been identified as an important resource for children and adolescents in coping with stress. As such, support received from family members is a logical starting point for understanding the ways in which families contribute to coping with disasters. Unfortunately, we could not find any studies that examined social support provided by parents to children coping with disaster. This is a high priority for future research.

It is also possible that family members, in addition to providing valuable support, can in some instances impede coping of the children faced with disasters. Since disasters often strike parents as well as their children, in many instances parents may be affected psychologically by the event. For example, McFarlane (1987) found that children's adjustment to a devastating brush fire was related to the degree of psychological distress experienced by their parents. Earls, Smith, Reich, and Jung (1988) also found a relation between parental psychological symptoms and children's reactions to a major flood. This pattern is similar to the association of parental psychological response to stress and children's adjustment found in families confronted with more normative levels of day-to-day stress (Compas, Howell, Phares, Williams, & Ledoux, 1989). Thus, parental distress may impede the ability of parents to assist their children in coping with both major and minor levels of stress. Further, Handford, Mayes, Mattison, Humphrey, Bagnato, Bixler, and Kales (1986) found that, although neither mothers' nor fathers' psychological symptoms were related to their children's reactions to the Three Mile Island nuclear accident, the *discrepancy* between the two parents' symptoms was related to the intensity of their children's reactions. Greater differences between the two parents' levels of psychological symptoms were associated with more intense reactions to the disaster by their children.

It is widely assumed that the family provides the primary context in which children naturally acquire ways of coping with stress. Based on a general social-learning-theory model, parents are viewed as models for coping who influence the children's coping behavior through observational learning processes. Unfortunately, there are no data available on parents and children that bear on the question. Modeling and direct instruction are frequently combined in interventions to teach problem-solving skills and emotion management techniques to assist children in coping with illness (e.g., Manne, Redd, Jacobsen, Gorfinkle, Schorr, & Rapkin, 1990). If similar processes operate in families on a natural basis, it is likely that parents' active problem-focused coping strategies are more readily observable to children than are emotion-focused coping techniques. Problem-focused coping is more likely to involve behavioral strategies that the child can observe and emulate, whereas many important emotion-focused coping skills involve covert cognitive processes and are unlikely to be verbalized by parents. To the extent that parents do serve as important models of coping for their children, this would underscore the importance of helping parents acquire effective coping skills and enlisting them in teaching these skills to their children (e.g., Jay & Elliott, 1990). This certainly represents a high priority for future research.

In addition to processes of modeling and observational learning, it is assumed that families affect the coping behaviors of their members through rules and regulatory mechanisms. Drawing on the work of Reiss and his colleagues (Reiss, 1981; Reiss, Oliveri, & Curd, 1983), Fiese and

Sameroff (1989) have discussed the importance of family paradigms, family stories, and family rituals in the regulation of the family and in shaping the experiences and behaviors of individual family members. Most pertinent to the process of coping with disasters, these family regulatory mechanisms provide rules for acceptable or preferred coping behavior in the family. These rules may be as specific as defining prescribed coping behaviors and roles for individual family members. For example, in some families, children might be encouraged to share their feelings with a family member. In others families, however, emotional expression might be prohibited. Further, it appears that mothers and fathers take on different roles in coping with some types of stress, such as childhood illness (e.g., Hauser, Jacobson, Wertlieb, Weiss-Perry, Follansbee, Wolsdorf, Herskowitz, Houlihan, & Rajapark, 1986).

Finally, there is the notion of the family as a system. This is the broadest perspective on the role of the family in coping with disasters, and perhaps a perspective that encompasses the other aspects of family functioning discussed above. The potential significance of family systems theory for child stress has been discussed (e.g., Compas, 1987; Kazak, 1989). Our intent here is to highlight the ways in which a systemic perspective might enhance our understanding of the ways that children, adolescents, and their families cope with disaster.

From a family systems perspective, questions regarding family coping can be asked in two ways. First, researchers may ask, "How is this *family* coping with the disaster or traumatic event?" In this case, the coping process is operationalized and measured at the level of the family unit. For example, the Family Environment Scale (Moos & Moos, 1986) and other measures of family functioning are frequently used to assess the responses of families to stress (e.g., Davies, 1988). This approach provides useful information on characteristics of families that are associated with good versus poor psychological outcomes. However, the use of aggregate-level measures of family functioning has two limitations as measures of family coping. First, these are measures of perceived family functioning that are appropriate only for adults and are completed only by parents, virtually always the mother. Second, they describe the functioning of the family as a whole without reference to the actions of specific family members.

A second approach to analyzing coping in a family system involves the examination of reports on or observations of the coping of each family member. Systemic processes and interpretations are then derived from the aggregated data on all family members. For example, Hauser *et al.* (1986) observed the interactions in families with children recently diagnosed with a chronic illness (insulin-dependent diabetes mellitus) and in families of children with acute illnesses or injuries. These families were observed while they tried to achieve resolution on a standard set of family problems. Diabetic children and their parents displayed significantly more behaviors that could be considered reflective of effective coping (enabling behaviors) as well as behaviors that could adversely affect coping (constraining behaviors) (Hauser et al., 1986). Observational data of this type are particularly useful to assess coping behaviors that involve direct interactions among family members.

Family processes may also affect the coping behaviors of family members outside direct family interactions. That is, the tendency for a parent or child to use various problem- or emotion-focused strategies in personal efforts to cope with a pediatric problem may be influenced by family roles and by the individual coping behaviors of others in the family. We are pursuing this possibility in our analyses of parents' and children's responses to individual coping interviews concerning parental cancer. Our preliminary analyses indicate that there may well be significant relations among family members in the ways that they choose to cope with a parent's cancer (Ey, Worsham, & Compas, 1992). For example the use of emotion-focused coping by the patient is significantly correlated with the use of more emotion-focused coping by the spouse, r (74) = .23, p = .054. In contrast, patients' use of coping strategies that are dual-focused (i.e., addressing both problem- and emotion-focused functions in a single coping effort) is inversely related to children's use of emotion-focused coping, r (16) = $-.44$, $p <$ .08, and is inversely related to children's use of dual-focused coping, r (16) = $-.47$, $p <$ .06. Although the direction of influence of one family member's coping behavior on another must await future analyses of our longitudinal data from these families, these preliminary analyses suggest the potential links between the coping efforts of spouses and parents and children. Obtaining data of this type requires the use of individual indices of the coping behavior of each family member on measures that are developmentally appropriate for children and adults and that also yield comparable data across different individuals. Children and their parents may cope with disasters in very different ways. Whether these differences serve complementary or incompatible functions for family members warrants attention in future research.

IMPLICATIONS FOR CHILDREN COPING WITH DISASTER

Recent research on coping in children, adolescents, and families has generated a solid foundation for future investigations of coping in a variety of special populations. Foremost among these special groups are children and adolescents who have been exposed to disasters. Based on this research, we would like to offer a definition of coping from a developmental and familial perspective. The vast majority of recent research has been guided by the process-oriented model of Lazarus and Folkman (1984). Building on their definition of coping, it will be essential to consider that coping efforts change as a function not only of situational and temporal factors related to the stressor, but as a function of the developmental level of the individual as well. Further, both appraisals of stress and appraisals of coping resources are influenced not only by the cognitive processes of the individual but by the perceptions of other family members who are affected by the stressful circumstances. Consideration of developmental and family contributions to the coping process will make research on coping even more focal and more useful in the study of children's reactions to disasters.

Future research on children coping with disaster will benefit from addressing several issues discussed above. First, it will be necessary to assess coping and psychological symptoms at multiple points in time to examine stability, changes, and patterns in coping and maladjustment associated with disasters. A process approach to studying children's coping with disasters could contribute much to the understanding of the way that children adapt to the complete course of traumatic events over time. Second, it will be important to examine different types of coping, including more detailed analyses of the subtypes of problem- and emotion-focused coping. More fine-grained analyses of different types of coping should prove helpful in discerning which types of coping are most effective in which situations. Third, an examination of the developmental consistencies and differences in children's coping with disaster should be a high priority for future research. The impact of disasters on children and adolescents may vary as a function of their coping skills and resources. Finally, the ways in which the coping and adjustment of parents and other family members contribute to or deter effective coping by children needs to be determined. Consideration of developmental and family factors in the process of children's coping with disasters will help both researchers and practitioners in answering the question: What about the children?

ACKNOWLEDGMENTS. Preparation of this manuscript was supported by National Institute of Mental Health Grant MH43819.

REFERENCES

Altshuler, J. L., & Ruble, D. N. (1989). Developmental changes in children's awareness of strategies for coping with uncontrollable stress. *Child Development*, *60*, 1337–1349.

Band, E. B. (1990). Children's coping with diabetes: Understanding the role of cognitive development. *Journal of Pediatric Psychology, 15,* 27–41.

Band, E. B., & Weisz, J. R. (1988). How to feel better when it feels bad: Children's perspectives on coping with everyday stress. *Developmental Psychology, 24,* 247–253.

Benedek, E. D. (1985). Children and disaster: Emerging issues. *Psychiatric Annals, 15,* 168–172.

Cohen, R., & Ahren, F. (1980). *Handbook for mental health care of disaster victims.* Baltimore: Johns Hopkins University Press.

Compas, B. E. (1987). Coping with stress during childhood and adolescence. *Psychological Bulletin, 101,* 393–403.

Compas, B. E., & Worsham, N. (1991, Apr.). *When mom or dad has cancer: Developmental differences in children's coping with family stress.* Paper presented at the conference of the Society for Research on Child Development, Seattle.

Compas, B. E., Forsythe, C. J., & Wagner, B. M. (1988). Consistency and variability in causal attributions and coping with stress. *Cognitive Therapy and Research, 12,* 305–320.

Compas, B. E., Malcarne, V. L., & Fondacaro, K. M. (1988). Coping with stressful events in older children and young adolescents. *Journal of Consulting and Clinical Psychology, 56,* 405–411.

Compas, B. E., Howell, D. C., Phares, V., Williams, R. A., & Ledoux, N. (1989). Parent and child stress and symptoms: An integrative analysis. *Developmental Psychology,* 550–559.

Compas, B. E., Banez, G. A., Malcarne, V. L., & Worsham, N. (1991). Perceived control and coping with stress: A developmental perspective. *Journal of Social Issues, 47,* 23–34.

Compas, B. E., Malcarne, V. L., & Banez, G. A. (1992). Coping with psychosocial stress: A developmental perspective. In B. Carpenter (Ed.), *Personal coping: Theory, research and application.* New York: Praeger.

Curry, S. L., & Russ, S. W. (1985). Identifying coping strategies in children. *Journal of Clinical Child Psychology, 14,* 61–69.

Davies, B. (1988). The family environment in bereaved families and its relationship to surviving sibling behavior. *Children's Health Care, 17,* 22–31.

Dollinger, S. J. (1986). The need for meaning following disaster: Attributions and emotional upset. *Personality and Social Psychology Bulletin, 12,* 300–310.

Earls, F., Smith, E., Reich, W., & Jung, K. G. (1988). Investigating psychopathological consequences of a disaster in children: A pilot study incorporating a structured diagnostic interview. *Journal of the American Academy of Child and Adolescent Psychiatry, 27,* 90–95.

Ey, S. S. (1992). *Cancer patients' coping and psychological adjustment within the family context.* Unpublished doctoral dissertation, University of Vermont, Burlington.

Ey, S., Worsham, N. L., & Compas, B. E. (1992). *When mom or dad has cancer: 3. Interrelations among family members coping with parental cancer.* Unpublished manuscript, University of Vermont, Burlington.

Fiese, B. H., & Sameroff, A. J. (1989). Family context in pediatric psychology: A transactional perspective. *Journal of Pediatric Psychology, 14,* 293–314.

Folkman, S., & Lazarus, R. S. (1985). If it changes it must be a process: A study of emotion and coping during three stages of a college examination. *Journal of Personality and Social Psychology, 48,* 150–170.

Handford, H. A., Mayes, S. D., Mattison, R. E., Humphrey, F. J., Bagnato, S., Bixler, E. O., & Kales, J. D. (1986). Child and parent reactions to the Three Mile Island nuclear accident. *Journal of the American Academy of Child Psychiatry, 25,* 346–356.

Hauser, S. T., Jacobson, A. M., Wertlieb, D., Weiss-Perry, B., Follansbee, D., Wolfsdor, J. I., Herskowitz, R. D., Houlihan, J., & Rajapark, D. C. (1986). Children with recently diagnosed diabetes: Interactions with their families. *Health Psychology, 5,* 273–296.

Jay, S. M., & Elliott, C. H. (1990). A stress inoculation program for parents whose children are undergoing painful medical procedures. *Journal of Consulting and Clinical Psychology, 58*, 799–804.

Kazak, A. E. (1989). Families of chronically ill children: A systems and social-ecological model of adaptation and change. *Journal of Consulting and Clinical Psychology, 57*, 25–30.

Lazarus, R. S., & Folkman, S. (1984). *Stress, appraisal and coping.* New York: Springer.

Lystad, M. H. (1984). Children's responses to disaster: Family implications. *International Journal of Family Psychiatry, 5*, 41–60.

Lystad, M. H. (1985). Human response to mass emergencies: A review of mental health research. *Emotional First Aid, 2*, 5–18.

Manne, S. L., Redd, W. H., Jacobsen, P. B., Gorfinkle, K., Schorr, O., & Rapkin, B. (1990). Behavioral intervention to reduce child and parent distress during venipuncture. *Journal of Consulting and Clinical Psychology, 58*, 565–572.

McFarlane, A. C. (1987). Posttraumatic phenomena in a longitudinal study of children following a natural disaster. *Journal of the American Academy of Child and Adolescent Psychiatry, 26*, 764–769.

McFarlane, A. C., Policansky, S. K., & Irwin, C. (1987). A longitudinal study of the psychological morbidity in children due to a natural disaster. *Psychological Medicine, 17*, 727–738.

Miller, S. M. (1980). When is a little information a dangerous thing? Coping with stressful life-events by monitoring vs. blunting. In S. Levine & H. Ursin (Eds.), *Coping and health* (pp. 145–169). New York: Plenum Press.

Moos, R. H., & Moos, B. S. (1986). *Family Environment Scale Manual.* Palo Alto, CA: Consulting Psychologists Press.

Murphy, L. B., & Moriarity, A. E. (1976). *Vulnerability, coping and growth.* New Haven: Yale University Press.

Peterson, L. (1989). Coping by children undergoing stressful medical procedures: Some conceptual, methodological, and therapeutic issues. *Journal of Consulting and Clinical Psychology, 57*, 380–387.

Peterson, L., Harbeck, C., Chaney, J., Farmer, J., & Thomas, A. M. (1990). Children's coping with medical procedures: A conceptual overview and integration. *Behavioral Assessment, 12*, 197–212.

Reiss, D. (1981). *The family's construction of reality.* Cambridge: Harvard University Press.

Reiss, D., Oliveri, M. E., & Curd, K. (1981). Family paradigm and adolescent social behavior. In H. D. Grotevant & C. R. Cooper (Eds.), *Adolescent development in the family: New directions for child development* (Vol. 22, pp. 77–91). San Francisco: Jossey-Bass.

Rothbaum, F., Weisz, J. R., & Snyder, S. S. (1982). Changing the world and changing the self: A two-process model of perceived control. *Journal of Personality and Social Psychology, 42*, 5–37.

Rubonis, A. V., & Bickman, L. (1991). Psychological impairment in the wake of disaster: The disaster-psychopathology relationship. *Psychological Bulletin, 109*, 384–399.

Seroka, C. M., Knapp, C., Knight, S., Siemon, C. R., & Starbuck, S. (1986). A comprehensive program for postdisaster counseling. *Social Casework: The Journal of Contemporary Social Work, 67*, 37–44.

Spivack, G., & Shure, M. B. (1982). The cognition of social adjustment: Interpersonal cognitive problem-solving thinking. In B. B. Lahey & A. E. Kazdin (Eds.), *Advances in clinical child psychology* (Vol. 5, pp. 323–372). New York: Plenum Press.

Titchener, J. L., & Ross, W. D. (1974). Acute and chronic stress as determinants of behavior, character, and neurosis. In S. Arieti & E. B. Brody (Eds.), *American handbook of psychiatry: Vol. 3. Adult clinical psychiatry* (2nd. ed., pp. 39–60).

Weisz, J. R., Rothbaum, F. M., & Blackburn, T. C. (1984). Standing out and standing in: The psychology of control in America and Japan. *American Psychologist, 39*, 955–969.
Wertlieb, D., Weigel, C., & Feldstein, M. (1987). Measuring children's coping. *American Journal of Orthopsychiatry, 57*, 548–560.
Wills, T. A. (1986). Stress and coping in early adolescence: Relationships to substance use in urban school samples. *Health Psychology, 5*, 503–529.
Worsham, N. L., Ey, S., & Compas, B. E. (1992). *When mom or dad has cancer: 2. Developmental consistencies and differences in coping with family stress.* Manuscript submitted for review.
Wortman, C. B., & Silver, R. C. (1989). The myths of coping with loss. *Journal of Consulting and Clinical Psychology, 57*, 349–357.

2

Posttraumatic Stress Disorder in Children and Adolescents

JANE M. KEPPEL-BENSON and THOMAS H. OLLENDICK

Prior to the 1950s, there was little systematic investigation into the effects of traumatic events on children or adolescents. Excepting the early work of Anna Freud on the effects of war on children (see Freud & Burlington, 1943), little scientific interest was evident. This is not to suggest that children and adolescents were free of trauma; to the contrary, their lives were characterized by considerable turmoil that today would be described as "out of the range of usual human experience" (American Psychiatric Association, 1987, p. 250). However, consistent with the "adultmorphic" conception of children that was prevalent at the time, children were viewed as miniature adults capable of handling the multitude of stresses to which they were subjected (Ollendick & Hersen, 1989).

In contrast, adult reactions to overwhelming stressors have been documented for many years. Terms such as *shell shock, traumatic neurosis,* and *nervous shock* existed prior to 1900 (Erichson, 1882; Trimble, 1985), and the diagnosis of "gross stress reaction" appeared in the first edition of the *Diagnostic and Statistical Manual* (DSM-I; American Psychiatric Association, 1952). The nomenclature used to describe adult reactions to stress has continued to evolve in the last decade, with the emergence of terms such as *survivor syndrome,* used to describe psychological sequelae of survivors from Nazi persecution; *post-Vietnam syndrome* for war veterans; and *rape-*

JANE M. KEPPEL-BENSON and THOMAS H. OLLENDICK • Department of Psychology, Virginia Polytechnic Institute and State University, Blacksburg, Virginia 24060.

Children and Disasters, edited by Conway F. Saylor. Plenum Press, New York, 1993.

trauma syndrome for victims of rape (Burgess & Holmstrom, 1974; Trimble, 1985). In the third edition of the *Diagnostic and Statistical Manual* (DSM-III; 1980), the American Psychiatric Association (APA) coined the term *posttraumatic stress disorder* (PTSD) and described the basic symptoms present in the current criteria. In the revised third edition of the manual (DSM-III-R; American Psychiatric Association, 1987), posttraumatic symptoms specific to children were added. This chapter focuses on this set of symptoms and related consequences of trauma in children and adolescents. We will describe the requirements for diagnosis, illustrate the symptoms with various examples from the literature, and suggest areas of future study.

MAKING THE DIAGNOSIS

According to its current criteria, posttraumatic stress disorder requires the experience of a traumatic event that is "outside the range of usual human experience" (e.g., a serious threat to one's life of physical integrity, the sudden destruction of one's home or community, witnessing the torture or death of a loved one; APA, 1987). Such events are deemed so severe that preexisting psychopathology is not necessary for victims to experience significant psychological sequelae (Eth & Pynoos, 1985b). That is, the event itself is so extreme that almost anyone would experience significant psychopathology and subsequent problems in adjustment. Other events, which are also stressful (e.g., going to school, the divorce of one's parents), are common events and do not meet criteria for a traumatic stressor (i.e., out of the realm of usual human experience).

Posttraumatic symptoms have been described in children and adolescents exposed to events including sexual abuse (Kiser, Ackerman, Brown, Edwards, McColgan, Pugh, & Pruitt, 1988; McLeer, Deblinger, Atkins, Foa, & Ralphe, 1988; Wolfe, Gentile, & Wolfe, 1989); natural disasters (Lonigan, Shannon, Finch, Daugherty, & Taylor, 1991; McFarlane, 1987); political unrest and war (Arroyo & Eth, 1985; Saigh, 1989); transportation accidents (Keppel & Ollendick, 1991; McCaffrey & Fairbank, 1985; Yule & Williams, 1990); and homicide (Malmquist, 1986; Pynoos & Nader, 1988; Pynoos, Frederick, Nader, Arroyo, Steinberg, Eth, Nunez, & Fairbanks, 1987).

One of the key variables in determining the impact of such events of children and adolescents is the child or adolescent's subjective interpretation of the trauma. Some children exposed to traumatic events appear to be unaffected by such events and do not develop adverse symptoms. Other children and adolescents develop some posttraumatic symptomatology, yet not all of the symptoms required for the diagnosis of PTSD. Still others exhibit all of the requisite symptoms but demonstrate them only in the acute phase, with a diminution of symptoms over the course of several days or weeks following the traumatic event. In all of these instances, we would not be describing posttraumatic stress disorder *per se.*

A diagnosis of PTSD is warranted when, following the experience of a trauma, an individual demonstrates a number of symptoms in three major categories: reexperiencing the event, avoiding aspects of the event or showing a general numbing of responsiveness, and becoming hyperaroused when in the presence of relevant stimuli. Furthermore, these symptoms must persist for a period of at least one month in order to meet the diagnosis of posttraumatic stress disorder. Children must demonstrate at least one of the reexperiencing symptoms, at least three of the avoidance or numbing symptoms, and at least two of the hyperarousal symptoms as described below (APA, 1987).

PTSD SYMPTOMATOLOGY

Reexperiencing Symptoms

Reexperiencing symptoms include recurrent and intrusive thoughts, dreams, or flashbacks of the trauma; repetitive traumatic play; and intense distress at reminders of the traumatic event. These symptoms are the hallmark of the diagnosis and set it apart from other anxiety disorders. Traumatized children and adolescents may experience distressing memories or have persistent recollections of the trauma in which they remember and replay aspects of the trauma over and over in their minds. For example, 14 months after a sniper attack at an elementary school in California, children on the playground where 1 child was killed and 13 were injured described continued thoughts and images of the deceased child, injured and bleeding classmates, bullets striking in the pavement, sounds of gunfire, and cries for help (Nader, Pynoos, Fairbanks, & Frederick, 1990). Intrusive recollections occur spontaneously, are typically not under a child's control, and cause victims significant psychological distress and discomfort.

Frequently, reexperiencing occurs in the form of horrifying nightmares. Although nightmares are common during childhood (Hartmann, Russ, Oldfield, Sivan, & Cooper, 1987), posttraumatic nightmares occur more frequently and include events that are trauma-specific. Pynoos *et al.* (1987) reported that over 75% of children involved in the sniper attack who suffered serve PTSD symptoms reported bad dreams involving the trauma. In fact, nightmares and sleep difficulties were the symptoms that best differentiated severe PTSD reactions from moderate reactions. Trauma-specific nightmares may change to bad dreams about other frightening things (e.g., ghosts, monsters) some time after the traumatic event (APA, 1987).

Children may also experience a sudden acting or feeling as if the trauma were re-occurring. Environmental cues such as sounds or smells similar to those present during the trauma may trigger children to feel as if the event were happening all over again. Such flashback experiences are reported to occur less frequently in children than in adults (APA, 1987; Lyons, 1987). However, in studies which have assessed the phenomenon, the percentages of children who have reported them range from 0% (Terr, 1979) to 100% (Malmquist, 1986).

The early PTSD literature suggested that, instead of flashbacks, young children were more likely to actively demonstrate memories of the trauma in their play. Terr (1979) first described posttraumatic play in children of Chowchilla, California, who were held captive for 11 hours and then "buried alive" for 16 hours. In this instance, three armed men hijacked their bus and transferred the children and their bus driver to two darkened vans in which the victims were driven around for 11 hours. The kidnappers then forced the group into a tractor-trailer, in which they were "buried alive" for 16 hours, until two of the boys finally dug them out. Terr noted that some of these children repeatedly played bus driver, kidnapping, or other trauma-related games. One 5-year-old girl began to bury her Barbie dolls just as she had been buried in the tractor-trailer (Terr, 1981).

As in the cases described above, posttraumatic play has oftentimes been described as "unproductive," repetitive play in which the child is stuck reliving the trauma and is unable to establish psychological distance from the traumatic event (Terr, 1981). However, trauma-related play can be therapeutic, as children may be assisted in working through the traumatic aspects of the event. For example, children may be coached to change the themes of their play (or they may spontaneously alter them) to move from the position of a helpless victim to that of a hero. A report of children exposed to hurricane Hugo in South Carolina revealed that many of the children played "hurricane" games until they were able to resolve their fears (Saylor, Swenson, & Powell, 1992).

Intrusive memories are often frightening for children and can make concentration difficult. Intrusions usually occur in quiet situations or those in which a child is functioning independently. Therefore, quiet times at school, times when alone at home, or times of falling asleep at night may be prime times for difficult, intrusive memories of trauma.

Avoidance or Numbing Symptoms

In the second set of criteria necessary for the diagnosis of PTSD, the characteristic symptoms of avoidance or numbing of responsiveness include: avoidance of thoughts and feelings associated with the trauma, avoidance of reminders of the event, an inability to recall aspects of the trauma, decreased interest in significant activities (in children, this may take the form of loss of previously acquired developmental skills), feeling detached or estranged from others, a restricted range of feelings, and a sense of a foreshortened future.

The pain involved in remembering and recounting aspects of a trauma makes a child or adolescent's reluctance to discuss it understandable. The very nature of the event leads traumatized individuals to avoid thoughts or feelings associated with it. Avoidance can be intentional, or it may occur without the conscious effort or awareness of the child. Often, avoidance can resemble resistance or noncompliance, such as in the case of an obviously distressed child (sulking, whimpering, despondent) who responds to a therapist's inquiry by insisting that she is "just fine." Frederick (1985, 1986) suggests that therapists proceed sensitively with traumatized children, encouraging a discussion of the trauma, but permitting protective defenses and guiding them at a pace which they can tolerate.

In addition to avoidance of thoughts or feelings, children may avoid activities which remind them of the traumatic event. A 12-year-old boy with PTSD following an automobile accident refused to accompany his mother on car trips to visit his sister as they would have to pass by the site of their automobile accident, which occurred 8 months earlier. Another 8-year-old who had been struck by a car 14 months earlier did not participate in trick-or-treating on Halloween because he was afraid of crossing streets (Keppel-Benson, 1992).

Sometimes, avoidance may include amnesia about important aspects of the trauma (APA, 1987). Adults who have been sexually abused as children, recall events that they have "forgotten" for up to 30 years. Such massive denial is theorized to protect the victim against intolerable levels of emotional upset (Horowitz, 1983). Most studies of traumatized children do not report evidence of amnesia. In fact, many children are reported to vividly describe aspects of traumatic events, such as being assaulted or witnessing the homicide or sexual assault of a parent (Malmquist, 1986; Pynoos & Nader, 1989), even when they are as young as 3 (Jones & Krugman, 1986). In a recent study, however, Yule and Williams (1990) describe the case of a 13-year-old girl involved in a ferryboat disaster off the coast of England. The girl was sitting in the cafeteria of the ferry with her mother when the boat capsized. The two were catapulted through a glass partition and fell into the water, where the mother drowned. Although the girl was near her mother for some time before she drowned and spent a total of two hours in the water before being rescued, she was unable to recall many details of the event after falling into the water.

Following a trauma, children also may show a general numbing of responsiveness. In some cases, this symptom may be manifested in a decreased interest in activities that were once exciting or reinforcing (e.g, hobbies, after-school activities). In other cases, children may show a decline in the maintenance of relationships that were once treasured. With young children, decreased responsiveness can be evidenced in the regression of developmental skills. For example, Pruett (1979) described the symptoms of a 3½-year-old boy and his 2-year-old sister who witnessed the shotgun murder of their mother by their father and his subsequent suicide attempt. Both children lost previously acquired toileting skills, and the boy requested to be fed instead of feeding himself. According to the children's maternal grandmother, the boy seemed to have "forgotten how to do anything for himself" (Pruett, 1979, p. 648). Such developmental regression is most frequently reported in children under age 7.

Decreased responsiveness in the form of emotional withdrawal may also occur following trauma. Vietnam veterans suffering from PTSD often report emotional withdrawal from life, not being able to feel happiness, sadness, and other emotions as keenly as they once did. Marital relationships also suffer as they are less able to trust and more likely to remain at a distance from others (Smith, 1985). This type of emotional numbing is difficult to evaluate in children, however. Because children are less adept at expressing such abstract emotions as "detachment," and because they are less likely to show negative emotions for extended periods of time (or extreme variability in their emotions), parents and other adults may not notice a child's emotional withdrawal even when it is present.

Finally, the last symptom in this cluster is a sense of a foreshortened future. This symptom refers to children developing more limited expectations about their future, such as never marrying, reaching adulthood, or having a career (APA, 1987). Some children involved in the Chowchilla kidnapping were reported to display these decreased expectations (Terr, 1983a,b). However, this finding is rarely reported in the literature.

Increased Arousal Symptoms

The third set of PTSD symptoms consists of those symptoms associated with increased arousal. Hyperarousal is characterized by sleep difficulties, irritability, difficulty concentrating, hypervigilance, and physiological reactivity to trauma-related stimuli. Difficulty sleeping was reported in all of the children who experienced the ferryboat disaster (Yule & Williams, 1990). These children and those in other disasters (Dollinger, 1986; Ollendick & Hoffman, 1982) often find concentration to be more difficult, which may result in a decline in performance at school. Irritability and outbursts of anger may occur because of heightened fears of losing control, blaming others for what happened to them, or increased agitation as a result of their own feelings of guilt (Milgram, 1989).

Children may display symptoms of hyperarousal when exposed to events that symbolize or resemble aspects of the trauma. Children who have been in car accidents are reported by their parents to "put on the brakes" in the back seat when the driver must stop suddenly (Keppel & Ollendick, 1991). Yule and Williams (1990) describe an 8-year-old boy who became terrified while riding on a double-decker bus. When the bus swayed as it turned a corner, the boy thought he was going to tip over like he did in the ferryboat three months earlier. Interestingly, this increased reactivity is alternated with the decreased or avoidant symptoms described earlier. Both phenomena are exercises of extremes and facilitate the diagnosis of the disorder.

Vietnam veterans diagnosed with PTSD can be distinguished from veterans without the disorder by more dramatic increases in heart rate and blood pressure when exposed to trauma-related stimuli (Pallmeyer, Blanchard, & Kolb, 1986). Such psychophysiological reactions have not been investigated in studies of children but would be an important contribution to the literature.

OTHER RELATED SYMPTOMS

Investigations of children and adolescents exposed to trauma frequently document other common symptomatology. Children and adolescents are reported to experience more trauma-related fears than normal control children (Dollinger, O'Donnell, & Staley, 1984; Wolfe et al., 1989; Yule, Udwin, & Murdoch, 1990), particularly with respect to fears of a recurrence of the trauma (Pynoos & Nader, 1988; Saylor et al., 1992). The experience of guilt has been reported for children who were unable to aid a victim or had to endure pleas for help from others whom they could not help. Pynoos and Nader (1987) report the tremendous sense of guilt experienced by an adolescent who was frozen in fear as he watched his mother's sexual assault. Similarly, the same authors report the guilt experienced by a sixth-grade boy who, prior to the sniper attack, had sent his younger brother to get their cousin. Both were pinned on the playground under the gunman's fire (Pynoos & Nader, 1988).

Traumatized children have also been found to display more behavioral disturbances than normative samples (Cohen & Mannarino, 1988; Friedrich, Urquiza, & Beilke, 1986; McLeer et al., 1988), but fewer behavioral disturbances than other clinical samples (Cohen & Mannarino, 1988). In many instances, their scores on frequently used measures of anxiety, depression, self-concept, and family functioning are not significantly different from the scores of normative samples (Cohen & Mannarino, 1988; Kiser et al., 1988; Wolfe et al., 1989; Yule & Udwin, 1991). These findings suggest that PTSD is a distinct diagnostic condition, which may not be detected on general measures of psychopathology that do not specifically measure PTSD symptomatology.

FACTORS AFFECTING SYMPTOM EXPRESSION

Traumatic Event

The nature of traumatic stressors varies tremendously. Some traumatic events are one-time occurrences, referred to as acute or *Type I traumas.* Other stressors are repeated, long-standing, or chronic, referred to as *Type II traumas* (Famularo, Kinscherff, & Fenton, 1990; Terr, 1991). Terr (1991) suggests that children exposed to Type I traumas evidence the typical PTSD symptoms of repetition, avoidance, and hyperalertness and are more likely to have intact recollections of the traumatic events, without amnesia. Children exposed to Type II traumas, on the other hand, are more likely to demonstrate long-standing characterological problems, increased detachment from others, sadness, restricted range of affect, and dissociation. Memories of Type II traumas are also less likely to be vivid, as children are more likely to blur memories of events that occur repeatedly over time.

In addition to the duration or chronicity of the trauma, factors such as the degree of exposure, the life threat involved, the prospect of loss, and the event of physical injury have been found to correlate modestly with adjustment following trauma. For example, Pynoos et al. (1987) found the degree of children's exposure to the sniper and his victim to be a significant predictor of subsequent adjustment. The degree of exposure was defined by the child's proximity to the murdered child (e.g., on the playground with the victim, in the school building, in the neighborhood, at home, absent and out of the vicinity of the school). Similarly, higher levels of persisting symptoms have been found to be associated with higher degrees of disaster exposure during the Buffalo Creek disaster. In this instance, the collapse of a slag mining dam and subsequent flood caused the deaths of 125 people and left thousands homeless for a prolonged period of time (Gleser, Green, & Winget, 1981). The element which may underlie the relationship between exposure and symptomatology is the degree to which the children felt their own lives were in danger. The degree of life threat has been shown to be a predictor of adult victims of sexual assault as well (Kilpatrick, Saunders, Amick-McMullan, Best, Veronen, & Resnick, 1989). Of course, this relationship is not always direct, as the child's subjective experience and interpretation of the event must also be taken into consideration.

Previous Traumatic Experiences

Prior experiences of traumatic and/or stressful events will have an impact on a child's adjustment. The sheer number of stressors impinging on children, their families, or their communities will increase the subjective experience of distress in geometric rather than arithmetical proportions (Rutter, 1979). If a second trauma occurs, it is likely to bring back memories of a previous one, even if the second trauma does not occur to them. For children involved in violent attacks or natural disasters, news of similar events can cause a recurrence of memories and feelings that had laid dormant for some time.

Premorbid Functioning and Developmental Considerations

Additionally, conditions that existed prior to the trauma must also be considered. Some important pre-trauma variables include preexisting psychopathology, cognitive development, and psychosocial development. Prior emotional conditions are likely to increase a child's vulnerability to stressful life events. Similarly, stressful events are likely to exacerbate preexisting or related symptomatology. A case presented by Gillis (1991) illustrates this reciprocal influence. At age 5, a young girl was diagnosed with separation anxiety disorder. Three years later, she experienced a sniper attack at her school. She responded with symptoms including heightened clingingness, sleep disturbance, and school phobia. In this case, the presence of separation anxiety disorder likely increased the child's vulnerability to related anxiety symptoms, while the experience of the sniper attack increased previously existing symptoms.

The cognitive developmental level of children also influences their responses to trauma. Cognitive development influences a child's interpretation of traumatic events, as well as his/her ability to report symptoms. For example, children who have witnessed or experienced sexual assaults often have a keen comprehension of the violent, aggressive aspects of the trauma, but they may be confused by the sexual aspects of the attack (Pynoos & Eth, 1985; Pynoos & Nader, 1987). Also, in contrast to adults, young children may be less aware of the realistic threat of harm implied in particular stressful situations and of the realistic coping options available to them (Milgram, 1989). Some reports suggest that preschoolers are more likely to fantasize about superheros or powerful others swooping down to help them in a traumatic situation. On the contrary, adolescents, who have the cognitive ability to accurately appraise the traumatic situation and their responses to it, may be more likely to experience guilt about not being able to stop the event, particularly given their tendency toward an inflated sense of power, control, and autonomy (Eth & Pynoos, 1985b).

Some clinical research suggests that children's responses to trauma or their reports of symptoms, reliably vary across preschoolers, school-aged children, and adolescents. Eth and Pynoos (1985a) report that preschoolers are more likely than older children to show internalizing behaviors such as separation anxiety, somatic complaints, and social withdrawal; School-aged children are reported to experience many of the classic symptoms of PTSD (e.g., reexperiencing symptoms, avoidance, and hyperarousal) and in some cases, decreased school performance. Adolescents are most likely to exhibit both internalizing and externalizing behavioral extremes (Lyons, (1987). Symptomatic adolescents may show increased anxiety, decreased energy, and greater dysphoria, as well as aggressive behavior, substance abuse, and acting-out behavior (Eth & Pynoos, 1985a).

As noted in the diagnostic criteria, traumatic events may cause developmental regression or loss of previously acquired developmental skills. The developmental tasks required of children at the time of exposure to trauma, or in the months following, may influence their response to the event. For example, adolescents, whose primary developmental task relates to identity formation (Erickson, 1963), may be more likely to respond to traumatic events with failure to address pertinent issues related to identity, such as occupational choices, value commitments, and personal philosophies. The lack of progression along the continuum of development, as well as developmental regression, are important indicators of distress which vary across the age range.

Posttrauma Variables

Lastly, factors relating to the recovery environment also appear to affect a child's response to trauma. Parental reactions to trauma have been reported to be the best predictor of a child or adolescent's adjustment (McFarlane, 1987). As young children are less familiar with the world around them, they rely on adult appraisals of threat and danger. It follows, then, that if parents communicate emotional distress to children, the children may be more likely to respond in kind (Milgram, 1989; Sullivan, Saylor, & Foster, 1991).

In addition to parents, other emotional supports are important for the adjustment of children and adolescents. It has been suggested that the plight of individuals involved in traumatic events may only begin with his or her exposure to the trauma (Janoff-Bulman & Frieze, 1983). Following the trauma, children and adolescents have to answer and adhere to procedures dictated by doctors, police, medical examiners, lawyers, and others. Often, the process of "secondary victimization" occurs, in which a social stigma adheres to the survivor (Ayalon, 1983). Examples of this phenomenon are reported in cases of childhood sexual abuse, incest, homicide, and war. Terr (1991) reports that, when a psychological shock mandates long-standing adjustment (e.g., when a shock leaves a child homeless, handicapped, disfigured or causes prolonged hospitalization and pain), co-existing conditions such as depression may result. Existing evidence suggests that the broader and deeper the network of social support, the greater the chance of ameliorating the negative effects of stressful life events (Cohen & Wills, 1985).

FUTURE DIRECTIONS

While our knowledge of responses of children to trauma has increased tremendously in the last 20 years, several areas of research remain undeveloped. Cross-cultural research of traumatized children, for example, is meager. Despite some indications of the cross-cultural validity of the PTSD diagnosis (Macksoud, 1991; Saigh, 1989), research is lacking about the influence of cultural contexts on trauma response. Similarly, research examining the influence of developmental level on children's responses to trauma also is limited.

One of the recent advances in examining developmental level is the use of methods that directly assess children's responses. Rather than rely on adult interpretations of children's responses to trauma, researchers have begun to ask the children themselves about their thoughts and feelings. Because the subjective interpretation of the trauma is essential to understanding the posttraumatic response, children's thoughts and feelings need to be directly assessed. Moreover, teachers and parents are often unaware of the impact of a trauma on children's mood and concentration (Keppel-Benson 1992; Yule & Williams, 1990). Parents may tend to minimize or deny their children's responses to trauma. Furthermore, if parents were involved in the trauma, they may discourage discussion of the trauma by their children because of their own avoidance symptoms.

These developmental considerations may lead to refinements of the

PTSD diagnostic criteria. For children, questions remain about the validity of including foreshortened-future or flashback experiences in the diagnostic criteria. For adults, as well as children, the differentiation between acute and chronic trauma and the respective sequelae needs further refinement. In particular, chronic trauma may be more closely aligned with dissociative disorders than with anxiety disorders.

Improvements in research methodology will provide an empirical basis for these refinements in diagnosis (see Garmezy, 1986, for a review of various research designs and their strengths and weaknesses). Methods which involve comparison groups, multimethod assessment, and diagnostic interviews are likely to lead to a better understanding of the features of PTSD in children.

REFERENCES

American Psychiatric Association. (1952). *Diagnostic and statistical manual of mental disorders*. Washington, DC: Author.
American Psychiatric Association. (1980). *Diagnostic and statistical manual of mental disorders*. (3rd ed.; DSM-III). Washington, DC: Author.
American Psychiatric Association. (1987). *Diagnostic and statistical manual of mental disorders*. (3rd ed., rev.; DSM-III-R). Washington, DC: Author.
Arroyo, W., & Eth, S. (1985). Children traumatized by Central American warfare. In S. Eth & R. S. Pynoos (Eds.), *Posttraumatic stress disorder in children* (pp. 103–120). Washington, DC: American Psychiatric Press.
Ayalon, O. (1983). Coping with terrorism: The Israeli case. In D. Meichenbaum & M.E. Jaremko (Eds.), *Stress reduction and prevention*. New York: Plenum Press.
Burgess, A. W., & Holmstrom, L. L. (1974). Rape trauma syndrome. *American Journal of Psychiatry, 131*, 981–986.
Cohen, J., & Mannarino, A. (1988). Psychological symptoms in sexually abused girls. *Child Abuse and Neglect, 12*, 571–577.
Cohen, S., & Wills, T. A. (1985). Stress, social support, and the buffering hypothesis. *Psychological Bulletin, 98*, 310–357.
Dollinger, S. J. (1986). The measurement of children's sleep disturbances and somatic complaints following a disaster. *Child Psychiatry and Human Development, 16*, 148–153.
Dollinger, S. J., O'Donnell, J. P., & Staley, A. A. (1984). Lightning-strike disaster: Effects on children's fears and worries. *Journal of Consulting and Clinical Psychology, 52*, 1028–1038.
Erichson, J. E. (1882). *On concussion of the spine: Nervous shock and other obscure injuries of the nervous system in their clinical and medico-legal aspects*. London: Longmans, Green.
Erickson, E. (1963). *Childhood and society* (2nd ed.) New York: Norton.
Eth, S., & Pynoos, R. (1985a). Developmental perspectives on psychic trauma in childhood. In C. R. Figley (Ed.), *Trauma and its wake*. New York: Brunner/Mazel.
Eth, S., & Pynoos, R. (Eds.). (1985b). *Post-traumatic stress disorder in children*. Washington, DC: American Psychiatric Press.
Famularo, R., Kinscherff, R., & Fenton, T. (1990). Symptom differences in acute and chronic presentation of childhood post-traumatic stress disorder. *Child Abuse and Neglect, 14*, 439–444.

Frederick, C. (1985). Children traumatized by catastrophic situations. In S. Eth & R. S. Pynoos (Eds.), *Post-traumatic stress disorder in children*. Washington, DC: American Psychiatric Press.

Frederick, C. (1986). Post-traumatic stress disorder and child molestation. In A. W. Burgess and C. R. Hartman (Eds.), *Sexual exploitation of patients by health professionals*. New York: Praeger.

Freud, A., & Burlington, D. T. (1943). *War and children*. New York: Foster Parents' Plan for War Children.

Friedrich, W. N., Urquiza, A. J., & Beilke, R. L. (1986). Behavior problems in sexually abused young children. *Journal of Pediatric Psychology, 11*, 47–57.

Garmezy, N. (1986). Children under severe stress: Critique and commentary. *Journal of the American Academy of Child Psychiatry, 25*, 384–392.

Gillis, H. M. (1991). Assessment and treatment of post-traumatic stress disorder in childhood. In P. A. Keller and S. R. Heyman (Eds.), *Innovations in clinical practice: A source book* (Vol. 10). Sarasota, Fl: Professional Resource Exchange.

Gleser, G. C., Green, B. L., & Winget, C. (1981). *Prolonged psychosocial effects of disaster: A study of Buffalo Creek*. New York: Academic Press.

Hartmann, E., Russ, D., Oldfield, M., Sivan, I., & Cooper, S. (1987). Who has nightmares? *Archives of General Psychiatry, 44*, 49–56.

Horowitz, M. J. (1983). Psychological response to serious life events. In S. Breznitz (Ed.), *The denial of stress*. New York: International Universities Press.

Janoff-Bulman, R., & Frieze, I. H. (1983). A theoretical perspective for understanding reactions to victimization. *Journal of Social Issues, 38*, 1–17.

Jones, D., & Brugman, R. (1968). Can a three-year-old child bear witness to her sexual assault and attempted murder? *Child Abuse and Neglect, 10*, 253–258.

Keppel, J. M., & Ollendick, T. H. (1991, Aug.). Children injured in automobile accidents: A focus on psychological adjustment. In R. W. Belter (Chair), *Short- and long-term effects of trauma in children and adolescents*. Symposium conducted at the meeting of the American Psychological Association, San Francisco.

Keppel-Benson, J. M. (1992). *Posttraumatic stress among children in automobile accidents*. Unpublished doctoral dissertation, Virginia Polytechnic Institute and State University, Blacksburg.

Kilpatrick, D. G., Saunders, B. E., Amick-McMullan, A., Best, C., Veronen, L. J., & Resnick, H. S. (1989). Victim and crime factors associated with the development of crime-related posttraumatic stress disorder. *Behavior Therapy, 20*, 199–214.

Kiser, L. J., Ackerman, B. J., Brown, E., Edwards, N. B., McColgan, E., Pugh, R., & Pruitt, D. B. (1988). Post-traumatic stress disorder in young children: A reaction to purported sexual abuse. *Journal of American Academy of Child and Adolescent Psychiatry, 27*, 645–649.

Lonigan, C. J., Shannon, M. P., Finch, A. J, Daugherty, T. K., & Taylor, C. M. (1991). Children's reactions to a natural disaster: Symptom severity and degree of exposure. *Advances in Behavior Research and Therapy, 13*(3), 135–154.

Lyons, J. A. (1987). Posttraumatic stress disorder in children and adolescents: A review of the literature. *Developmental and Behavioral Pediatrics, 8*, 349–356.

Macksoud, M. (1991, Aug.). *The war experiences of Lebanese children*. Paper presented at the annual meeting of the American Psychological Association, San Francisco.

Malmquist, C. P. (1986). Children who witness parental murder: Posttraumatic aspects. *Journal of the American Academy of Child Psychiatry, 25*, 320–325.

McCaffrey, R. J., & Fairbank, J. A. (1985). Posttraumatic stress disorder associated with transportation accidents: Two case studies. *Behavior Therapy, 16*, 406–416.

McFarlane, A. C. (1987). Posttraumatic phenomena in a longitudinal study of children following a natural disaster. *Journal of the American Academy of Child and Adolescent Psychiatry, 26,* 764–769.

McLeer, S. V., Deblinger, E., Atkins, M. S. Foa, E. B., & Ralphe, D. L. (1988). Post-traumatic stress disorder in sexually abused children. *Journal of American Academy of Child and Adolescent Psychiatry, 27,* 650–654.

Milgram, N. (1989). Children under stress. In T. H. Ollendick & M. Hersen (Eds.), *Handbook of child psychopathology* (2nd ed.). New York: Plenum Press.

Nader, K., Pynoos, R. S., Fairbanks, L., & Frederick, C. (1990). Children's PTSD reactions one year after a sniper attack at their school. *American Journal of Psychiatry, 147,* 1526–1530.

Ollendick, T. H., & Hersen, M. (Eds.). (1989). *Handbook of child psychopathology* (2nd ed.). New York: Plenum Press.

Ollendick, D. G., & Hoffman, M. (1982). Assessment of psychological reactions in disaster victims. *Journal of Community Psychology, 10,* 157–167.

Pallmeyer, T. P., Blanchard, E. B., & Kolb, L. C. (1986). The physiology of combat-induced post-traumatic stress disorder in Vietnam veterans. *Behavior Research and Therapy, 24,* 656–652.

Pruett, K. D. (1979). Home treatment for two infants who witnessed their mother's murder. *Journal of the American Academy of Child Psychiatry, 18,* 647–657.

Pynoos, R. S., & Eth, S. (1985). Children traumatized by witnessing acts of personal violence: Homicide, rape, or suicidal behavior. In S. Eth & R. Pynoos (Eds.), *Posttraumatic stress disorder in children.* Washington, DC: American Psychiatric Press.

Pynoos, R. S., & Nader, K. (1987). Children who witness the sexual assault of their mothers. *Journal of American Academy of Child and Adolescent Psychiatry, 27,* 567–572.

Pynoos, R. S., & Nader, K. (1988). Psychological first aid and treatment approach to children exposed to community violence: Research implications. *Journal of Traumatic Stress, 1,* 445–473.

Pynoos, R. S., & Nader, K. (1989). Children's memory and proximity to violence. *Journal of the American Academy of Child and Adolescent Psychiatry, 28,* 236–241.

Pynoos, R. S., Frederick, C., Nader, K., Arroyo, W., Steinberg, A., Eth, S., Nunez, F., & Fairbanks, L. (1987). Life threat and posttraumatic stress in school-age children. *General Archives of Psychiatry, 44,* 1057–1063.

Rutter, M. (1979). Protective factors in children's responses to stress and disadvantage. In M. W. Kent & J. E. Rolf (Eds.), *Primary prevention of psychopathology: Social competence in children* (Vol. 3). Hanover, NH: University Press of New England.

Saigh, P. (1989). The use of an in vitro flooding package in the treatment of traumatized adolescents. *Developmental and Behavioral Pediatrics, 10,* 17–21.

Saylor, C. F., Swenson, C. C., & Powell, P. (1992). Hurricane Hugo blows down the broccoli: Preschoolers' post-disaster play and adjustment. *Child Psychiatry and Human Development, 22,* 139–149.

Smith, J. A. (1985). Individual psychotherapy with Viet Nam veterans. In S. M. Sonnenberg, A. S. Blank, Jr., and J. A. Talbott (Eds.), *The trauma of war: Stress and recovery in Viet Nam veterans.* Washington, DC: American Psychiatric Press.

Sullivan, M. A., Saylor, C. F., & Foster, K. Y. (1991). Posthurricane adjustment of preschoolers and their families. *Advances in Behavior Research and Therapy, 13,* 163–171.

Terr, L. C. (1979). Children of Chowchilla; A study of psychic trauma. *Psychoanalytic Study of the Child, 34,* 547–623.

Terr, L. C. (1981). "Forbidden games": Post-traumatic child's play. *Journal of the American Academy of Child Psychiatry, 20,* 741–760.

Terr, L. C. (1983a). Chowchilla revisited: The effects of psychic trauma four years after a schoolbus kidnapping. *American Journal of Psychiatry, 140,* 1543–1550.

Terr, L. C. (1983b). Life attitudes, dreams, and psychic trauma in a group of "normal" children. *Journal of American Academy of Child Psychiatry, 22,* 221–230.

Terr, L. C. (1991). Childhood trauma: An outline and overview. *American Journal of Psychiatry, 148,* 10–20.

Trimble, M. R. (1985). Posttraumatic stress disorder: History of a concept. In C. R. Figley (Ed.), *Trauma and its wake: The study of posttraumatic stress disorder.* New York: Brunner/ Mazel.

Wolfe, V. V., Gentile, C., & Wolfe, D. A. (1989). The impact of sexual abuse on children: A PTSD formulation. *Behavior Therapy, 20,* 215–228.

Yule, W., & Williams, R. M. (1990). Post-traumatic stress reactions in children. *Journal of Traumatic Stress, 3,* 279–295.

Yule, W., & Udwin, O. (1991). Screening child survivors for posttraumatic stress disorders: Experiences from the "Jupiter" sinking. *British Journal of Clinical Psychology, 30,* 131–138.

Yule, W., Udwin, O., & Murdoch, D. (1990). The "Jupiter" sinking: Effects on children's fears, depression and anxiety. *Journal of Child Psychology and Psychiatry, 31,* 1051–1061.

3

Issues in the Assessment of Posttraumatic Stress Disorder in Children

A. J FINCH, Jr., and TIMOTHY K. DAUGHERTY

The assessment of posttraumatic stress disorder (PTSD) in children is of considerable interest because of the need for the rapid and accurate identification of children who are experiencing excessive stress following a natural or human-made disaster. Immediately following a disaster, the available resources must be efficiently used and mental health workers would like to be able to identify those individuals who are the most in need of services. In order to study or treat the disorder, we must be able to identify it. In addition, if we are going to treat the disorder and evaluate the effectiveness of the treatment, we need a reliable and valid measure of the disorder.

The purpose of the present chapter is to discuss the assessment of children's reactions to disaster. The authors will present a general discussion about methods of assessing behavioral and emotional adjustment in children. The advantages and disadvantages of the various methods will be discussed and measures which have been used in previous research in the area of children's reaction to disaster will be reviewed in light of their strengths and weaknesses.

A. J FINCH, Jr., and TIMOTHY K. DAUGHERTY • Department of Psychology, The Citadel, Charleston, South Carolina 29409.

Children and Disasters, edited by Conway F. Saylor. Plenum Press, New York, 1993.

POSTTRAUMATIC STRESS DISORDER IN CHILDREN

Before we begin a discussion of the assessment of PTSD in children following a natural disaster, we need to briefly review the symptoms of PTSD (for a more in-depth discussion of the clinical and diagnostic features of PTSD in children, see Keppel-Benson & Ollendick, 1993). In order to be diagnosed as having PTSD, the individual must have experienced an event outside the range of typical human experience, and this experience must be one which would be considered distressing to almost anyone. This event would be the particular disaster which the child had experienced.

In addition to having lived through the disaster, the individual must exhibit one of the following symptoms, which are related to reliving the trauma: (1) intrusive and recurrent distressing memories of the event, which may be manifested in children as repetitive play enacting the themes of the trauma; (2) recurrent dreams about the event which are distressing; (3) sudden feelings or action as if the trauma was occurring again; and (4) intense distress at exposure to events that represent or resemble aspects of the trauma. These symptoms vary from those which are known only to the individual (memories) to those that may be obvious to those around the person (distress to exposure).

The set of symptoms that is the most difficult to properly assess is the cluster of behaviors associated with avoidance. In PTSD, there must be at least three of the following avoidance symptoms: (1) attempts to avoid thoughts or feelings about the trauma; (2) attempts to avoid activities or situations that result in recollections of the trauma; (3) an inability to recall important aspects of the trauma; (4) a decreased interest in activities or in children, the loss of recently acquired developmental skills; (5) a feeling disconnected from others; (6) a restricted range of affect; and (7) a sense of a foreshortened future. These avoidance symptoms would make it very difficult for the person to respond positively when asked about the trauma. For example, a child might deny having symptoms associated with the trauma as a way of avoiding thinking about it. It could be argued that this type of avoidance makes the accurate assessment of PTSD in children impossible.

The final set of symptoms associated with PTSD has to do with increased arousal. Two of the following symptoms must be present: (1) difficulty sleeping; (2) irritability or outbursts of anger; (3) problems in concentrating; (4) hypervigilance; (5) an exaggerated startle response; and (6) physiological reactions to exposure to events associated with or symbolizing an aspect of the trauma. Again, these symptoms may or may not be obvious to those around the person, and in addition, some of the symptoms are frequently associated with other disorders (e.g., irritability is associated with depression).

TYPES OF MEASURES

A number of sources exist from which information can be obtained for the assessment of children after a disaster. In addition to the child, information may be obtained from parents, teachers, or peers, or from others familiar with the child. The following section addresses methods of obtaining the necessary information on which to base a diagnosis of posttraumatic stress disorder in children. Diagnoses should be based on all the available data, rather than on a single source of information. Any single measure serves as only one part of the data on which a diagnosis is to be based.

Rating Scales

Although there are a number of different types of rating scales, only those that are based on a cumulative, nonsystematic observation of the individual will be discussed here. For example, a teacher who has worked with a child over several weeks or months might be employed as a rater. Ratings differ from natural observations or time samples in that they are based on data that are accumulated casually and informally. In addition, ratings usually involve some interpretation and judgment rather than simple counting, they cover a longer observation period, and the observations are made under more naturalistic conditions.

Advantages of Rating Scales. The first advantage of rating scales is that they are relatively inexpensive in terms of the clinician's time. They can be completed by someone who is already familiar with the child over an extended period of time. Consequently, the rater can be someone who is familiar with the child's behavior, and the clinician has the advantage of this experience. The longer, more intimate perspective of such a rater may be particularly important and useful when the clinician or researcher is called in from the "outside" to assist in the disaster aftermath. Another advantage of rating scales is that many are relatively objective and behaviors can be described in terms that can be readily understood. As mentioned earlier, some interpretation and judgment can be used. Although the use of interpretation and judgment can be a potential source of error in the ratings, a great deal can be done to improve the accuracy of a rating scale by carefully defining the traits or characteristic being discussed. In addition, by closely tying the items to behaviors, ambiguity due to trait names can be reduced.

Disadvantages of Rating Scales. Ratings are subject to a number of measurement errors. The types of errors which can affect rating scales will be discussed in some detail because a number of these errors can be applied to other methods of measuring PTSD in children. The best known of the type of error associated with rating scales is the halo effect. The term *halo effect* refers to the tendency for raters to be unduly influenced by a single favorable or unfavorable characteristic, which sways the rater's opinion of the individual in other areas. A number of studies have indicated that children who are popular are rated as having a number of other desirable characteristics which they may or may not possess, while unpopular children tend to be rated as having a number of unsubstantiated negative characteristics (Foster & Ysseldyke, 1976). Other studies have suggested that children who have endured other sorts of trauma (e.g., cancer treatment) may be viewed in an unusually favorable light by teachers completing rating scales (Fryer, Saylor, Finch, & Smith, 1989). The best way to reduce the halo effect is to define traits as closely as possible in terms of specific behaviors. For example, an item like "appears nervous" is more prone to the halo effect than is "complains of stomachaches or headaches." Another technique that can be employed to reduce the halo effect involves reversing the favorable and unfavorable direction of different traits and thus emphasizing the distinctness of each trait.

Another source of error with rating scales is called the *error of central tendency*, which refers to the reluctance of raters to use the extreme points of rating scales. Some investigators have recommended employing an even number of points to help reduce this error source.

A final source of error with rating scales involves the tendency for raters to vary in their frame of reference. For example, many teachers who work with emotionally disturbed children become more tolerant of the children's behaviors. Consequently such a teacher might rate the same child much differently than would the regular classroom teacher who was not accustomed to working with such children. Following a natural disaster, informants may use the exposed population of children as their "normative" frame of reference, resulting in misleading scores that do not exceed those obtained by nonexposed populations. Emphasizing the need to rate the child with reference to the normal (non- or preexposed child) helps reduce this problem, but this source of error has been found to be one of the most difficult with which to deal.

Rating scales have a number of other disadvantages that are more related to their nature than to sources of error. First, with reference to posttraumatic stress, ratings do not attend to the subjective experiences and feelings of the child since they are usually completed by someone other than the child. Because many of the symptoms of PTSD are subjective experiences, they may not be observable by the rater.

Another problem that is related to rating scales is the fact that they frequently employ untrained raters. For example, the parents of a child may lack the reading ability and/or the experience with rating scales to properly complete the form. There are several strategies that the examiner can employ to circumvent this problem. First, by keeping the rating scale as closely related to behaviors as possible, the examiner can ensure that too much inference or judgment is not required. In addition, the examiner can help the parent complete a couple of the items to ensure that the individual understands the items and the format of the rating scale. Of course, each of these procedures requires more time of the examiner, thus reducing one the advantages of rating scale.

Specific Rating Scales. We will now turn to specific rating scales or behavior checklists and discuss their use. The following discussion is not exhaustive but will focus on some of the more respected and frequently cited measures. The Children's Behavior Questionnaires (Rutter, Tizzard, & Whitmore, 1970) were designed to screen for behavior problems at home and at school through parent and teacher report scales. The two questionnaires each include 26 examples of behavioral problems, to which the reporter responds 0 ("Does not apply"), 1 ("Applies somewhat"), or 2 ("Certainly applies"). Typically, item responses are summed to a total, and scores of 9 or above are taken to suggest a risk of behavioral or emotional disturbance. However, factor-analytic studies have suggested up to six factors rather than a single one (McFarlane, 1987; McGee, Williams, Bradshaw, Chapel, Robins, & Silva, 1985; Venables, Fletcher, Dalais, Mitchell, Schulsinger, & Mednick, 1983). Several studies using the questionnaires have supported the idea that children with posttraumatic stress symptomatology may be at risk, in general, for behavioral and emotional problems (Galante & Foa, 1986; McFarlane, 1987; McFarlane, Policansky, & Irwin, 1987). However, McFarlane (1987) found no one-to-one correspondence between PTSD and factor scores on the Rutter *et al.* questionnaires, suggesting that the questionnaires are not appropriately used as a screening device for PTSD *per se* (McFarlane, 1987).

The Child Behavior Checklist (CBCL; Achenbach & Edelbrock, 1983) assesses social competence and behavioral problems in children from ages 4 to 18. Both parent and teacher report scales are available. The reporter is asked to indicate which of 118 behavioral descriptors are not true (0), sometimes true (1), or often true (2) of the child. The factor structure of the instrument varies somewhat with age and gender, though the second-order factors, Externalizing and Internalizing, are relatively stable. The psychometric properties of the CBCL are generally quite strong as regards its use in behavioral psychopathology (Achenbach & Brown, 1991). However, reliability and validity must be established for each distinct use of an instrument (Novick, 1985), and rather little is known about the CBCL's properties in screening for PTSD in children.

The CBCL has been successfully used in distinguishing abused children with PTSD from abused children without PTSD (McLeer, Deblinger, Atkins, Foa, & Ralphe, 1988), and appears sensitive to PTSD treatment effects (Deblinger, McLeer, & Henry, 1990). However, supporting studies have focused on gross behavioral disturbance and do not suggest that the CBCL can differentially screen for PTSD versus other forms of childhood psychopathology. To address differential validity, Wolfe, Gentile, and Wolfe (1989) have identified 20 items from the CBCL, on rational grounds, that are associated with symptoms of PTSD. These investigators reported an internal consistency of .89 for the scale, based on data from 68 sexually abused children (Wolfe et al., 1989). Though a potentially promising application of the CBCL, the use of the Wolf et al. (1989) items to screen for PTSD needs to be studied further.

The Conners Teacher Rating Scale (Conners, 1969) and the Revised Behavior Problem Checklist (Quay & Peterson, 1983) have similarly been used in research on childhood PTSD, and, as is the case with the CBCL and the Rutter et al. questionnaires, these checklists are sensitive to associated behavior problems but are yet unable to differentially screen for PTSD (e.g., Handford, Mayes, Mattison, Humphrey, Bagnato, Bixler, & Kales, 1986) as opposed to general psychopathology or behavioral-emotional distress.

Peer Nominations

Peer nomination scales involve having a group of children in a specified setting (e.g., a certain classroom, unit, or cottage) nominate one or more individuals who are described by a certain characteristic. For example, the item might read "Gets angry easily." In this case, each child in the class would respond by circling the names of any members of the class who could be described as getting angry easily. Since each item must be followed by a full class list, forms can be very lengthy.

Advantages of Peer Nominations. Much as sociometric measures have the advantage of obtaining information from the individuals who know the child the best (other children), so do peer nominations. Sociometric measures of popularity are the best predictors of later adjustment in children, and it would seem likely that peer nomination measures will prove equally as useful. Parents may not observe or report the high levels of posttraumatic stress symptoms in their children that the children themselves report after a disaster (e.g., Belter, Dunn, Foster, Imm, & Jeney-Gammon, 1990). It is possible that children may be more aware of their peers' distress and less inhibited about noting it, as compared to adults in the postdisaster environment. In addition to employing raters who are very familiar with the child, peer nomination procedures are inexpensive in terms of the amount of time required for the examiner to collect the measures.

Disadvantages of Peer Nominations. As was mentioned previously with rating scales, peer nomination has the problem that much of the subjective experience associated with posttraumatic stress may not be observable to others, even the child's peers. However, it could be argued that more of this information would be available to the peers than would be available to parents or other adults. In addition, if a disaster such as a school shooting has affected some children and not others, the raters may not be "blind"or unbiased as they make their peer nominations.

Another set of problems associated with peer nomination measurement, particularly after a disaster, has to do with ethical issues. When an entire class has to complete a form that can include information on every other child in the class, one becomes concerned about the multiple ethical considerations. In addition to protecting confidentiality, the researcher must consider that measurement is often reactive, such that completing the form may change how children treat one another. Requesting negative nominations or ratings of negative behavior may, for instance, appear to encourage negative evaluations of peers, perhaps leading some children to become yet more socially alienated. Bell-Dolan, Foster, and Sikora (1989) studied the effects of sociometric testing on children and found no negative effects when the testing was appropriately administered. Still, the peer nomination format should be used only after careful consideration of its impact and risks.

As was mentioned in relation to rating scales, a potential problem in peer nomination procedures is the halo effect: the tendency for a rating on one item to influence ratings on other items. For example, most positive attributes tend to be positively correlated with popularity, whereas most negative attributes are correlated with each other. One way to reduce this problem is to have items that are positive, negative, and neutral on the same measure.

Finally, in considering the use of peer nominations, one should be aware of the amount of time needed to score the forms, as each must be reviewed individually. With the widespread availability of computers, this limitation can be reduced somewhat. To date, no known studies have used peer nomination to study children's reactions to disaster. However, this method of assessment would appear to have potential.

Structured Interviews

The interview has long been the infrastructure on which the diagnostic evaluation is based. Within the last few years, there has been increased interest in and attention to improving the reliability and validity of the clinical interview. One of the main themes in this area has been structured interviews that are designed to reduce the "information variance" as an error factor. Structured interview measures of PTSD are clinical ratings that are made following a standardized interview with the child and/or the parent. Most of the standardized structured-interview measures that are currently available are comprehensive diagnostic measures and are not specifically designed to inquire into posttraumatic stress in isolation. They differ from the usual clinical interview in that they are structured according to what questions will be asked and what sequence the questions will follow. In attempting to reduce the amount of variability in the information obtained, they provide a group of standardized questions that are asked by the interviewer. One of the problems with the traditional interview has to do with the interviewer making decisions based on limited information which may result in certain areas not being investigated. Structured interviews help to ensure that a wide range of information is obtained in a systematic manner. These interviews vary in the degree to which they depend on clinical judgment, the degree to which they are structured, and the level of expertise required of the interviewer.

Advantages of Structured Interviews.   There are several major advantages to clinical interviews. First, they may allow the maximum use of clinical judgment and highly trained personnel. Just as one cannot measure taste and smell without human judgment, it could be argued that there are many clinical issues that require human (clinical) judgment. Still, the use of clinical judgment introduces considerable variance into measurement because various examiners ask different questions and therefore base their judgment on different information. The *structured* clinical interviews have attempted to reduce the amount of clinician variance obtained from interviews by providing the examiner with a standard set of decision rules to guide questions. Clinician variance is reduced while clinical insights are maintained through the use of structured interviews.

An advantage of some structured clinical interviews is that they can be conducted by minimally trained individuals and retain their reliability. This flexibility may be of considerable importance when there is a need to screen a large number of individuals following a disaster. Local volunteers can be trained quickly, and the interviews can begin with minimal delay.

Disadvantages of Structured Interviews. Just as clinical judgment can be an advantage of using a structured interview, it may present a problem. The trouble with clinical judgment is that not everyone has good clinical judgment and not everyone arrives at the same judgment. Consequently, problems in reliability and validity increase as the degree of clinical judgment allowed in a structured interview rises. In a structured clinical interview, there are ways of improving reliability and validity. The amount of structure in the interview is important. The more structured and objective the interview, the more reliable it is likely to be. A number of the interview measures have approached the problems of reliability and validity by being very structured. Of course, something is lost by making the interview too structured. Clinical judgment tends to be minimized when the interview schedules are more structured. If the interviewer is highly trained and is also a very good clinician, considerable information may be lost.

Specific Structured Interviews. Much early research on childhood reactions to traumatic stress relied on unstructured clinical observations (e.g., Terr, 1981). Although these observations provided useful insights into the nature of PTSD in children, reliable standardized means of assessment begged existence for use in larger scale research. The advent of structured interviews has made possible the rapid, standardized gathering of large amounts of diagnostic data, often by persons with limited professional training. The two most promising instruments sensitive to children with PTSD appear to be the DICA and the DISC.

The Diagnostic Interview for Children and Adolescents (DICA-R) includes supplemental questions for diagnosing PTSD in children. The parent (Reich, 1991a) and child (1991b) versions of the interview allow multi-informant data collection. The DICA-R is highly structured and can be administered by nonspecialists with relatively brief training. Some preliminary data on the DICA-R have been published (Earls, Smith, Reich, & Jung, 1988; Stoddard, Norman, & Murphy, 1989), but its reliability and validity are yet uncertain.

The Diagnostic Interview Schedule for Children (DISC) also has a module for diagnosing PTSD (DISC2.1 PTSD Module; Fisher & Kranzler, 1990). The DISC interviews, the most structured of those available, were designed for epidemiological research using laypersons as interviewers. The psychometric properties of the DISC appear problematic with pre-adolescents, but the DISC, like other interviews, must be considered *in development* (Edelbrock, Costello, Dulcan, Kalas, & Conover, 1985).

Several specific interviews have been developed by PTSD researchers (e.g., Famularo, Kinscherf, & Fenton, 1990; Pynoos & Eth, 1986). Rather than continuing to develop alternatives, the field may be better served by ardently seeking to validate the many options that exist. Though still in development, the DICA and the DISC remain the optimal choice for researchers, particularly when lay interviewers are involved.

Projective Assessment

During the sixties and seventies, projective assessment fell into disfavor within much of psychology. With the behavioral movement and the increased emphasis on "science," many of the projective techniques that had played such an important role in the development of psychology were abandoned or at least forced into the closet. This was a necessary developmental step for psychology. However, we are now entering a new stage, and it is time for us to reexamine projective assessment. In fact, this process has been taking place, and the advancements in the last few years have been extensive.

Disadvantages of Projective Assessment. There have been a number of problems with projective techniques. First, there have been questions of reliability, which have taken several forms. Reliability of scoring is frequently an issue. Because much of the material obtained by projective techniques is in "raw" form, it has to be coded in some way that can be quantified. This coding may be very complex and difficult. For example, Exner (1986) has developed the Comprehensive System for the Rorschach. This system has numerous variables, as well as definitions for coding these variables. Despite the herculean efforts of Exner and his colleagues, it is difficult to reach acceptable interscorer reliability without considerable training.

Other issues of reliability have to do with interpretation. Do two examiners interpret the same data to mean the same thing? Again, if we take the Rorschach as an example, there are at least two diametrically opposed systems of interpretation. First, there is the structural approach, which is represented by Exner and his colleagues. In this approach, there is an attempt to remain very close to the empirical data that are available and to be cautious in the interpretation. In contrast to this structural approach, there is the conceptual approach, which comes more from the phenomenological tradition and is represented by Lerner (1991). The conceptual approach begins with a theoretical position and interprets the responses of the individual in the context of the theory. With regard to the reliability of interpretation, do the structural and the conceptual approaches result in the same interpretations? Limited work has been done in this area, but the potential for a lack of correspondence would appear high.

Another concern with projective techniques has been focused on issues of validity. Do projective techniques measure what they are supposed to measure? This issue has been at the heart of much of the criticism level at projective testing. Limited use of projective assessment in evaluating the effects of trauma has been attempted to date.

Advantages of Projective Assessment. The projective hypothesis suggests that individuals will organize an ambiguous situation in terms of previous experiences and internal needs. Projective assessment capitalizes on this tendency by presenting the individual with an ambiguous test demand and carefully monitoring the response. Projective testing may be useful, in the postdisaster environment, in either of two cases.

First, very young children may lack the language to respond reliably and validly to many available objective tests. Projective techniques provide the opportunity to communicate in an alternative medium (e.g., through drawings, play, and storytelling). For example, Abrams (1991) suggested that "kinesthetic damage," the symbolic expression of a threat to bodily integrity, in the drawings of young children may be pathognomic of trauma. Saylor, Swenson, and Powell (1992) reported posthurricane drawings and play in preschoolers that seemed to be projective representations of their experiences and fears. Controlled research is needed to support these anecdotal findings.

Second, some experiences and impulses may be defended against, so that the key symptoms of PTSD become inaccessible through direct objective assessment. The PTSD symptoms of numbing and avoidance may fall into this category. Theoretically, projective tests circumvent the defense mechanisms. Dollinger and Cramer (1990) found evidence supporting the hypothesis that defense mechanisms protect child victims from further trauma. Thus, a well-defended child victim of trauma may escape detection by objective measures.

Quantifying projective data is not impossible, but it may be a tedious task. Case-study and anecdotal data suggest that visual art (e.g., drawing) and oral art (e.g., storytelling) may be useful in both assessment and intervention (Klingman, Koenigsfeld, & Markman, 1987; Lystad, 1984). Dollinger (1985) demonstrated that it is possible to develop an apparently reliable system for coding thematic apperception responses to trauma-specific pictures. Still, techniques that are flexible enough to allow for the collection of normative data from a variety of populations are needed.

Self-Report Measures

Self-report measures are measures that ask individuals to respond to a number of statements as they apply to themselves. Traditionally, such measures have been of true-false, yes-no, rating, or option selection format.

Advantages of Self-Report Measures. Self-report measures have the advantage of obtaining information from the individual who is of interest and have the potential to access the subjective feelings that are part of PTSD. For example, fears, intrusive thoughts, and overwhelming feelings related to the disaster may be experienced by the child privately though not disclosed or demonstrated to others. From a practical standpoint, self-report measures are inexpensive for the examiner in that the subject can complete them without the examiner or with the assistance of less expensive personnel.

Disadvantages of Self-Report Measures. There have been a number of arguments against the use of self-report measures. These arguments have centered around the lack of correspondence between scores obtained on self-report measures and observable behaviors. When the results of the self-report differ from those from other sources, the researcher or clinician is faced with having to determine which information to accept. The problem is particularly prominent in child populations since the language of children is not as developed as that of the adult which limits their ability to report subjective feelings. In addition, the child may be unwilling or unable to report accurately. We have been struck by the number of children who seem to be unable or unwilling to express or label their feelings despite the fact that they appear to be attempting to cooperate in other ways. There are a number of reasons for this observation. Children may be hesitant to share information due to their past history of having been punished because of their feelings or because many of their feelings are painful. In the postdisaster environment, there may be an implicit or explicit message from already burdened parents about whether the child should express or admit to feelings about the trauma (Belter, Dunn, & Jeney, 1991). Whether this hesitancy to express painful experiences is conscious or unconscious is probably dependent on the individual child.

Finally, in our work, we have found that there are a large number of children who are unable to label or identify feelings. This inability does not appear to be due to defensiveness on their part but rather to be associated with an actual deficit. *Alexithymia* is the term that has been suggested to describe this inability to express feelings (Apfel & Sifneos, 1979). Research in this area has been basically nonexistent in children.

Specific Self-Report Measures

Self-Report Measures of Central Features of PTSD. The Impact of Events Scale (IES; Horowitz, Wilner, & Alvarez, 1979) is a 15-item scale initially developed for adults, with both self-report and clinician-report versions. The scale putatively measures two features of PTSD: intrusion (7 items) and avoidance (8 items). The response format requires the subjects to indicate the frequency of symptoms as "Not at all" (0), "Rarely" (1), "Sometimes" (3), or "Often" (5). Total scores are computed by the summing of item responses for each subscale.

Internal consistencies for both the intrusion subscale (.88) and the avoidance subscale (.89) have been reported for adult subjects (Zilberg, Weiss, & Horowitz, 1982). Similarly, test–retest reliability reportedly ranges from .86 to .90 (Zilberg et al., 1982). At least three studies (Jones & Ribbe, 1991; Malmquist, 1986; Yule & Williams, 1990) have used the IES to assess children's reactions to trauma. However, the psychometric properties of the IES have yet to be adequately established for child and adolescent populations.

The Reaction Index (RI; Frederick, 1985a) is a 20-item inventory of symptoms based primarily on diagnostic criteria in the third edition of the American Psychiatric Association's *Diagnostic and Statistical Manual* (DSM-III; APA, 1980) and in the revised third edition of the manual (DSM-III-R; APA, 1987). The RI can be administered in an interview format or in a paper-and-pencil self-report format. The age range for the RI spans from age 5 (Pynoos, Frederick, Nader, Arroyo, Steinberg, Eth, Nunez, & Fairbanks, 1987) to adulthood (Frederick, 1987). Responses vary from 0 to 4 ("None of the time," "Little of the time," "Some of the time," "Much of the time," or "Most of the time"), and a total score is calculated by a summing of the responses. Also, a dichotomous (symptom present vs. absent) format has been used (Frederick, 1985b) and may be particularly appropriate for subjects with cognitive limitations. Though Pynoos et al. (1987) reported a three-factor structure (using a principle components analysis of a 16-item version of the RI), most investigators have treated the RI as unifactorial (Applebaum & Burns, 1991; Bradburn, 1991; Frederick, 1985b; Nader, Pynoos, Fairbanks, & Frederick, 1990).

The unifactorial RI has reasonably good internal consistency (.85; Lonigan, Shannon, Finch, Daugherty, & Taylor, 1991) and interrater reliability (.95, Applebaum & Burns, 1991; .77, Frederick, 1987), though the five reverse-coded items may tend to add little common variance. Daugherty, Finch, Shannon, and Lonigan (1991) suggested that, given the cognitive demands of the response format, individual researchers and clinicians using the RI should consider modifying the instrument so that all items are coded in the same direction. If using the RI as an informant-report measure, researchers may wish to maintain the reverse coding in order to reduce the halo effect (see above).

Evidence for the concurrent validity of the RI is mounting. Frederick (1985b) reported that RI scores correlated with known cases of PTSD at a .95 level in adults and a .91 level in children. Furthermore, RI scores are predictably related to the amount of exposure to the trauma (Bradburn, 1991; Lonigan et al., 1991; Nader et al., 1990; Pynoos et al., 1987).

The Children's PTSD Inventory (Saigh, 1989) is a self-report measure with a dichotomous response format. The four subtests of the inventory are designed to measure traumatization, unwanted trauma-related ideation, general affect, and diverse symptoms.

In field trials, the instrument obtained a true positive rate of 84% (kappa = .78, $p < .01$), in support of its valid use as a screen for PTSD in children (Saigh, 1989). The inventory appears to be worthy of continued investigation in the search for psychometric support.

The Fear Survey Schedule for Children (FSSC; Scherer & Nakamura, 1968) is an 80-item self-report scale. Ollendick's revision of the FSSC (the FSSC-R) (1983) is comprised of the same 80 items with a 3-point response format (as opposed to the 5-point format of the original scale) that takes into consideration the cognitive limitations of young and mentally retarded children. Five factors have emerged from factor analysis (Ollendick, King, & Frary, 1989): fear of failure and criticism, fear of the unknown, fear of injury and small animals, fear of danger and death, and medical fears.

Good internal consistency and short-term reliability have been reported for the FSSC-R (Ollendick et al., 1989), and it appears to produce results consistent with the original version. Thus, a fair amount of past research may be applicable to the evidence for the revised instrument's valid use for children. Furthermore, some data support its valid use in the measurement of PTSD-related fears in children (Ollendick, Yule, & Ollier, 1990).

The Louisville Fear Survey for Children (LFSC; Miller, Barrett, Hampe, & Noble, 1972) is an 81-item self-report or parent-report scale. Form B of the LFSC has been expanded to include 104 items, putatively the "most exhaustive list of fears" available in a fear instrument (Dollinger, O'Donnell, & Staley, 1984). Five factors emerge from a factor analysis of

Form B: fear of physical injury, fear of animals, fear of public places, night fears, and school-related fears (Staley & O'Donnell, 1984).

Good internal consistency has been reported for both forms of the LFSC (Dollinger et al., 1984; Staley & O'Donnell, 1984), but temporal reliability has yet to be determined. Dollinger et al. (1984) provided some support for the valid use of both forms of the LFSC in assessing phobic reactions of children following a natural disaster (a lightning strike). In doing so, however, theoretically derived rather than empirically derived factors were used (Dollinger et al., 1984). It is worth noting that the five empirical factors of the LFSC appear to differ from the five empirical factors of the FSSC-R; the selection of an instrument may depend largely on which types of fears one suspects will be present.

Self-Report Measures of Associated Features of PTSD. PTSD is classified as an anxiety disorder, and children's self-reported negative affectivity following trauma has been explored in a number of studies. However, most research has failed to find elevated anxiety scores among trauma-exposed children. For example, the Children's Manifest Anxiety Scale (CMAS; Castenada, McCandless, & Patermo, 1956) and its revision (RCMAS; Reynolds & Richmond, 1978) did not appear to differentiate the general population from children exposed to war (Ziv & Israeli, 1973), nautical accidents (Yule & Udwin, 1991), nuclear accidents (Handford et al., 1986), and natural disaster (Lonigan et al., 1991). Similar findings exist for the State-Trait Anxiety Inventory for Children (STAIC; Spielberger, 1973) and for the Children's Depression Inventory (CDI; Kovacs, 1983).

Still, some researchers have found significant elevations on these general measures and other measures among trauma-exposed children (Deblinger et al., 1990). The construct of PTSD would suggest that state measures of anxiety and depression might be most appropriately employed to evaluate the syndrome itself, while trait anxiety measures might suggest a premorbid vulnerability (Daugherty et al., 1991).

The Minnesota Multiphasic Personality Inventory (MMPI; Hathaway & McKinley, 1951) can be administered to adolescents as young as approximately 13 if they have sixth-grade reading ability (Archer, 1987). Keane, Malloy, and Fairbank (1984) developed a combat-related PTSD subscale of MMPI items and also noted that an 8-2 code type (with elevated F scale) was common among PTSD veterans. Although the Keane subscale may be of dubious utility for noncombat PTSD, the typical profile pattern for adolescent PTSD sufferers may be similar to what Keane et al. reported for adults (Earl, 1991; Frederick, 1985a). The utility of the MMPI-2 (Butcher, Dahlstrom, Graham, Tellegen, & Kraemer, 1989) in identifying adolescent sufferers of PTSD has yet to be explored.

Physiological Measures

Physiological measures such as galvanic skin response, heart rate, and respiration rate have been used in the study of anxiety for an extended period of time. However, limited use has been made of physiological measures in studying the effects of disaster in children.

Advantages of Physiological Measures.   One of the main advantages of physiological measures is that they avoid response bias. The measurement is very objective, and the examiner is not dependent on the report of any respondent. Closely related to this advantage is the fact that physiological measures provide a window into experiences which do not involve language. As has been mentioned, some children have limited verbal skills and may not be able to describe how they are feeling. Physiological measures do not require any verbal response of the child.

Another advantage of physiological measures is that they avoid the problems associated with the child's attempting to avoid thinking about the experience. By exposing the child to stimuli associated with the trauma and taking physiological measures, the examiner is able to objectively record reactions.

Disadvantages of Physiological Measures.   Physiological measures are not without their problems. First, they generally require very expensive equipment that is highly sensitive. Movement of instruments frequently results in their having to be recalibrated. In addition, the subject has to remain relatively still during the procedure to reduce the amount of "artifact" in the readings. Such a requirement is very difficult for young children.

Specific Physiological Measures.   PTSD, or at least some of its symptoms, may be mediated through neurophysiological channels. In reviewing the literature, Pynoos (1990) cited evidence of a number of neuroendocrine changes that could affect arousal states (including sleep, concentration, mood, and startle response).

Dollinger (1982) developed a parent-report checklist based on the Missouri Child Behavior Checklist. The Sleep Disturbance scale was expanded to 20 items, and the Somatization scale was expanded to 16 items. Data is available on a general clinic sample (Dollinger, 1982) and on a sample of children exposed to a lightning-strike disaster (Dollinger, 1986). Parental reports of sleep disturbance tend to be elevated for trauma-exposed children (e.g., Sullivan, Saylor, & Foster, 1991). However, these reports may be more closely correlated with fears of sleep itself than with actual changes in the physiological pattern of sleep (Dollinger, 1986). Weisenberg, Schwartzwald, Waysman, Solomon, and Klingman (1992), for example, found no evidence of physiological sleep disturbance among Israeli children as a result of the ballistic missile attacks during the Gulf War. In fact, neither parental report nor objective "actigraph" data suggested any significant change in physiological sleep quality.

Ornitz and Pynoos (1989) studied the inhibitory startle modulation of seven children with PTSD and compared it with age norms. They found impaired modulation 17 to 21 months posttrauma when they used stimuli unrelated to the trauma. Ornitz and Pynoos stated that these findings suggest an underlying, enduring change in brain stem circuits involving a sort of neurophysiological regression. The inhibitory startle modulation paradigm may be promising, but more research is clearly needed to ultimately explore its reliable and valid application to the assessment of childhood PTSD.

CONCLUSION

The assessment of PTSD symptomatology in children can be approached using any of several different methods of measurement, with a number of options available within each method. Ideally, the choice of method (and the instrument within the method) is guided by a careful consideration of the advantages and disadvantages inherent in the method as well as of the empirically determined psychometric properties of the specific instrument. Postdisaster environments are not ideal. Time pressure and disaster-related limitations on resources may give rise to research that is not well integrated into the extant literature.

At one time, planning for disaster research appeared oxymoronic. Planning is, however, possible and is probably best done in an inter-institutional context. The development of *multimethod* batteries that include some common elements (across different disaster types) and unique elements (instruments specifically sensitive to the sequelae of a certain disaster) is advised. Interinstitutional collaboration may make it possible to not only develop assessment strategies that are in place prior to disasters but may also facilitate efficient assessment following a disaster (e.g., local professionals implement with the resource support of nonexposed professionals).

With respect to the selection of instruments for a postdisaster assessment battery, validation becomes a primary concern. Many researchers have developed instruments specifically for their studies (e.g., Blom, 1986), perhaps in response to the lack of a psychometrically sound instrument that is sensitive to all symptoms of the PTSD diagnosis with the flexibility to handle a range of traumas across ages. The number of instruments is large. Rather than patterning more instruments on the latest clinical definition of PTSD, it may behoove researchers to drive the diagnostic process by seeking to validate the use of the existing measures. In this way, differential patterns may become more readily evident, and controlled empiricism can determine *diagnostic* validity.

REFERENCES

Abrams, M. T. (1991). *Kinesthetic damage responses in projective batteries of abused children.* Paper presented at the annual meeting of the Society for Personality Assessment, New Orleans.

Achenbach, T. M., & Brown, J. S. (1991). *Bibliography of published studies using the child behavior checklist and related materials.* Burlington: Department of Psychiatry, University of Vermont.

Achenbach, T. M., & Edelbrock, C. S. (1983). *Manual for the child behavior checklist and revised child behavior profile.* Burlington: Department of Psychiatry, University of Vermont.

American Psychiatric Association. (1980). *Diagnostic and statistical manual of mental disorders* (3rd ed.; DSM-III). Washington, DC: Author.

American Psychiatric Association. (1987). *Diagnostic and statistical manual of mental disorders* (3rd ed., rev.; DSM-III-R). Washington, DC: Author.

Apfel, R. J., & Sifneos, P.E. (1979). Alexithymia: Concept and measurement. *Psychotherapy and Measurement, 32,* 180–190.

Applebaum, D. R., & Burns, G. L. (1991). Unexpected childhood death: Posttraumatic stress disorder in surviving siblings and parents. *Journal of Clinical Child Psychology, 20,* 114–120.

Archer, R. P. (1987). *Using the MMPI with adolescents.* Hillsdale, NJ: Erlbaum.

Bell-Dolan, D. J., Foster, S. L., & Sikora, D. M. (1989). Effects of sociometric testing on children's behavior and loneliness in school. *Developmental Psychology, 25,* 306–311.

Belter, R. W., Dunn, S. E., Foster, K. Y., Imm, P. S., & Jeney-Gammon, P. (1990, April) *The impact of catastrophic natural disaster on children and adolescents.* Paper presented at the meeting of the Southeastern Psychological Association, Atlanta.

Belter, R. W., Dunn, S. E., & Jeney, P. (1991). The psychological impact of Hurricane Hugo on children: A needs assessment. Presented at the Association for Advancement of Behavior Therapy meeting, San Francisco.

Blom, G. (1986). A school disaster—Intervention and research aspects. *Journal of the American Academy of Child Psychiatry, 25,* 336–345.

Bradburn, I. S. (1991). After the earth shook: Children's stress symptoms 6–8 months after a disaster. *Advances in Behavior Research and Therapy, 13,* 173–179.

Butcher, J. N., Dahlstrom, W. G., Graham, J. R., Tellegen, A., & Kraemer, B. (1989). *Manual for the Restandardized Minnesota Multiphasic Personality Inventory: MMPI-2. An interpretive and administrative guide.* Minneapolis: University of Minnesota Press.

Castenada, A., McCandless, B., & Palermo, D. (1956). The children's form of the Manifest Anxiety Scale. *Child Development, 27,* 317–326.

Conners, C. K. (1969) A teacher rating scale for use in drug studies with children. *American Journal of Psychiatry, 126,* 884–888.

Daugherty, T. K., Finch, A. J, Shannon, M. P., & Lonigan, C. J. (1991). *Assessment and prediction of children's reaction to natural disaster.* Paper presented at the annual meeting of the Society for Personality Assessment, New Orleans.

Deblinger, E., McLeer, S. V., & Henry, D. (1990). Cognitive behavioral treatment for sexually abused children suffering post-traumatic stress: Preliminary findings. *Journal of the American Academy of Child and Adolescent Psychiatry, 29,* 747–752.

Dollinger, S. J. (1982). On the varieties of childhood sleep disturbance. *Journal of Clinical Child Psychology, 11,* 107–115.

Dollinger, S. J. (1985). Lightning-strike disaster among children. *British Journal of Medical Psychology, 58,* 375–383.

Dollinger, S. J. (1986). The measurement of children's sleep disturbances and somatic complaints following a disaster. *Child Psychiatry and Human Development, 16,* 148–153.

Dollinger, S. J., & Cramer, P. (1990). Children's defensive responses and emotional upset following a disaster: A projective assessment. *Journal of Personality Assessment, 54,* 116–127.

Dollinger, S. J., O'Donnell, J. P., & Staley, A. A. (1984). Lightning-strike disaster: Effects on children's fears and worries. *Journal of Consulting and Clinical Psychology, 52,* 1028–1038.

Earl, W. L. (1991). Perceived trauma: Its etiology and treatment. *Adolescence, 26,* 97–104.

Earls, F., Smith, E., Reich, W., & Jung, K. G. (1988). Investigating psychopathological consequences of a disaster in children: A pilot study incorporating a structured diagnostic interview. *Journal of the American Academy of Child and Adolescent Psychiatry, 27,* 90–95.

Edelbrock, C., Costello, A. J., Dulcan, M., Kalas, R., & Conover, N. C. (1985). Age differences in the reliability of the psychiatric interview of the child. *Child Development, 56,* 265–275.

Exner, J. E. (1986). *The Rorschach: A comprehensive system* (Vol. 1). New York: Wiley.

Famularo, R., Kinscherf, R., & Fenton, T. (1990). Symptom differences in acute and chronic presentation childhood post-traumatic stress disorder. *Child Abuse and Neglect, 14,* 439–444.

Fisher, P., & Kranzler, E. (1990). *Post-traumatic stress disorder: Supplemental module for the DISC-2.1.* New York: Division of Child and Adolescent Psychiatry, New York State Psychiatric Institute.

Foster, G., & Ysseldyke, J. (1976). Expectancy and halo effects as a result of artificially induced bias. *Contemporary Educational Psychology, 1,* 37–45.

Frederick, C. J. (1985a). Children traumatized by catastrophic situations. In S. Eth & R. S. Pynoos (Eds.), *Post-traumatic stress disorders in children* (pp. 73–99). Washington, DC: American Psychiatric Press.

Frederick, C. J. (1985b). Selected foci in the spectrum of posttraumatic stress disorders. In J. Laube & S. Murphy (Eds.), *Perspectives on disaster recovery* (pp. 110–130). Norwalk, CN: Appleton-Century-Crofts.

Frederick, C. J. (1987). Psychic trauma in victims of crime and terrorism. In G. R. VandenBos & B. K. Bryant (Eds.), *Master lecture series.* Washington, DC: American Psychological Association.

Fryer, L. L., Saylor, C. F., Finch, A. J., & Smith, K. E. (1989). Helping the child with cancer: What school personnel want to know. *Psychological Reports, 65,* 563–566.

Galante, R., & Foa, D. (1986). An epidemiological study of psychic trauma and treatment effectiveness for children after a natural disaster. *Journal of the American Academy of Child Psychiatry, 25,* 357–363.

Handford, H., Mayes, S., Mattison, R., Humphrey, F., Bagnato, S., Bixler, E., & Kales, J. (1986). Child and parent reaction to the Three Mile Island nuclear accident. *Journal of the American Academy of Child Psychiatry, 25,* 346–356.

Hathaway, S. R., & McKinely, J. C. (1951). *The Minnesota Multiphasic Personality Inventory Manual*. New York: Psychological Corporation.

Horowitz, M., Wilner, N., & Alvarez, W. (1979). Impact of events scale: A measure of subjective stress. *Psychosomatic Medicine, 41*, 209–218.

Jones, R. T., & Ribbe, D. P. (1991). Child, adolescent, and adult victims of residential fire: Psychosocial consequences. *Behavior Modification, 15*, 560–580.

Keane, Malloy, & Fairbank (1984). Empirical development of an MMPI subscale for the assessment of combat-related posttraumatic stress disorder. *Journal of Consulting and Clinical Psychology, 52*, 888–891.

Keppel-Benson, J., & Ollendick, T. H. (1993). Posttraumatic stress disorder in children and adolescents. In C. F. Saylor (Ed.), *Children and disasters*. New York: Plenum Press.

Klingman, A., Koenigsfeld, E., & Markman, D. (1987). Art activity with children following disaster: A preventive oriented crisis intervention modality. *Arts in Psychotherapy, 14*, 153–166.

Kovacs, M. (1983). *The Children's Depression Inventory: A self-rated depression scale for school-aged youngsters*. Unpublished manuscript, University of Pittsburgh.

Lerner, P. M. (1991). *Psychoanalytic Theory and the Rorschach*. Hillsdale, NJ: The Analytic Press.

Lonigan, C. J., Shannon, M. P., Finch, A. J, Daugherty, T. K., & Taylor, C. M. (1991). Children's reactions to a natural disaster: Symptom severity and degree of exposure. *Advances in Behavior Research and Therapy, 13*, 135–154.

Lystad, M. H. (1984). Children's responses to disaster: Family implications. *International Journal of Family Psychiatry, 5*, 41–60.

Malmquist, C. P. (1986). Children who witness parental murder: Posttraumatic aspects. *Journal of the American Academy of Child and Adolescent Psychiatry, 25*, 320–325.

McFarlane, A. C. (1987). Post-traumatic phenomena in a longitudinal study of children following a natural disaster. *Journal of the American Academy of Child and Adolescent Psychiatry, 26*, 677–690.

McFarlane, A. C., Policansky, S. K., & Irwin, C. (1987). A longitudinal study of the psychological morbidity in children due to a natural disaster. *Psychological Medicine, 17*, 727–738.

McGee, R., Williams, S., Bradshaw, J., Chapel, J. Robins, A., & Silva, P. (1985). The Rutter Scale for completion by teachers: Factor structure and relationships with cognitive abilities and family adversity for a sample of New Zealand children. *Journal of Child Psychology and Psychiatry, 26*, 727–739.

McLeer, S. V., Deblinger, E., Atkins, M. S., Foa, E. B., & Ralphe, D. L. (1988). Posttraumatic stress disorder in sexually abused children. *Journal of the American Academy of Child and Adolescent Psychiatry, 27*, 650–654.

Miller, L. C., Barrett, C. L., Hampe, E., & Noble, H. (1972). Factor structure of childhood fears. *Journal of Consulting and Clinical Psychology, 39*, 264–268.

Nader, K., Pynoos, R. S., Fairbanks, L., & Frederick, C. J. (1990). Children's PTSD reactions one year after a sniper attack at their school. *American Journal of Psychiatry, 147*, 1526–1530.

Novick, M. (1985). *AERA/APA/NCME Standards for Educational and Psychological Testing*. Washington, DC: American Psychological Association.

Ollendick, T. H. (1983). Reliability and validity of the Revised Fear Survey Schedule for Children (FSSC-R). *Behavior Research and Therapy, 21*, 685–692.

Ollendick, T. H., King, N. J., & Frary, R. B. (1989). Fears in children and adolescents: Reliability and generalizability across gender, age, and nationality. *Behavior Research and Therapy, 27*, 19–26.

Ollendick, T. H., Yule, W., & Ollier, K. (1990). Fears in British children and their relationship to manifest anxiety and depression. *Journal of Child Psychology and Psychiatry and Allied Professions, 32,* 321–331.

Ornitz, E. M., & Pynoos, R. S. (1989). Startle modulation in children with posttraumatic stress disorder. *American Journal of Psychiatry, 146,* 866–870.

Pynoos, R. S. (1990). Post-traumatic Stress Disorder in children and adolescents. In B. D. Garfinkle, G. A. Carlson, & E. B. Weller (Eds.), *Psychiatric disorders in children and adolescents.* Philadelphia: W. B. Saunders.

Pynoos, R. S., & Eth, E. (1986). Witness to violence: The child interview. *Journal of the American Academy of Child and Adolescent Psychiatry, 25,* 306–318.

Pynoos, R. S., Frederick, C. J., Nader, K., Arroyo, W., Steinberg, A., Eth, S., Nunez, F., & Fairbanks, L. (1987). Life threat and posttraumatic stress in school-age children. *Archives of General Psychiatry, 44,* 1057–1063.

Quay, H. C., & Peterson, D. R. (1983). *Manual for the Revised Behavior Problem Checklist.* Coral Gables, FL: University of Miami.

Reich, W. (1991a). *Diagnostic Interview for Children and Adolescents—Child Version.* Unpublished manuscript. Washington University School of Medicine.

Reich, W. (1991b). *Diagnostic Interview for Children and Adolescents—Parent Version.* Unpublished manuscript. Washington University School of Medicine.

Reynolds, C. R., & Richmond, B. O. (1978). "What I Think and Feel": A revised measure of children's manifest anxiety. *Journal of Abnormal Child Psychology, 6,* 271–280.

Rutter, M., Tizzard, J., & Whitmore, K. (1970). *Education, health and behavior.* London: Longmans.

Saigh, P. A. (1989). The development and validation of the Children's Posttraumatic Stress Disorder Inventory. *International Journal of Special Education, 4,* 75–84.

Saylor, C. F., Swenson, C. C., & Powell, P. (1992). Hurricane Hugo blow down the broccoli: Preschoolers' post-disaster play and adjustment. *Child Psychiatry and Human Development, 22,* 139–149.

Scherer, M. W., & Nakamura, C. Y. (1968). A Fear Survey Schedule for Children (FSS-FC): A factor analytic comparison with manifest anxiety. *Behavior Research and Therapy, 6,* 173–182.

Spielberger, C. D. (1973). *Preliminary manual for the State-Trait Anxiety Inventory for Children.* Palo Alto, CA: Consulting Psychologists Press.

Staley, A. A., & O'Donnell, J. P. (1984). A developmental analysis of mother's reports of normal children's fears. *Journal of Genetic Psychology, 144,* 165–178.

Stoddard, F. J., Norman, D. K., & Murphy, J. M. (1989). A diagnostic outcome study of children with severe burns. *The Journal of Trauma, 29,* 471–477.

Sullivan, M. A., Saylor, C. F., & Foster, K. Y. (1991). Post-hurricane adjustment of preschoolers and their families. *Advances in Behavior, Research, and Therapy, 13,* 163–172.

Terr, L. (1981). Psychic trauma in children: Observations following the Chowchilla school-bus kidnapping. *American Journal of Psychiatry, 138,* 14–19.

Venables, P. Fletcher, R., Dalais, J., Mitchell, D., Schulsinger, F., & Mednick, S. (1983). Factor structure of the Rutter Children's Behavior Questionnaire in a primary school population in a developing country. *Journal of Child Psychology and Psychiatry, 22,* 375–392.

Weisenberg, M., Schwartzwald, J., Waysman, M., Solomon, Z., & Klingman, A. (1992). *Coping of school-aged children in the sealed room during scud missile bombardment and postwar stress reactions.* Unpublished manuscript, Department of Mental Health, Medical Corps, Israel Defense Forces (in Hebrew).

Wolfe, V. V., Gentile, C., & Wolfe, D. A. (1989). The impact of sexual abuse on children: A PTSD formulation. *Behavior Therapy, 20,* 215–228.

Yule, W., & Udwin, O. (1991). Screening child survivors for post-traumatic stress disorders: Experiences from the "Jupiter" sinking. *British Journal of Clinical Psychology, 30,* 131–138.

Yule, W., & Williams, R. M. (1990). Post-traumatic stress reactions in children. *Journal of Traumatic Stress, 3,* 279–295.

Zilberg, N. J., Weiss, D. S., & Horowitz, M. (1982). Impact of events scale: A cross validation study and some empirical evidence supporting a conceptual model of stress response syndromes. *Journal of Consulting and Clinical Psychology, 50,* 407–414.

Ziv, A., & Israeli, R. (1973). Effects of bombardment on the manifest anxiety levels of children living in the kibbutz. *Journal of Consulting and Clinical Psychology, 40,* 287–291.

4

Concepts of Death and Loss in Childhood and Adolescence
A Developmental Perspective

LINDA J. GUDAS

Professionals who deal with children who have experienced a significant loss face the overwhelming task of understanding their concerns and helping them struggle with their feelings. Children's mourning is directly related to developmental efforts to make sense of and attempts to master the concept and experience of death. Clinicians working with children on such issues need to define a framework of grieving that is specific to children and that incorporates an understanding of the levels of comprehension of death in children at various ages and stages of growth and development. Such a framework could be applied to children experiencing loss through the death of a loved one, as well as loss experienced in the traumatic effects of war, technical or natural disasters, or violence.

Marked controversy exists in the literature as to when and to what degree children have the capacity to understand death and to mourn. This chapter will review researchers' efforts to resolve that disagreement. Methodological issues and suggestions for further research will be discussed. Brief consideration will be give to bereaved children in the context of disasterous situations.

LINDA J. GUDAS • Department of Psychiatry, The Children's Hospital, Harvard Medical School, Boston, Massachusetts 02115.
Children and Disasters, edited by Conway F. Saylor. Plenum Press, New York, 1993.

TERMINOLOGY OF GRIEF

Grief, mourning, and *bereavement* are terms used in the literature to describe the process that occurs when an individual experiences the loss of a significant person or object. These words are often used synonymously and without specific definition.

Sigmund Freud's 1917 definition of mourning, based on his work with adult patients, is the most often quoted term to define and describe what occurs following a loss. According to Freud (1917/1957), *mourning* refers to a gradual relinquishment of libidinal ties to the mental representation of the lost object through the painful process of decathexis. This is carried out by repeatedly confronting memories of the lost one with the reality of the loss. The emotional task following loss, then, is to detach energy, memories, and hope from what has been lost.

Those authors who describe a clear differentiation between grief, mourning, and loss (Bowlby, 1960, 1980; Furman, 1974; Rando, 1988) tend to agree on their definitions, although they acknowledge that these terms are often used interchangably. Grief, the subjective state of bereavement, refers to the process of experiencing the psychological, social, and physical reactions that follow loss and accompany mourning. Mourning refers to the psychological work set in motion by the loss. Furman (1974), however, believes that true grief and mourning can occur only when the loss is through death. Furman's position differs from that of many others (A. Freud, 1960; S. Freud, 1917/1957; Rando, 1988; Sekaer, 1987), who believe genuine grief does occur with all kinds of losses (e.g., through divorce or relocation), not just death. Despite differences in terminology, clinicians who have worked directly with children suffering a death or loss often note that these children experience the powerful feelings of sadness, pain, and anger commonly associated with grief and mourning.

A HISTORICAL REVIEW OF CHILDREN'S AWARENESS OF DEATH AND LOSS

A review of the literature on death and loss highlights the differences of opinion about the capacity of children and adolescents to grieve and mourn and the age and stage of development in which a child comprehends a concept of death. These differences stem, in part, from varying theoretical perspectives and methodological disparities among studies.

The early contributions to the literature regarding children's understanding of death came from studies during or shortly after World War II. Anthony (1940) studied children in England in the early part of the war.

She formulated a stage-based theory of children's understanding of the word *dead*, which follows an age-related hierarchy beginning with a complete lack of awareness and progressing to a logical and accurate description of the word. Nagy (1948) studied 378 Hungarian children, most of whom had direct death experience during wartime. Nagy's classification of children's understanding of death involves three stages. In Stage I (under the age of 5), children perceive no definite death, for death is reversible. The preschooler either denies death or recognizes physical death but cannot separate it from life. Death is a departure, a separation, a sleep, and also a living on under altered circumstances. In Stage II (ages 5–9), death is personified. Each child creates his or her own image of a death-man, always invisible, always remote from them. Death resides outside the child and is not conceptualized as a universal phenomenon. In Stage III (age 9 and older), death is regarded as a cessation of bodily activities. Once the child understands that death is a process operating within the body, its inevitability and universality are realized.

Thus, these studies first identified a developmental sequence in children's understanding of death. What these early investigators failed to recognize was the extent to which children's ideas about death are derived from their cultural traditions, coping styles, and environment (Bowlby, 1980; Koocher, 1973, 1981). For example, with rare exception (Lonetto, 1980), personification responses have not been replicated in studies of American children (Kane, 1979; Koocher, 1973; Reilly, Hasazi, & Bond, 1983).

From the European children of the World War II era also came some of Anna Freud's work on the responses of young children to the separation from and loss of the mother. A. Freud and Burlingham (1943, 1944) observed the distressful behaviors of very young children separated from their parents by the bombings and referred specifically to these behaviors as grief. Although these authors acknowledged "the depth and seriousness of this grief of a small child" (1943, p. 51), they were reluctant to state that the children experienced the psychological work necessary for what they considered "true mourning":

> This childish grief is short-lived. Mourning of equal intensity in an adult person would have to run its course throughout a year; the same process in the child between 1 and 2 years will normally be over in 36–48 hours. (p. 51)

To what degree the specific environmental stressors of disaster and war affected the children's grief is not clear.

A. Freud and Dann (1951) studied six orphaned 3-year-old children cared for in the Hampstead Nursery following their release from a concentration camp. Striking behaviors were observed in these children, such as the absence of jealousy, rivalry, and competition with one another; unusual emotional dependence on one another; an inability to engage in age-appropriate play; and a marked impersonal aggression toward and attachment to adults. Although Freud's work directly addressed neither age- nor stage-related concepts, she and her colleagues documented grief reactions in children which qualitatively differ from that of adults. Based on the population of children in the Hampstead Nursery, she described and extended the bereavement process beyond the "short-lived" acute grief period previously described.

In 1944, Lindemann wrote a seminal article on the symptomatology and management of acute grief. The population studied consisted of 101 adults, including individuals who had lost a relative during a nightclub fire, during the course of treatment, and in the armed services. Lindemann's description of "normal" versus "pathological" grief reactions became a standard for observation and assessment. Many of these adults, however, might today be described as experiencing posttraumatic stress disorder. Although based on adult findings, two outcomes of this study are particularly relevant to children. Case examples cited by Lindemann support Deutsch's earlier position (1937) that a childhood loss has a significant effect on adult grief, thus acknowledging the long-term impact of bereavement on a young child. In addition, Lindemann (1944) connected the experience of separation and loss with grief:

> It must be understood that grief reactions are just one form of separation reactions. . . . We were at first surprised to find genuine grief reactions in patients who had not experienced a bereavement but who had experienced a separation. (p. 438)

Until well into the 1950s, little additional material was written regarding children's awareness of death or their capacity to mourn. The basic developmental findings set forth by Anthony, Nagy, and A. Freud were undisputed, and childhood response to loss was simply not considered authentic grief.

The psychoanalytic literature through the 1960s essentially halted the exploration of mourning in children and, undoubtedly, affected the growth of a developmental theory of children's understanding of death. Classical psychoanalytic theorists strongly argued that true mourning could not occur until the end of adolescence. Wolfenstein (1966) stated that identity formation (i.e., the decathexis of internalized parental images) must be completed before grieving is possible and concluded that children deny the painful affect of loss through defensive phenomena and lack the reality testing necessary to mourn. She based this conclusion, in part, on her observations of children's "short sadness span," of the tendency to "slip" into the present tense when referring to the deceased, and of mistaking someone else for the deceased. According to Deutsch (1937), children have neither the intellectual ability to grasp the reality of death nor an adequate formation of object-relatedness to mourn. In a review of the psychoanalytic literature, Miller (1971) summarized:

> The response of children to the death of an emotionally meaningful person is . . . strikingly similar to pathological forms of mourning as they have been described in adults. While the primary function of the mourning process "is to detach the survivors' memories and hopes from the dead" (Freud, 1913), the reactions to object loss in children are seen as having an equally precise but contrary aim, namely to avoid the acceptance and emotional meaning of the death. (p. 701)

Most of the papers written through the 1960s that addressed the capacity of children to understand death and to mourn effectively were rooted in adult-oriented Freudian beliefs. They were centered on case studies of children in psychotherapeutic treatment or disasterous wartime circumstances who had lost a parent. These writings were based on small numbers of children of different ages. However, the rich clinical vignettes of the children's behavior provided important material for future reference and study.

A. Freud (1960) and Miller (1971) proposed that the principal dissenter from the consensus on the nature of children's responses to death and loss was John Bowlby. Bowlby (1960, 1961) emphasized attachment behavior in children separated from their mothers. He proposed that these children experienced a three-phase sequence of behavior—protest, despair, and detachment—that is characteristic of all forms of mourning. Drawing on evolution theory, Bowlby (1961) explained that, in all species, the immediate response to every separation or loss from the loved object is an immediate, automatic, and strong affect (protest and anger) whose motive is recovery of the lost object. There is no discrimination of those separations that are retrievable from those that are not. Bowlby (1961) warned:

> To regard the defensive process following childhood loss as an alternative to mourning is to miss both that defensive processes of similar kind but of lesser degree and later onset enter also into healthy mourning, and also that what is pathological is not so much the defensive processes themselves as their intensity and prematurity of their onset. (p. 489)

Bowlby's early work (1960, 1961) was critical in acknowledging that children and infants as young as 6 months old who have lost a loved object experience grief, go through periods of mourning, and do so in ways associated with their developmental abilities.

As beginning research on childhood bereavement was emerging, a parallel body of knowledge on children's responses to hospitalization was growing. This research also described stages of protest, despair, and detachment in the children studied (Dimock, 1960; Geist, 1965; Robertson,

1958). Natterson and Knudson (1966) correlated Nagy's three chronological stages (1948) of the meaning of death with three primary fears of the hospitalized child (separation, castration or mutilation, and death anxiety). Natterson and Knudson's maturational scheme of fear fits into the developmental pattern of a child's sense of awareness: first, of the mother (the elemental fear of separation), then of his or her own body (fear of bodily harm), and finally, of the self in time (the more sophisticated fear of death itself). These studies were also embedded in psychoanalytic theory, and the references to developmental differences were general. However, this area of research focused an increased awareness on the young child's concerns about separation, loss, and death and enhanced many of Bowlby's beliefs (1960, 1961).

The limitations inherent in the psychoanalytic bias of previous works was recognized in the 1970s (Kerr, 1979), and alternative explanations of children's responses to illness, loss, and death were sought in the research. Empirical documentation emerged that sick and dying children face different issues than healthy children (Brodie, 1974), that older children have different concerns and perceptions than younger children (Campbell, 1975), and that the feelings and behaviors of children are in some way related to cognitive maturational levels (Campbell, 1975; Neuhauser, Amsterdam, Hines, & Steward, 1978).

Gradually, personal, social, and cognitive variables were deemed significant in the assessment of childhood loss. In her study of children whose parent had died, Furman (1974), stated that the first step in the mourning process is the individual's awareness, comprehension, and acknowledgment of the death of the loved one. Furman believed that the requirements for mourning involve memory, perception, and object constancy, which can occur by the end of the first year of life. However, Furman stressed that, although children as young as 2 do mourn, the youngest children in her study needed permission and educational help from an adult to recognize and tolerate their own affect and to confirm the concrete aspects of death. All of the children best understood death and took on the tasks of mourning when they felt personally safe, could rely on trusted caretakers, and had had a previous realistic encounter with death. Furman's work was instrumental in advancing the concept that children's grief is developmentally appropriate and normal.

REVIEW OF THE RECENT LITERATURE

Since the early 1970s, a steadily increasing interest in children's understanding of death and loss is documented in the literature (Speece & Brent, 1984). This research focused more on healthy children than on the clinical populations previously described. Many of these studies were heavily influenced by developmental theory and reflect the work of Jean Piaget, whose theory on children's intellectual development was gaining rapid recognition (Ginsburg & Opper, 1969; Gruber & Voneche, 1977; Piaget, 1960; Piaget & Inhelder, 1969). Researchers began making an effort to extend the physical and logical-mathematical domain of cognition set forth by Piaget to the psychosocial domain of children's concepts of such life events as illness (Bibace & Walsh, 1981; Perrin & Gerrity, 1981, 1984) and death (Cotton & Range, 1990; Kane, 1979; Koocher, 1973, 1981; Lonetto, 1980; Reilly *et al.*, 1983). These studies reflect a predictable developmental progression of cognitive processing that resembles the sequence described by Piaget.

Infancy

During infancy, until approximately age 2, the child is in the sensorimotor period of cognitive development (Gruber & Voneche, 1977; Piaget, 1960), where exploration of the physical and interpersonal environment occurs chiefly through perceptual and motor functions. The major cognitive task of this period is the establishment of object permanence. The first psychosocial task is the establishment of trust, where the child acquires a sense of others and self as being reliable and nurturant (Erikson, 1964). Beginning in the first few months of life, primitive distress is seen at the withdrawal of nurturance and gradually becomes specific to the loss of mother (Rando, 1988). By the middle of the first year of life, recognition and elementary search occurs for lost objects. By 17 months, the child can retain an image and have memory of an object (Bowlby, 1980). Ellis (1989) stated that the beginning concepts of death can be observed in the child's play (e.g., "All gone" and "Peek-a-boo"). Most authors believe that children of this age do not comprehend all dimensions of death. Clearly, the research is limited by children's language capacity, and thus responses can be assessed only through behavioral observation. Stambrook and Parker (1987), however, stated that evidence exists that infants and toddlers can, under certain circumstances (e.g., a direct experience with death), understand death to be final earlier than is typically suggested. Bowlby's research (1960, 1961, 1980) describing protest, despair, and detachment remains the standard for the expression of grief in this age.

Preschool

Between the ages of, roughly, 2 and 6 or 7, the child is in the preoperational stage of cognitive development (Gruber & Voneche, 1977; Piaget, 1960). Cause-and-effect relationships have not yet been established. Thinking is prelogical, magical, egocentric, and circular. The child does not clearly understand concepts of time, space, measurement, or movement.

Most studies regarding death and loss in young children use direct interviews as the primary source of data. Additional supportive measures (e.g., drawings, play, and Piagetian conservation tasks) have also been used (Speece & Brent, 1984). With the acquisition of language, children's ideas about the various dimensions or components of the death concept (irreversibility, finality, universality, causality, and nonfunctionality) can begin to be measured and empirically validated. In her study of 3- to 12-year-olds, Kane (1979) found that the death concept grows most rapidly and regularly from ages 3 to 5, undoubtedly reflecting the children's emerging communication skills.

Preoperational children construct reality on the physically observable world, are limited by their own experiences, and realize death in the here-and-now. As preoperational children think magically and egocentrically, they neither fully appreciate the universality of death (Stambrook & Parker, 1987) nor their personal mortality. A gradual awareness of finality and dysfunctionality (i.e., the cessation of body functions) occurs, but young children become aware of the loss of visible, noncognitive abilities (e.g., eating and speaking) before the loss of more subtle, internal, abstract abilities (e.g., feeling, smelling, dreaming) (Hoffman & Strauss, 1985; Kane, 1979). As the child struggles with finality, he or she allows degrees of death; for example, someone buried is "more dead" (Yates & Bannard, 1988). Due to their animistic thinking, ideas about what is alive and what is dead are related and often confused. These children in general view death as Nagy (1948) proposed in Stage I: a life under changed circumstances, a separation or departure, sleep, or as similar to being sick. These circumstances are those with which the child is familiar. Without a concept of constancy, death is perceived as temporary and irreversible (Koocher, 1973, 1981; Lonetto, 1980). Berzonsky (1987) and Speece and Brent (1984) warn, however, that the research assumes that the child comprehends life and death as mutually exclusive, distinct states. The conclusion that young children view death as reversible may thus overestimate their abilities.

Studies on grief and mourning patterns in preschool children report the child's use of a variety of mechanisms to deal with loss, including sadness, regression, hopelessness, denial, and animistic fantasies. Kranzler, Shaffer, Wasserman and Davies's study (1990) of 3- to 6-year-olds whose parent had died demonstrated that the children expressed a full range of affect, not simply sadness or anhedonia. Furman (1974) noted that remembering in young bereaved children is accompanied by physical activity (e.g., hyperactivity). Reenactment or posttraumatic play may be observed (Terr, 1990), especially if the child experienced significant trauma associated with the death.

Bowlby (1980) believed that young children are able to mourn in a way that clearly parallels that of adults, with the longing, sadness, and anger that accompany grief. Specific to this age, however, is the belief that death can happen by simultaneous occurrence of related or nonrelated events. Young children may believe they can cause death to happen due to their lack of conceptualization of cause and effect. Self-blame and guilt occur, often resulting in a regression in basic ego functions (Furman, 1974).

Until children develop a better control of their impulses and fears, they may make use of an imaginary companion as a transitional phenomenon. Working in the service of defense and ego mastery such companions concretize in percept for the child what cannot be grasped in concept (Sekaer, 1987; Yates & Bannard, 1988). Young children also use identification with the deceased as a means of coping. Identification (e.g., putting on a treasured hat of the deceased) is useful for the child if it helps conserve the loved object and integrates the past and the future, but it may become a problem if it is pervasive or if it interferes with the grieving process (e.g., if the child takes on symptoms of the deceased's illness). Young children's grief responses are often intermittent and show marked affective shifts over brief periods of time. Such children's questions about death are asked in a repeated, often unrelenting manner. This behavior is the child's attempt to assimilate and master the experience with death, as neither conservation of affect nor perception is well established. The developmental appropriateness and normality of the coping behavior of these children contrasts starkly with Wolfenstein's assertion (1966) that the child is unable to mourn before adolescence.

School Age

Between the ages of 6–7 and 12, children learn to perform concrete operations, mental actions that have the added property of being reversible (Gruber & Voneche, 1977). Causal and logical explanations are understood, and children grasp the concepts of time, space, and measurement (Piaget, 1960). However, their thinking remains concrete, and they cannot yet reflect on all the possible outcomes of a situation. A major developmental shift at this time is the emergence of a clear differentiation between the self and others, as children learn to distinguish the phenomena that are internal in and external to themselves (Bibace & Walsh, 1981).

During this period, children gradually abandon their animistic-magical interpretations of death in favor of biological ones (Lonetto, 1980). Almost all school-aged children achieve an understanding of the various dimensions of the death concept (Childress & Wimmer, 1971; Cotton & Range, 1990; Kane, 1979; Lansdown & Benjamin, 1985; Orbach, Talmon, Kedem, & Har-Even, 1987; Reilly et al., 1983; Speece & Brent, 1984).

Psychosocially, the school years are a period of building independent skills and personal accomplishments (Erikson, 1964). These skills are frequently the most vulnerable in times of stress. Grief responses may manifest themselves in school or learning problems, reactions often linked to preoccupation with the deceased or related worries (Koocher, 1986). School-aged bereaved children, with their understanding of permanence and personal mortality, tend to experience more anxiety, more overt symptoms of depression, and more somatic complaints than younger children (Gudas, 1990). Phobias, identification with the deceased, and hypochondriasis may also occur (Rando, 1988).

Children's cognitive reasoning about death undergoes dramatic and often uneven shifts during this period. Children can recognize finality in general, yet comprehension of the specific death of a loved one or themselves is difficult (Rando, 1988). As children begin to question any hope of reunion on earth with the deceased, they are often left with feelings of extreme anger (at the loved one and those adults who could not save the deceased), anxiety, and helplessness. In this period of latency, when talking about painful events is difficult, children are capable of depressive symptomatology and potential suicidal ideation.

Adolescence

With the onset of formal operations at 11–12 years, children begin to analyze information systematically, to isolate variables, and to generate hypotheses (Ginsburg & Opper, 1969). They can think symbolically; construct theories, ideals, and metaphors; and analyze both a situation and their own thoughts.

The concept of death has rarely been studied in adolescents, perhaps because of the untested assumption that adolescents "understand death and that once 'mature' understandings are established . . . they remain unchanged throughout life" (Stambrook & Parker, 1987, p. 150). Although adultlike responses to death and grief may be established, they are complicated by developmental issues such as resistance, alienation from adults, separation from their parents, and independence (Rando, 1988).

Adolescents develop an increasing awareness of illness and death in terms of internal physiological structures and systems, and realize the complex interactions between host and environment in illness and death (Bibace & Walsh, 1981). Conceptualization of death is understood as an inevitable process of the life cycle (Koocher, 1973, 1981).

The intense physiological changes of this period, coupled with a developing sense of personal identity (Erikson, 1964), make adolescents prone to increased bodily interest and narcissism. "Immortality is implied in their attitude that there will always be time" (Sarwer-Foner, 1972, p. SS52). The threat of personal mortality or the loss of loved ones may be so great that denial becomes a major defense. Adolescents' omnipotence may be viewed as counterphobic to the fear of the reality of death. Faced with a loss (whether death or another loss, such as the breakup of a relationship), the adolescent's grief may be expressed in death-defying, risk-taking behaviors such as substance abuse.

Heightened bodily concerns leave the adolescent vulnerable to somatization as a result of any stress. Responses to grief not only may result in symptoms limited to the more immediate perceptions seen in younger children (e.g., stomachaches) but may also revolve around highly sophisticated syndromes (e.g., lack of energy and eating disorders). The use of metaphorical and symbolic thought allows adolescents to use and identify psychosomatic responses and the conversion of emotion to parts of the body.

The quality of life takes on meaning as the adolescent develops ideals and morals and thinks futuristically. A shattering of life assumptions (see Janoff-Bulman, 1985) can lead to depression, resentment, mood swings, and rage as the adolescent seeks the answers to such questions as "If the world is meaningful, and if I am a good person, why did this happen?" Alternately, the realities of dying (pain and loss of function) may lead the adolescent to philosophical explanations (e.g., "being at peace") to ease the loss. For summary of age- and stage-related concepts, please refer to Table 1.

METHODOLOGICAL ISSUES

Investigations on the topic of children, death, and loss are fraught with methodological difficulties. Stambrook and Parker (1987) described this research as "directionless" and commented that replication of and clarification of results from previous studies are lacking. Kane (1979), for example, stated that her critical review of Nagy's 1948 study was the first attempted in almost 40 years. Developmental trends have been examined by different methods, samples of children, theoretical perspectives, and measuring techniques. Generalizability, therefore, is difficult to obtain.

Early attempts at assessment of children's responses to death and loss were obtained primarily from a population of children who experienced the separation or death of a parent. These children were gathered from

Table 1. Developmental Concepts of Death and Loss

	Infancy	Preschool	School age	Adolescence
Age	0–2	2–6	6–12	Teenage
Cognitive development	Sensorimotor	Preoperational	Concrete-operational	Formal operational
Psychosocial development	Trust	Use of language	Independence	Identity formation
Death perception	Establish object–concept permanence	Death as temporary Animistic thinking	Death as irreversible	Death as part of physiological life cycle
Common grief reactions	Protest Despair Detachment	Sadness Regression Helplessness Identification Affective shifts Play reenactment Magical thinking	School and learning problems Phobias Depression Hypochondriasis Anger Identification	Denial Depression Somatization Anger Philosophical questions Mood swings

either a clinical population or were in highly distressing environments. The more recent literature has begun to expand the study of the impact of death and loss on ill and dying children (Bluebond-Langer, 1989; Koocher, 1986), on healthy children who have lost a sibling (Pollock, 1986; Schumacher, 1984), and even on the loss of pets (Blue, 1986). Furman (1974) and Schumacher (1984) commented that losses of different degree, type, and intensity are difficult to compare. Thus, the study of different kinds of death experiences would enhance the literature. The research lacks in its descriptions of the nature of the death (e.g., chronic or acute) as well as of the circumstances surrounding the death (Kranzler et al., 1990). Experiences such as how well the surviving family members respond to the loss (Cotton & Range, 1990; Kranzler et al., 1990; Payton & Krocker-Tuskan, 1988; Stambrook & Parker, 1987; Yates & Bannard, 1988), what and when the child is told about the loss (Bowlby, 1980; Cotton & Range, 1990; McNeil, 1983), to what degree the child is involved in grieving rituals (Weller, Weller, Fristed, Cain & Bowes, 1988; Kranzler et al., 1990), whether other stresses coincide with the bereavement (Furman, 1974; Yates & Bannard, 1988), and the developmental impact of previous associations with death (Stambrook & Parker, 1987) have an enormous influence on the child's reactions and are important confounding variables generally not clarified in the studies.

The available research has focused on white, urban, middle-class children of average to above-average intelligence (Speece & Brent, 1984). Comparisons of children of different color, culture, and socioeconomic status would provide insight into cross-cultural similarities and differences regarding grief reactions and concepts of death. Only recently have such differences been considered (Florian & Kravetz, 1985; Hul, Chan, & Chan, 1989; Payton & Krocker-Tuskan, 1988; Schonfield & Smilansky, 1989). Religious orientation of the children has generally not been provided. The children's mourning process as well as their concepts of death (e.g., finality and irreversibility) may well be influenced by this variable. Gender differences have also been ignored. Boys and girls do differ in their grief reactions (Gudas, 1990; Kranzler *et al.*, 1990), although gender may not have as great an effect on the attainment of death concepts.

The developmental literature on children's concepts of death has several methodological weaknesses. Stambrook and Parker (1987) emphasized that inferring a longitudinal process from cross-sectional data confounds the effects of age with the effects of experience. Orbach *et al.* (1987) stated that the developmental studies do not measure the same components of the death concept (e.g., finality) and use different definitions of each component. Different measures (interviews, tasks, questionnaires, case studies); type, order, and language level of the questions; and statistical analyses have been used (Berzonsky, 1987; Orbach *et al.*, 1987). The wide variation (from 50% to 100% of the children) in the statistical criteria of age attainment for acquisition of components of the death concept makes the reliability and validity of comparisons of studies questionable (Speece & Brent, 1984).

Studies are lacking which address the order of acquisition of the various dimensions of the concept. Researchers should also consider the acquisition of the death concept in both humans and other organisms to address such questions as wether the concept is organized differently and when a general concept is formed (Berzonsky, 1987; Orbach *et al.*, 1987; Speece & Brent, 1984). Regarding the use of Piagetian stages, differences in the procedures used to assess developmental stage are found (Speece & Brent, 1984). Whether or not Piagetian stage attainment by itself is a sufficient and/or necessary predictor variable needs further exploration (Reilly *et al.*, 1983). What is needed is "a model of development that simultaneously accounts for both increases in subject-matter knowledge and the development of context-independent reasoning abilities" (Speece & Brent, 1984, p. 1683). The question of age versus stage attainment is also debated, although Cotton and Range (1990) and Koocher (1981) have stated the cognitive developmental level is more useful than age or IQ (McLoughlin, 1986) in the prediction of responses to the formation of death concepts.

This developmental literature requires systematic research based on standardized, developmentally specific instruments and interviews.

Finally, studies on children's responses to death and loss should not be undertaken without considering individual differences. No two children grieve or perceive death in exactly the same way.

DEATH, LOSS, AND DISASTER

Furman's 1974 statement that "No author explores the interferences which result from the coincidence of bereavement and other stressful life experiences . . . or threats to survival" (p. 249) remains generally true in regards to the simultaneous occurrence of death and disaster in children. Bereavement and trauma such as war, technical or natural disasters, or acts of group violence interfere with the impact of grieving and complicates recovery and resolution. In such tragic situations, secondary losses occur, such as the disruption of the community, family reorganization, and the destruction of personal possessions. The effect of the 1992 riots in Los Angeles following the *Rodney King* verdict demonstrate such secondary losses. The consistency, security, and comfort of the familiar routines so critically important to bereft children often disappear in times of disaster (Furman, 1974; Siegel, Mesagno, & Christ, 1990).

Children exposed to both death and disaster are frequently denied the opportunity for or discouraged from grieving all their losses. These children experience what is referred to as *unsanctioned* or *disenfranchised grief* (Doka, 1989; Ellis, 1989; Rando, 1988), where grief is not openly acknowledged, publicly mourned, or socially supported. This lack of recognition of the child's grief can result from adults' lack of awareness of the psychological impact of loss in children; adult denial of the horror which they, too, experience; or the conflict which adults face in dealing with their grief and the needs of the child (Benedek, 1985; Furman, 1974; Harrison, Davenport, & Dermott, 1967).

The grief responses of children and adolescents to multiple losses are significant and can have long-term effects. In a longitudinal study of 25 kibbutz children who lost their fathers in the October War of 1973, Elizur and Kaffman (1983) found that almost half the children suffered from bereavement reactions that involved serious, prolonged emotional disorders for as long as 42 months following the parental death. Moses (1991) described the impact of war on children as involving survivor guilt, shame, fear of abandonment and betrayal, concerns about lack of protection from adults, and anxiety that their rescuers would turn against them. Terr (1990) studied young children who were kidnapped and buried alive in a school bus. She noted that children who concurrently experience trauma and threat of death are prone to depression, paranoid thinking, and/or character change. Several authors (Schwartz, 1982; Terr, 1990; Wortman & Silver, 1989) have commented that children in traumatic, disastrous conditions come to view the world as a place where things they value can be taken away in a moment. A casualness about the worth of human life may occur. Once a seemingly impossible event happens, everything else becomes possible for the child. The result is a sense of helplessness and pessimism.

Studies repeatedly emphasize that children's and adolescents' ability to mourn successfully depends strongly on the presence of a secure relationship with a trusted adult who provides consistency and comfort, who shares in the child's grief, and who offers prompt, accurate information about the child's losses (Benedek, 1985; Bowlby, 1980; DeAngeles, 1991; Furman, 1974; Payton & Krocker-Tuskan, 1988). This critical variable implies that mental health professionals should be available following disasters, both to assist parents to understand and meet their children's needs and to establish relationships directly with the child victims and survivors.

Carrying on research in conditions of widespread conflict, dangerous environments, or community disruption presents multiple problems (Benedek, 1985; Chimienti, Nasr, & Khalifeh, 1989). However, it is important to begin looking at the impact of such conditions on the children, especially when major losses occur.

CONCLUSION

In 1967, Harrison *et al.* stated, "Our society has never had much in the way of identifiable guidelines to follow in dealing with children's confrontations with death" (p. 596). More than 25 years later, the literature is beginning to explore such guidelines, and researchers and clinicians are at an exciting point in addressing the changing attitudes toward and understanding of the concepts of death and loss in children and adolescents. Professionals should continue to look systematically and within a developmental framework at children's and adolescents' expressions of grief, their questions about death, and their unique forms of coping with loss.

Children and adolescents do feel pain and anguish when death and loss occur. We must learn to understand what they know and feel so they do not grieve alone.

ACKNOWLEDGMENTS. The author wishes to thank Gerald Koocher for his review of this manuscript.

During the preparation of this manuscript, the author was supported in part by Grant No. MH41791 from the National Institute of Mental Health, G. P. Koocher, Principal Investigator.

REFERENCES

Anthony, S. (1940). *The children's discovery of death*. New York: Hartcourt, Brace.

Benedek, E. D. (1985). Children and disaster: Emerging issues *Psychiatric Annals, 15,* 168–172.

Berzonsky, M. D. (1987). A preliminary investigation of children's conceptions of life and death. *Merrill-Palmer Quarterly, 33,* 505–513.

Bibace, R., & Walsh, M. E. (1981). Children's conceptions of illness. In R. Bibace & M. E. Walsh (Eds.), *New directions for child development: Children's conceptions of health, illness and bodily function* (No. 14, pp. 31–47). San Francisco: Jossey-Bass.

Blue, G. F. (1986). The value of pets in children's lives. *Childhood Education, 63,* 84–90.

Bluebond-Langer, M. (1989). Worlds of dying children and their well siblings. *Death Studies, 13,* 1–16.

Bowlby, J. (1960). Grief and mourning in infancy and early childhood. *Psychoanalytic Study of the Child, 15,* 9–52. New York: International Universities Press.

Bowlby, J. (1961). Childhood mourning and its implications for psychiatry. *American Journal of Psychiatry, 18,* 481–498.

Bowlby, J. (1980). *Attachment and loss: Vol. 3. Loss, sadness and depression.* New York: Basic Books.

Brodie, P. (1974). Views of healthy children toward illness. *American Journal of Public Health, 64,* 1156–1159.

Campbell, J. D. (1975). Illness is a point of view: The development of children's concepts of illness. *Child Development, 46,* 92–100.

Childress, P., & Wimmer, M. (1971). The concept of death in early childhood. *Child Development, 42,* 1299–1301.

Chimienti, G., Nasr, J. A., & Khalifeh, I. (1989). Children's reactions to war-related stress. *Social Psychiatry and Psychiatric Epidemiology, 26,* 282–287.

Cotton, C. R., & Range, L. M. (1990). Children's death concepts: Relationship to cognitive functioning, age, experience with death, fear of death, and hopelessness. *Journal of Clinical Child Psychology, 19,* 123–127.

DeAngeles, T. (1991). Impact of war trauma hits children hardest. *APA Monitor, 22,* 8–9.

Deutsch, H. (1937). Absence of grief. *Psychoanalytic Quarterly, 6,* 12–22.

Dimock, H. G. (1960). *The child in hospital.* Philadelphia: F. A. Davis.

Doka, K. J. (1989). *Disenfranchised grief.* Lexington, MA: Lexington Books.

Elizur, E., & Kaffman, M. (1983). Factors influencing the severity of childhood bereavement reactions. *American Journal of Orthopsychiatry, 53,* 668–676.

Ellis, R. R. (1989). Young children: Disenfranchised grievers. In K. J. Doka (Ed.), *Disenfranchised grief* (pp. 201–211). Lexington, MA: Lexington Books.

Erikson, E. (1964). *Childhood and society.* New York: Norton.

Florian, V., & Kravetz, S. (1985). Children's concepts of death: A cross-cultural comparison among Muslims, Druze, Christians and Jews in Israel. *Journal of Cross-cultural Psychology, 16,* 174–189.

Freud, A. (1960). Discussion of Dr. John Bowlby's paper. *Psychoanalytic Study of the Child, 15,* 53–62. New York: International Universities Press.

Freud, A., & Burlingham, D. (1943). *War and children.* New York: Medical War Books.

Freud, A., & Burlingham, D. (1944). *Infants without families*. New York: International Universities Press.

Freud, A., & Dann, S. (1951). An experiment in group upbringing. *Psychoanalytic Study of the Child, 6*, 127–168. New York: International Universities Press.

Freud, S. (1913/1957). Totem and Taboo. *Standard Edition, 13* (pp. 1–161). London: Hogarth Press.

Freud, S. (1917/1957). Mourning and melancholia. In J. Strachey (Ed.), *The standard edition of the complete psychological works of Sigmund Freud* (Vol. 14, pp. 243–258). London: Hogarth Press.

Furman, E. (1974). *A child's parent dies*. New Haven: Yale University Press.

Geist, H. (1965). *A child goes to the hospital*. Springfield, IL: Thomas.

Ginsburg, H., & Opper, S. (1969). *Piaget's theory of intellectual development*. Englewood Cliffs, NJ: Prentice-Hall.

Gruber, H. E., & Voneche, J. J. (Eds.). (1977). *The essential Piaget*. New York: Basic Books.

Gudas, L. J. (1990, Aug.). Children's reactions to bereavement: A developmental perspective. In D. E. Balk (Chair), *The many faces of bereavement: Counseling and research*. Symposium conducted at the 98th Annual Convention of the American Psychological Association, Boston.

Harrison, S. I., Davenport, C. W., & McDermott, J. F. (1967). Children's reactions to bereavement. *Archives of General Psychiatry, 17*, 593–597.

Hoffman, S., & Strauss, S. (1985). The development of children's concepts of death. *Death Studies, 9*, 469–482.

Hul, C. H., Chan, I. S., & Chan, S. (1989). Death cognition among Chinese teenagers: Beliefs about consequences of death. *Journal of Research in Personality, 23*, 99–117.

Janoff-Bulman, R. (1985). The aftermath of victimization: Rebuilding shattered assumptions. In C. R. Figley (Ed.), *Trauma and its wake* (pp. 15–31). New York: Brunner/Mazel.

Kane, B. (1979). Children's concepts of death. *Journal of Genetic Psychology, 13*, 141–153.

Kerr, N. J. (1979). The effect of hospitalization on the developmental tasks of childhood. *Nursing Forum, 18*, 108–130.

Koocher, G. P. (1973). Childhood, death, and cognitive development. *Developmental Psychology, 9*, 369–375.

Koocher, G. P. (1981). Children's conceptions of death. In R. Bibace & M. Walsh (Eds), *New directions for child development: Children's conceptions of health, illness, and bodily function* (No. 14, pp. 85–99). San Francisco: Jossey-Bass.

Koocher, G. P. (1986). Coping with a death from cancer. *Journal of Consulting and Clinical Psychology, 54*, 623–631.

Kranzler, E. M., Shaffer, D., Wasserman, G., & Davies, M. (1990). Early childhood bereavement. *Journal of the American Academy of Child and Adolescent Psychiatry, 29*, 573–520.

Lansdown, R., & Benjamin, G. (1985). The development of the concept of death in children aged 5–9 years. *Child Care, Health, and Development, 11*, 13–20.

Lindemann, E. (1944). Symptomatology and management of acute grief. *American Journal of Psychiatry, 101*, 141–148.

Lonetto, R. (1980). *Children's conceptions of death*. New York: Springer.

McLoughlin, I. J. (1986). Bereavement in the mentally handicapped. *British Journal of Hospital Medicine, 36*, 256–260.

McNeil, J. N. (1983). Young mothers' communication about death with their children. *Death Education, 6*, 323–339.

Miller, J. B. M. (1971). Children's reactions to the death of a parent: A review of the psychoanalytic literature. *Journal of the American Psychoanalytic Association, 19*, 997–719.

Moses, S. (1991). Hidden children break the silence. *APA Monitor, 22*, 1, 24–25.

Nagy, M. (1948). The child's theories concerning death. *Journal of Genetic Psychology, 7*, 3–27.
Natterson, J. M., & Knudson, A. G. (1966). Observations concerning fear of death in fatally ill children and their mothers. *Psychosomatic Medicine, 22*, 456–465.
Neuhauser, C., Amsterdam, B., Hines, P., & Steward, M. (1985). Children's concepts of healing: Cognitive development and locus of control factors. *American Journal of Orthopsychiatry, 48*, 335–341.
Orbach, I., Talmon, O., Kedem, P., & Har-Even, D. (1987). Sequential patterns of five subconcepts of human and animal death in children. *Journal of the American Academy of Child and Adolescent Psychiatry, 26*, 578–582.
Payton, J. B., & Krocker-Tuskan, M. (1988). Children's reactions to loss of parent through violence. *Journal of the American Academy of Child and Adolescent Psychiatry, 27*, 563–566.
Perrin, E. C., & Gerrity, P. S. (1981). There's a demon in your belly: Children's understanding of illness. *Pediatrics, 67*, 841–849.
Perrin, E. C., & Gerrity, P. S. (1984). Development of children with a chronic illness. *Pediatric Clinics of North America, 31*, 19–31.
Piaget, J. (1960). *The child's conception of the world*. Paterson, NJ: Littlefield, Adams.
Piaget, J., & Inhelder, B. (1969). *The psychology of the child*. New York: Basic Books.
Polloch, G. H. (1986). Childhood sibling loss: A family tragedy. *Pediatric Annals, 15*, 851–855.
Rando, T. A. (1988). *Grieving: How to go on living when someone you love dies*. Lexington, MA: Lexington Books.
Reilly, T. P., Hasazi, J. E., & Bond, L. A. (1983). Children's conceptions of death and personal mortality. *Journal of Pediatric Psychology, 8*, 21–31.
Robertson, J. (1958). *Young children in hospital*. New York: Basic Books.
Sarwer-Foner, G. J. (1972). Denial of death and the unconscious longing for indestructability and immortality in the terminal phase of adolescence. *Canadian Psychiatric Association Journal, 17*, SS51–SS57.
Schonfield, D. J., & Smilansky, S. (1989). A cross-cultural comparison of Israeli and American children's death concepts. *Death Studies, 13*, 593–604.
Schumacher, J. D. (1984). Helping children cope with a sibling's death. *Family Therapy Collections, 8*, 82–94.
Schwartz, R. E. (1982). Children under fire: The role of the schools. *American Journal of Orthopsychiatry, 52*, 409–419.
Sekaer, C. (1987). Toward a definition of "childhood mourning." *American Journal of Psychotherapy, 41*, 201–219.
Siegel, K., Mesagno, F. P., & Christ, G. (1990). A prevention program for bereaved children. *American Journal of Orthopsychiatry, 60*, 168–175.
Speece, M. W., & Brent, S. B. (1984). Children's understanding of death: A review of three components of a death concept. *Child Development, 55*, 1671–1686.
Stambrook, M., & Parker, K. C. (1987). The development of the concept of death in childhood: A review of the literature. *Merrill-Palmer Quarterly, 33*, 133–157.
Terr, L. (1990). *Too scared to cry: Psychic trauma in childhood*. New York: Harper & Row.
Weller, E. B., Weller, R. A., Fristed, M. A., Cain, S. E., & Bowes, J. M. (1988). Should children attend their parents funeral? *Journal of the American Academy of Child and Adolescent Psychiatry, 27*, 559–562.
Wolfenstein, M. (1966). How is mourning possible? *Psychoanalytic Study of the Child, 20*, 93–123. New York: International Universities Press, 93–123.
Wortman, C. B., & Silver, R. C. (1989). The myths of coping with loss. *Journal of Consulting and Clinical Psychology, 57*, 349–357.
Yates, T. T., & Bannard, J. R. (1988). The "haunted" child: Grief, hallucinations, and family dynamics. *Journal of the American Academy of Child and Adolescent Psychiatry, 27*, 573–581.

5

Impact of Natural Disasters on Children and Families

RONALD W. BELTER and MITSUKO P. SHANNON

INTRODUCTION

Addressing the impact of natural disasters on children and their families poses a need to identify the manner in which natural disasters differ from other disasters (unnatural or human-made), as well as the manner in which children might be affected differently from adults. This chapter will define these distinctions as the foundation for discussing the research that has been conducted on natural disasters and their impact on children and families.

A disaster of any sort is identified by the characteristics of the disaster event and the scope and extent of physical, social, and psychological damage caused. An event which is outside the realm of everyday experience, affects a large number of people, and causes damage serious enough to pose demands or threats which exceed the victims' resources and ability to cope can be classified as a disaster. From this definition of disaster, it is relatively simple to produce a definition of a natural disaster as one caused by the forces of nature, rather than by the actions or products of humans. With this definition, one can easily classify numerous disastrous

RONALD W. BELTER and MITSUKO P. SHANNON • Department of Psychiatry and Behavioral Sciences, Medical University of South Carolina, 171 Ashley Avenue, Charleston, South Carolina 29245.

Children and Disasters, edited by Conway F. Saylor. Plenum Press, New York, 1993.

events in this category: e.g., earthquakes, hurricanes, tornadoes, cyclones, volcanic eruptions, floods, lightning strikes, forest and brush fires.

However, the distinction between natural disasters and other disasters is not always clear-cut. This is apparent in those situations in which nature and humans join forces to create a disaster. Human action or neglect can sometimes create a natural disaster. For example, a flood caused by the collapse of a dam has all the features of a natural disaster, but is possibly linked to human error in the dam construction. On the other hand, a naturally occurring event such as lightning can be disastrous due to poor judgement of playing golf, sailing, or standing under a tree during a thunderstorm. Such "natural" disasters, including fires, which have a human element as a causative factor, will be discussed in this chapter.

Special Features of Natural Disasters

The distinction between natural and other disasters is important in considering the damaging impact of a disaster and an individual's or community's efforts to cope with it and adjust in the aftermath. In a purely natural disaster, there will be little opportunity to realistically direct blame and responsibility to a guilty party, as there often is in human-made disasters. As a result, expression and discharge of emotion may be impeded to some extent, since there is no individual, group, or corporate entity toward whom victims can direct anger and frustration. Some individuals may turn these feelings inward and assume responsibility for not being prepared or for taking the wrong action. On the other hand, in a natural disaster which includes a human causative element, some individuals may externalize these feelings to an excessive degree.

From a cognitive standpoint, it may be more difficult for some individuals to make sense of the purely natural disaster by way of identifying a cause or rationale for the disaster. As a result, achieving closure and resolution may be more difficult as the individual continues to struggle with the question "Why?" or "Why me?" Conversely, some individuals may find comfort in the notion that it was "just fate" or "the will of God."

Full resolution and closure in a purely natural disaster is not likely to be complicated by the criminal prosecution of a perpetrator or a negligent party, nor by civil suits to recover damages from the responsible party. However, complications arising from disputes with insurance carriers over coverage for damage caused in a natural disaster may find their way into court. Such litigation may prove helpful to some individuals in having justice done or receiving compensation, an opportunity not usually available to victims of purely natural disasters. For others it may only prolong and accentuate the distress, and the absence of extended court battles may be a blessing for those who just want to put the disaster behind them.

While distinguishing between natural and other disasters identifies the common elements shared by natural disasters, there are important factors which differentiate various types of natural disasters. The first is the nature of the damage caused, which includes physical, social, and psychological damage. Not all natural disasters result in physical injury and/or loss of life, and by the same token, not all of them cause significant material damage to property and possessions. For example, a lightning strike may cause injury and death without property damage, and proper evacuation before a hurricane or flood can prevent injury with devastating property damage. Social damage can vary over a wide spectrum of disruption of functioning of the various systems with which an individual interacts. Different disasters may displace families from their homes, children from their schools, or parents from their employment. Other community systems such as the health care system, utilities and communication systems, transportation, and systems for normal distribution of necessary commodities may be affected in different ways. Variation in psychological damage caused by disasters accompanies variations in physical damage and social damage, posing different types of stress and barriers to coping with that stress.

The scope and extent of damage caused is another factor on which natural disasters can vary. Not every disaster causes widespread damage. By contrast to large-scale disasters such as hurricanes and earthquakes, which may devastate an entire region, other disasters may affect a relatively small proportion of the community. A large-scale disaster may accentuate the damage by affecting a larger number of people and depleting community resources for assistance. However, such an extensive impact may result in a sense of shared experience which unites victims in support of each other. While resources for assistance may not be depleted in a disaster with less extensive damage, victims may have to deal with feeling unjustly singled out from nonvictims. They may also feel a sense of being special as a result of extra attention and resources made available to them.

Finally, natural disasters vary in the amount of prior warning and preparation time afforded to those who are affected. Today, hurricane warnings afford ample time to secure property and evacuate to safety. Conditions ripe for tornadoes and floods can also be forecast, but tornadoes and flash floods still occur without prior warning. Earthquakes still remain unpredictable and strike without any warning. This factor of sudden onset or prior warning of a disaster can accentuate or mute surprise and shock reactions. Prior warning is a critical factor in preparatory action which can reduce the physical, social, and psychological damage caused in a natural disaster.

Developmental Issues for Child Disaster Victims

In addition to the common and distinctive characteristics of natural disasters discussed above, the common and distinctive characteristics of child victims of natural disasters merit consideration. Basic issues of stress and coping, PTSD, and grief have been addressed from a developmental perspective in previous chapters of this book. However, in relation to the distinctive features of natural disasters, a few specific points are important to address.

At any age, a child's comprehension of the natural disaster may be complicated by his/her magical belief system, religious beliefs, and level of moral development. Ascribing blame to a nonhuman entity (God, Mother Nature, or some other anthropomorphized natural force) may impact on acceptable and successful ways of expressing emotions. Can a child be comfortably angry with God? Should a parent encourage clearly erroneous, fantasized notions the child has? While some children are prone to seek and blame external causes, others are prone to internalize when such external causes are not readily apparent. Under the circumstances of a natural disaster, a young child may be particularly vulnerable to believing that he/she is being punished for being bad. As the child struggles to achieve a cognitive understanding of a natural disaster, there is often not a clear and concrete explanation which fits the child's developmental level. Developmental theories would suggest that a child's comprehension of and emotional adjustment to a natural disaster depend on the characteristics of the disaster as discussed earlier, key developmental factors and characteristics of the child, and the extent to which the child's significant others and systems are affected by the natural disaster.

RESEARCH ON NATURAL DISASTERS AND CHILDREN

Although there is a respectable body of research describing significant short- and long-term effects in adults, there have been relatively few studies of the impact of natural disasters on children. The quality of this research has varied considerably as the sophistication and rigor of research design have improved over time. The review of the literature which follows is organized according to the type of research method employed.

Nonstandardized Methods

The earliest studies of the effects of natural disasters on children are characterized by the use of interviews and other nonstandardized methods in describing clinical assessments of children affected by a disaster. The first of these was conducted after a tornado damaged a theater filled with children in Vicksburg, Mississippi, in 1953 (Block, Silber, & Perry, 1956). In less than 10 minutes, several children were killed as they watched a Saturday afternoon matinee. A total of 185 children, ranging in age from 2 to 15, were evaluated through interviews with 88 parents conducted one week after the tornado struck. The results based on "exploratory impressionistic overview" of the interviews made by two psychiatrists indicated that 113 children demonstrated no emotional disturbance, while 32 had mild emotional disturbance, and 24 had severe emotional disturbance. Behavior problems reported by the parents included increased dependency, regression, "tornado games," phobic symptoms, and avoidance symptoms. Emotional disturbance in the children was linked to factors which included awareness of the tornado, presence at the impact zone, personal injury as a result of the tornado, having a family member killed or injured, and exposure to parents who responded in a dissociative/demanding way. There were no differences between boys and girls on the ratings of emotional disturbance, but preschool children were less likely to be rated as disturbed than school-aged children.

In a second report focusing on the parents of the same children (Silber, Perry, & Block 1957), clinical impressions derived from parent interviews indicated that the parents themselves may have experienced difficulty dealing with the disaster. It also appeared that no particular pattern of child management was more effective than any other in decreasing symptoms of emotional disturbance in children. However, it appeared that consistency by the parent and the resumption of school resulted in a decrease in disturbances in children.

In 1962, a cyclone struck Oregon killing 46 people. Winds were estimated to be well over 100 mph, lasting over five hours, and causing over $170 million in material damage. A cyclone warning was issued five hours before impact. A descriptive study of this event and its impact on children described some of the general reactions reported by children in interviews and therapy contacts (Crawshaw, 1963). The impression was that children ages infant to eight years displayed reactions that were "a direct reflection of the parents' psychological state" (p. 159). Children ages 10 to 13 reported feeling excitement during the storm with no overt expression of fear or anxiety. Teen-aged children reported both excitement and anxiety.

In 1966, a tip-mining complex collapsed after several days of heavy rain in Aberfan, Wales, causing a massive landslide directly onto a primary school, killing 116 children and 28 adults. Although there had been concern about its proximity to the school, there was no advance warning of the disaster. In a descriptive study based on 400 interviews conducted over a four-year period following the disaster, Lacey (1972) evaluated 56 children and their parents who had been referred to the child guidance clinic. Clinical impressions indicated that the children exhibited emotional difficulties secondary to the disaster. The author observed that the children who were most affected had other anxiety-creating events in their backgrounds, such as a number of grief situations in the family's past.

In 1972, following an extended rainfall, a slag dam collapsed, sending a tidal wave of water through Buffalo Creek Valley in West Virginia, killing 125 people, and leaving 4,000 others homeless as it destroyed several communities. The flood was not entirely without warning, as the residents had apparently expressed some concern about potential flooding (Rangell, 1976). In her assessment of 11 of the children under the age of 12 who survived the disaster, Newman (1976) utilized projective techniques, such as the draw-a-person, three wishes, and storytelling techniques. Her clinical impressions suggested that the nature of emotional impairment was dependent on the child's developmental level at the time of the trauma, their perceptions of the reactions of their families, and direct exposure to the disaster.

Standardized Methods

The early clinical reports yielded valuable clinical impressions indicating that negative psychological experiences were common effects of natural disasters. There were also indications that these effects were possibly linked to a number of factors which included the extent of exposure to the disaster, personal injury to self or a significant other, predisaster history of stressful events, age or developmental level of the child, and the effectiveness of parental coping with the disaster. To further refine these impressions and collect more reliable and valid data that could be generalized to other populations, researchers began to employ more structured and standardized methods of inquiry. This group of studies is characterized by the use of structured and standardized methods with a single data source and with multiple data sources.

In the first of these studies, Milne (1977a,b) assessed the effects of cyclone Tracy, which devastated Darwin, Australia, in the early morning hours of Christmas Day in 1974. The storm destroyed between 5,000 and 8,000 houses, leaving only 500 that were habitable. The casualty list included 49 dead, another 16 lost at sea, and an unknown number missing and presumed dead. An original questionnaire was administered to 267 parents of children up to age 18 who actually experienced the cyclone (child N = 647). This questionnaire assessed the frequency of (1) behavior problems such as fear, repression, and aggression; (2) somatic complaints; and (3) school problems in the 7–10 months after the cyclone. The children's parents reported a higher prevalence of behavior problems in the preschool and primary-school children, with a lower prevalence observed with increasing age. Only fear of rain and wind was observed in a significant percentage of the entire sample (26%). Overall, behavior problems, somatic complaints, and school problems were reported more frequently among children who were evacuated after the cyclone but had not yet returned home and least frequently among children who had not evacuated.

In late 1982 and the spring of 1983, two housing subdivisions in a river flood plain near St. Louis were flooded, forcing evacuation of residents and causing significant property damage. Earls, Smith, Reich, and Jung (1988) used the Diagnostic Interview for Children and Adolescents (DICA) to evaluate 32 children, aged 6–17, in 20 households, one year after the flooding occurred. Data were collected in separate interviews with the child and the parent. The results showed that although there was a pattern of consistency in the parent and child reports (r = .38), the parents reported significantly fewer symptoms in their children than the children themselves reported. A strong association between the parent's own symptoms and the child's symptoms was noted, as the parents of children with a high number of self-reported symptoms reported a high number of symptoms in themselves. Of the 32 children, 19 were classed as having had a preexisting psychiatric disorder. All 9 of the children reporting flood-related symptoms had had preexisting psychiatric disorders. There was no relationship between the degree of exposure to the flood and the symptoms in either parents or children.

Two studies were conducted in Revere, Massachusetts, following a blizzard with a record snowfall and flood which paralyzed the region for a week in 1978. Seven to eight months prior to the disaster, Burke, Moccia, Borus, and Burns (1986) had collected data on 81 preschool children in a Head Start program with a Connors Teacher and Parent Questionnaire. Five months following the disaster, follow-up questionnaires were again distributed to the parents of these children with questionnaires for 64 of the children, 33 male and 31 female, returned. The following results were obtained: (1) Anxiety scores for boys increased while anxiety scores for girls decreased; (2) The entire group had significantly increased Aggressive Conduct subscale scores, indicating an increase in externalizing behaviors; (3) Scores on the School Behavior subscale decreased significantly, indicating improved adjustment to the pre-school environment; (4) Two subgroups of children demonstrated increased problems after the disaster, those with unspecified predisaster "special needs" and children who lived closer to the flooded area. (5) Parents' subjective rating of overall behavior indicated that there was no worsening of behavior.

The second study was conducted 10 months after the disaster with a sample of 47 fifth-grade Sunday school students, 19 from the flooded area and 28 from a nonflooded area (Burke, Borus, Burns, Millstein, & Beasely, 1982). Each subject was asked to write a story about "what this coming winter will be like", which was blindly rated by six clinicians for signs of depression, anxiety, and concern about the future. These ratings indicated that emotional distress was higher in the children from the flooded area, compared with the children from the nonflooded area. Analysis by gender revealed that this difference was true only for the girls, but not the boys, from the flooded area.

In 1980, a lightning-strike disaster occurred during a soccer game in southern Illinois. One child was killed, and several others were injured. There were two reports of the impact of this tragedy on the children who were present and survived. In the initial study (Dollinger, O'Donnell, & Staley, 1984), 29 children, aged 10–12, who survived the disaster were compared to a control group of 58 nontraumatized children matched for sex, age, and socioeconomic class drawn from a normative study of the Louisville Fear Survey for Children (LFSC). Data collection one to two months after the disaster involved interviews with the surviving children and their parents, a brief TAT-like projective task consisting of two lightning pictures, as well as the LFSC completed by the child and the parent. The results included the following: (1) interview-based ratings of increased emotional distress in the lightning strike group were related to the child's report of increased fears; (2) on both parent and child report, the lightning-strike group demonstrated more intense and frequent fears in general and, in particular, of storms; (3) mothers tended to report a lower frequency of specific fears than their children reported, and correlations between mother and child report were similar for both the study and the control groups ($r = .06$ to $.56$); and (4) the correlations between mother and child reports of the frequency of fear of storms was poor in both groups ($r = .09$ and $.19$); however, the correlation between mother and child reports of intensity of fear of storms was significantly higher for the study group ($r = .86$) than for the control group ($r = .38$). The indication is that the disaster enhanced the mothers' sensitivity to the intensity of this specific fear.

In addition to the procedure described above, in the second report the mothers were asked to complete an expansion of the Sleep and Somatization scales of the Missouri Children's Behavior Checklist (Dollinger, 1986). The results indicated that the children's adjustment improved over time, and children judged to be more emotionally upset by the trauma (based on interview data) exhibited increased sleep problems and somatic complaints as reported by their mothers.

Fires.   An Australian brush fire in 1983 left 14 people and over 200,000 livestock dead while burning approximately 300,000 acres of land. A longitudinal survey of child victims at 2, 8, and 26 months after the fire was described in a series of reports (McFarlane, 1987, 1988; McFarlane, Policansky, & Irwin, 1987). An initial total of 808 children (mean age = 8.2 years; 52.8% were male) were surveyed, although smaller groups of subjects were assessed at each of the points of data collection. At the 2-month point, Rutter Parent and Teacher Questionnaires were administered, along with general questionnaires that assessed such areas as personal loss and exposure. The 8- and 26-month questionnaires documented the continuing impact of the disaster. The symptoms reported by parents at the 2-month point were fewer than the symptoms reported at the 8- and 26-month point. The teachers' report indicated that educational underachievement and absenteeism were higher at the 26-month point than at the 8-month point. With regard to PTSD symptoms, (1) one third of the children continued to have a preoccupation with the brush fire at the 26-month point; (2) posttraumatic symptoms were not directly and consistently predictive of psychological disorders; (3) at 2 and 8 months, the children who showed increased anxiety and behavioral problems at school (but not at home) showed increased posttraumatic symptoms at the 26-month point; (4) family disruption after the fire (separation, changes in family function, and maternal preoccupation) was more of a posttraumatic stress determinant than the extent of direct exposure; and (5) the intensity of the posttraumatic symptoms observed by the parents at the 8-month point significantly correlated with the symptoms at the 26-month point.

It was postulated that adverse life events after the fire could have had an effect on continuing preoccupation with the disaster, as indicated by (1) increased morbidity from the 2-month to the 8-month to the 26-month point and (2) educational achievement decreased between the 8-month and 26-month points. However, the teachers' reports did not show an increase in problems over time. Children who had had school behavior problems at the 2- and 8-month points later quiesced at school. However, at the 8- and 26-month points, these same children were more of a problem at home and showed sustained morbidity across the entire 26-month postfire period.

Children and adolescents who were victims of four residential fires were evaluated by Jones and Ribbe (1991a). The study was conducted in two phases. The first phase evaluated eight children ranging in age from 4 to 16 years and their parents. Adult and child fire questionnaires were used to assess demographic data, behavior prior to and during the fire, and the consequences of the fire. All eight of the children were worried, sad, scared, or upset at the time of the fires. Five of the eight children were fearful of another fire or upset one month after the fire (one child did not respond). Parents' and children's perceptions of the fire were different with five out of eight children fearing injury versus only one out of seven parents. Also, seven out of eight children felt panic during the fire, but only one out of seven parents felt panic. This was a preliminary study that indicated an individual's psychological reaction to a fire could be documented and that PTSD symptoms were endorsed.

This led to a second study of 38 boys attending a private boarding school (Jones & Ribbe, 1991a). A fire had occurred in the dormitory, and 29 residents of the dorm were interviewed, as well as 13 boys who were not residents. The residents had a mean age of 16.7 years, and the nonresidents had a mean age of 16.5 years. Three instruments were used to interview the subjects four months after the fire: the State Trait Anxiety Inventory (STAI), the Horowitz Impact of Events Scale (HIES), and a semistructured diagnostic interview Diagnostic Interview for Children and Adolescents (DICA-6R-A) assessing major affective disorders, conduct disorders, oppositional disorders, overanxious disorders, and adjustment disorders. The results revealed that short-term PTSD symptomatology had increased in both the resident and the nonresident populations as measured by the HIES. However, levels of PTSD symptomatology as measured by the DICA were found to be much higher in the residents. Only two subjects met the full criteria for PTSD in the revised third edition of the American Psychiatric Association's *Diagnostic and Statistical Manual* (DSM-III-R; APA, 1987). The STAI results were below normative levels for both groups in state anxiety levels.

A third study was conducted following a wildfire that spread through a small city in Southern California on June 27, 1990 (Jones & Ribbe, 1991b). The fire was fueled by winds gusting up to 60 miles per hour and occurred quickly at approximately six o'clock in the evening, when nearly everyone was at home or returning from work, a situation causing a very difficult evacuation for rescue workers and fire fighters. The fire raged on for five days, leaving in its wake one fatality and over $250 million in damage. One month after the disaster, researchers identified and interviewed a group of 33 children and adolescents. Of these, 23 had been victims of the fire, and 10 were nonvictims, selected as a control group from the same city where the fire occurred. The study subjects ranged in age from 7 to 18 years of age; 13 were younger than 11. The control group ranged in age from 7 to 13; there was only one 13-year-old; and the remaining subjects in the group were less than 12 years of age. A longitudinal, cross-sectional study was conducted utilizing a semi-structured diagnostic interview (DICA), the Horowitz Impact of Events Scale, the State Trait Anxiety Inventory For Children, the Children's Behavioral Questionnaire for Completion by Parents, and the child form of the Fire Questionnaire. Only the results of the DICA, the HIES, and the Fire Questionnaire were reported. The overall level of PTSD symptoms assessed by the DICA was relatively mild for both groups. However, both the victim and control groups scored in the "high" range on the total HIES score. Data gathered from the HIES revealed a significant increase on the avoidance subscale in the study group. However, this effect was not seen on the DICA. There were no significant differences across developmental levels. Two children and one adolescent met the DSM-III-R criteria for PTSD. Information gathered from the fire questionnaire indicated that children and adolescents may have demonstrated a great deal of anxiety concerning their parents' safety, which may have exacerbated their symptomatology.

Earthquakes. On November 23, 1980, an earthquake struck a rural region of central Italy. Four thousand people died in 116 villages, while tens of thousands lost their homes. Because of the terrain and isolation of the villages, emergency relief was delayed for days for many victims. A study of the impact on children in six different villages (Galante & Foa, 1986) was broken into three phases: (1) at six months after the earthquake, preintervention testing of 300 children to select children at risk of developing "neurotic or antisocial disturbances," using the Rutter Behavioral Questionnaire for completion by teachers; (2) implementation of treatment with all the children in the first through fourth grades in one village who were judged to be at greatest risk according to the questionnaires ($n = 62$); and (3) posttreatment assessment 18 months after the earthquake. The findings were as follows: (1) the amount of destruction experienced by the children was not correlated with their at-risk scores; (2) at six months after the earthquake, at-risk scores were correlated with a death in the family for the children of only one of the villages; (3) this correlation no longer existed at the 18-month assessment; and (4) although there was a reported decrease in the at-risk scores of the children who received treatment, there was also a slight decrease in the at-risk scores of children in another village who received no treatment. Otherwise, the 18-month scores either stayed the same or increased in the other four villages.

The Loma Prieta earthquake struck the San Francisco Bay area in October 1989, killing 67 people and causing about $6 billion in property damage throughout the region. At least two studies of the emotional effects of the earthquake on children have been completed. Bradburn (1991) conducted a survey of 22 children, aged 10 to 12 years. Twelve were male and 17 were African-American. The Post-Traumatic Stress Reaction Index for Children (Frederick, 1985) was administered as well as the Individual Experience interview designed for this study to assess the subject's personal experience of the quake and perceptions of family response. The data were collected six to eight weeks after the disaster. More than half of the children reported feeling afraid and upset when thinking about the earthquake, having frequent reminders of it, and feeling more jumpy and nervous than they had before the earthquake. On the Reaction Index twenty-seven percent reported "moderate" levels of PTSD symptomatology, 36% reported "mild" symptoms, none endorsed "severe" levels. The most powerful predictor of PTSD symptoms was close proximity to the disaster area. Parental disturbance, previous traumatic experiences, and personal damage experienced did not predict PTSD symptoms.

The second study (Guerin, Junn, & Rushbrook, 1991; Junn, Guerin, & Rushbrook, 1990) assessed behavior problems exhibited in preschool children who experienced the Loma Prieta earthquake. The sample consisted of 56 preschool directors, 50 preschool teachers, 75 parents of 2- and 3-year-olds, and 35 parents of 4- and 5-year-olds. Over 50% of the preschool directors and/or teachers reported increasing behavioral problems, including increased clinging, difficulty separating from parents, disobedience, difficulty concentrating, and increased aggressiveness and activity level. On the Achenbach Child Behavior Checklist (CBC) and a questionnaire assessing personal experiences related to the earthquake, over 50% of the parents of the 2- and 3-year-olds reported sleep problems, attention seeking, dependency traits, whining, and low frustration tolerance. For the 4- and 5-year-olds, 50% or more of the parents reported increased whining, arguing, disobedience, and attention seeking. Several factors contributed to these increased behaviors, including being at home during the earthquake, being away from the parent during the earthquake, the marital status of the parent, the number of children in the family, and the amount of damage to the home. Overall, approximately 15% of these preschoolers had a least one elevated behavior-problem scale on the CBC two to six weeks after the disaster. The most common symptoms reported were somatic complaints (vomiting, headaches, and stomachaches) and sleep problems.

Hurricanes. In September 1975, hurricane Eloise struck the Florida panhandle. Two cities were initially threatened, but only one of them actually sustained significant damage, which resulted in the county's being declared a federal disaster area. A comparison of the impact of the hurricane on children in the two cities was conducted by Piotrowski and

Dunham (1983). A disaster sample of 269 fifth-graders was drawn from four public schools in the city hit by the hurricane. Of these, 184 had taken part in a previous study seven months earlier and had completed the Nowicki-Strickland Locus of Control Scale for Children. A nondisaster sample of 194 fifth-graders was drawn from two public schools in the city that was not hit by the hurricane. Each student completed the locus-of-control scale and a semantic differential scale to assess the student's evaluation of the concept *hurricane*. The 184 pretested subjects showed a change toward more internal scores, which is expected with increased age. The disaster subjects had significantly more internal scores than the nondisaster subjects. Finally, the disaster subjects and the more internally oriented subjects overall evaluated the concept *hurricane* more positively than the non-disaster and externally oriented subjects. The implication is that an internal orientation and a more positive view of the hurricane may have been fostered by the opportunity to exercise some kind of control through various means of coping with the disaster.

In September 1989, hurricane Hugo struck the South Carolina coast around Charleston with 175-mile-per-hour winds and a tidal surge of 12–23 feet. The storm left in its wake 35 people dead and $5.9 billion of property damage. Hundreds of homes and buildings were totally destroyed, 900,000 people were without electricity, and approximately 270,000 people were temporarily out of work. There was advance warning of the storm, and an evacuation order was issued 24 hours in advance. A series of studies was conducted in a comprehensive effort to assess the impact of the hurricane on several different groups of children and adolescents who were affected by the hurricane in different ways.

The first study (Sullivan, Saylor, & Foster, 1991; Saylor, Swenson, & Powell, 1992) collected data on 278 preschool children aged 1 year 11 months to 6 years 3 months, 54% of whom were male. Questionnaires completed by parents six weeks after the disaster included a modified Child Behavior Checklist and a questionnaire developed to assess the level of stress experienced before, during, and after the storm. The children were found to display a significant increase in the number and severity of problem behaviors after the hurricane, including dependent and demanding behavior, frustration, irritability, temper tantrums, and sleep difficulties. The children's prehurricane behavior problems, the total number of objective stressors experienced, and the parents' subjective level of stress were associated with an increase in the number of behavior problems. Developmental level was not a significant predictor of the children's reactions to the hurricane.

The long-term impact of the hurricane was assessed in a second sample of 161 pre-school-aged children, who were evaluated 14 months after the hurricane (Swenson, Powell, Foster, & Saylor, 1991). The children ranged in age from 2 to 6; 55% were male, and 99% were white. A control group of children in another southeastern city who had not experienced the hurricane was evaluated at the same time. This group of 21 children ranged in age from 2 to 6; 52% were female (19% did not indicate gender), and 91% were white. The parents of all the children completed four questionnaires designed for this study to assess hurricane-related experiences, life stressors, duration of symptoms, and problem behaviors. No differences were found between the control and study groups in the number or severity of problem behaviors over one year after the hurricane. However, in the children who experienced the hurricane, problem behavior did not decrease immediately after the storm. By parental report, 38% of the children displayed emotional or behavioral problems immediately after the hurricane; 29% continued to have problems three months after; 16% continued with problems six months after; 9% exhibited problems seven to nine months after; and only 6% still displayed such problems one year after the hurricane. Global ratings of behavioral difficulties in the children were found to be affected by the mother's level of distress after the hurricane, and increased parental distress was associated with higher ratings of behavioral problems.

A third sample of elementary-school students was evaluated in a study of 259 third-, fourth-, fifth-, and sixth-graders, 52% of whom were female (Dunn, 1991; Belter, Dunn, & Jeney, 1991; Belter, Foster, Imm, & Finch, 1991). Five months after the hurricane, each child and his or her parent completed five questionnaires that assessed behavioral difficulties and general emotional distress, PTSD symptoms, changes in family support, the material impact of the hurricane, and the coping strategies used by the children. The first four measures included a retrospective rating of circumstances before the hurricane as well as a current rating at five months after the hurricane. In this group of children, there was no evidence of significant behavioral difficulties or general emotional distress either before or after the hurricane. However, scores obtained on the Reaction Index of PTSD symptoms indicated that 89% of the children endorsed severe PTSD symptoms, and 69% of the parents reported severe PTSD symptoms in their children, based on the cut-off scores recommended by the author of the Reaction Index (Frederick, 1985). Finally, the children appeared to have used a wide array of primarily adaptive coping strategies after the hurricane. However, contrary to expectations, it was the children who reported the highest number of coping strategies who also reported the highest degree of PTSD symptoms.

The final hurricane Hugo study was a large-scale survey of 5,687 children in grades 5–12 in a rural county public school system (Lonigan,

Shannon, Finch, Daugherty, & Taylor, 1991; Daugherty, Shannon, Finch, & Lonigan, 1991). Of this sample, 51% were male and 67.3% were white. Each subject completed a trait anxiety measure (Revised Children's Manifest Anxiety Scale), a PTSD symptom self-report inventory (Reaction Index), and a questionnaire designed for the study to assess various experiences of the child related to the hurricane. The data were collected two to three months after the hurricane.

The results of this project revealed three classes of variables that predicted the extent to which the children endorsed PTSD symptoms. First were personal characteristics of the child at the time of the hurricane, including age, gender, race, and trait anxiety. Younger children, females, blacks, and children with higher levels of trait anxiety tended to endorse higher levels of PTSD symptoms. The second variable was the child's emotional experience during the hurricane. Here, the children who reported experiencing the hurricane with negative emotionality (e.g., sad, worried, and scared) scored higher on the PTSD index. Children who reported being excited during the hurricane did not show excessive symptoms. The third variable was the severity of exposure to the hurricane and its damage. Increased exposure, damage to the home, and a subjective rating of the severity of the storm were all related to a higher endorsement of PTSD symptoms.

DISCUSSION

The studies which have been conducted on children and adolescents to assess the psychological impact of natural disasters have all found emotional and behavioral consequences to varying degrees. The more recent, more rigorously designed studies have confirmed the clinical impressions of the earlier studies that psychological reactions to natural disasters are significant. Although the literature seems to raise more questions than have been answered, there are some general conclusions which appear to be supported.

First, it appears that, in general, diagnosable psychopathology is not commonly seen in the great majority of children who experience a natural disaster. However, when their inner concerns specifically related to the disaster are assessed, most children report significant levels of emotional distress. Thus, the immediate and direct psychological impact is significant for most children, who often report high levels of PTSD symptoms, but does not result in widespread diagnosable psychopathology.

Second, there is a general trend for the acute effects to diminish over time, with long-term effects for most children being minimal. However, this trend is not consistent, as the long-term effects of the Australian brushfires were reported to be more severe than the immediate acute effects. This appears to be the exception to the rule, as the other studies which addressed long-term follow-up reported a steady decline in stress reactions over time.

Third, in general, it appears that the more directly experienced and personally threatening or disruptive the disaster is, the greater the psychological impact on the child. This finding is consistent with other research in the area of trauma indicating that proximity to the traumatic event, threat of personal harm, and extent of loss are critical factors in the development of PTSD symptoms (Kilpatrick, Saunders, Amick-McMullen, Best, Veronen, & Resnick, 1989; Pynoos, Frederick, Nader, Arroyo, Steinberg, Eth, Nunez, & Fairbanks, 1987). Again, this trend was observed in most, but not all studies. The study of the St. Louis area flood and one of the San Francisco earthquake studies did not find exposure or personal damage to be directly related to stress reactions.

Fourth, in most studies, younger children were reported to be affected to a greater degree than older children and adolescents. This finding is intuitively reasonable and consistent with expectations that younger children are more vulnerable to stress which disrupts family stability and routine. The only study which found younger children to be less distressed was the Vicksburg tornado study, with conclusions based on subjective interview impressions, rather than on objective, standardized measures.

Fifth, children tend to report higher levels of specific symptoms and general emotional distress than their parents report in their children. This would suggest that under the circumstances of a natural disaster, parents have a tendency to underreport or be less aware of the extent to which their children are negatively affected. It may also be true that children tend to overreport their distress. In either case, it is clear that both perspectives need to be considered in assessing the impact of a natural disaster on children.

Sixth, there apparently is an association between the child's adjustment prior to the natural disaster and the extent to which the child experiences difficulty coping with the disaster. In summary, the child who is having difficulties of some sort before a natural disaster apparently is at greater risk for negative and prolonged reactions to the disaster.

Seventh, the extent to which the child's parents are negatively impacted by the disaster and have difficulty coping with it appears to be related to the impact of the disaster on the child. It would appear that parents having difficulty coping themselves convey that distress to their children and may thus exacerbate the reactions of their children. With regard to assisting the child in coping with a natural disaster, the parent who is unable to cope effectively may not be as available for effective coping and support for the child.

Although these conclusions appear to be fairly well established by the research that has been done to date, there is a great deal of work needed to further refine these findings. Research on the impact of natural disasters on children and families is still in an early stage. Since the late 1970s, as research efforts have become more sophisticated and rigorous, the results have revealed the complexity of the problem and uncovered widely diverse issues for further study and refinement. These issues relate to the nature of the impact of natural disasters on children as well as to the manner in which research is conducted.

There is clearly a need for further refinement of the distinctions among different types of disasters to determine the nature of their unique psychological impact on children and adolescents. The research that has been done has also underscored the importance of developmental issues which require further study. Another critical area of research is in the area of identification of the factors which mediate the psychological impact of a disaster. For example, predisaster functioning, internal coping resources, and external sources of support appear to contribute to the child's successful coping with the stress of a natural disaster. Likewise, access to these sources of support and utilization of coping resources is likely to be impacted by the disaster. Finally, the individual child's personal perception and experience of the disaster makes a unique contribution to the impact of the disaster, as does the parents' perception and experience.

Among the research issues to be addressed are the following. First, research on the impact of natural disasters on children has focused primarily on individuals who have been negatively affected and have displayed problematic reactions to the disaster. Yet, there are significant numbers of individuals who appear to cope well with the disaster and display considerable resilience in response to the stress. These individuals represent a group that should also be studied, to identify the factors which foster adaptive functioning and resilience in the face of disaster. Second, the research to date has emphasized the importance of comparison standards for assessing the impact of a natural disaster. The availability of predisaster baseline data or appropriate nonvictim control groups is essential in evaluating the effects of a disaster. Third, the importance of collecting data from multiple sources (e.g., self-report, parent report, teacher report) has been underscored to provide access to different, valid perspectives on the disaster experience. Fourth, it is important also to conduct longitudinal studies with periodic follow-up of victims to assess the long-term consequences and the process of healing. Finally, there is clearly a

need for development and refinement of better measures for assessing the
psychological processes and functions which are relevant.

REFERENCES

American Psychiatric Association. (1987). *Diagnostic and statistical manual of mental disorders*
(3rd ed., rev.; DSM-III-R). Washington, DC: Author.

Belter, R. W., Dunn, S. E., & Jeney, P. (1991). The psychological impact of hurricane Hugo on
children: A needs assessment. *Advances in Behaviour Research and Therapy, 13*(3), 155–161.

Belter, R. W., Foster, K. Y., Imm, P. S., & Finch, A. J. (1991). *Parent vs. child reports of PTSD
symptoms related to a catastrophic natural disaster.* Paper presented at the biennial meeting
of the Society for Research in Child Development, Seattle.

Block, D., Silber, E., & Perry, S. (1956). Some factors in the emotional reaction of children to
disaster. *American Journal of Psychiatry, 113*, 416–422.

Bradburn, I. S. (1991). After the earth shook: Children's stress symptoms 6–8 months after a
disaster. *Advances in Behaviour Research and Therapy, 13*(3), 173–179.

Burke, J., Borus, J., Burns, B., Millstein, & Beasley, M. (1982). Change in children's behavior
after a natural disaster. *American Journal of Psychiatry, 139*, 1010–1014.

Burke, J. D., Moccia, P., Borus, J. F., & Burns, B. J. (1986). Emotional distress in fifth-grade
children ten months after a natural disaster. *Journal of the American Academy of Child
Psychiatry, 25*, 536–541.

Crawshaw, R. (1963). Reaction to disaster. *Archives of General Psychiatry, 9*, 157–162.

Daugherty, T. K., Shannon, M. P., Finch, A. J, Jr., & Lonigan, C. J. (1991). *Assessment and
prediction of children's reaction to natural disaster.* Paper presented at the annual meeting of
the Society for Personality Assessment, New Orleans.

Dollinger, S. J. (1986). The measurement of children's sleep disturbances and somatic complaints following a disaster. *Journal of Consulting and Clinical Psychology, 52*, 1028–1038.

Dollinger, S. J., O'Donnell, J. P., & Staley, A. A. (1984). Lightning-strike disaster: Effects on
children's fears and worries. *Journal of Consulting and Clinical Psychology, 52*, 1028–1038.

Dunn, S. E. (1991). *The impact of a catastrophic natural disaster on children: PTSD symptomatology
and coping strategies.* Unpublished manuscript.

Earls, F., Smith, E., Reich, W., & Jung, K. G. (1988). Investigating psychopathological
consequences of a disaster in children: A pilot study incorporating a structured diagnostic interview. *Journal of the American Academy of Child and Adolescent Psychiatry, 27*, 90–95.

Frederick, C. J. (1985). Children traumatized by catastrophic situations. In S. Eth & R. S.
Pynoos (Eds.), *Post-traumatic stress disorders in children* (pp. 73–99). Washington, DC:
American Psychiatric Press.

Galante, R., & Foa, A. (1986). An epidemiological study of psychic trauma and treatment
effectiveness in children after a natural disaster. *Journal of the American Academy of Child
Psychiatry, 25*, 357–363.

Guerin, D. W., Junn, E., & Rushbrook, S. (1991). Preschoolers' reactions to the 1989 Bay Area
earthquake as assessed by parent report on the Child Behavior Checklist. In J. M. Vogel
(Chair), *Children's responses to natural disasters: The aftermath of hurricane Hugo and the 1989
Bay Area earthquake.* Symposium conducted at the biennial meeting of the Society for
Research in Child Development, Seattle.

Jones, R. T., & Ribbe, D. P. (1991a). Child, adolescent, and adult victims of residential fire:
Psychosocial consequences. *Behavior Modification, 15*, 560–580.

Jones R. T., & Ribbe, D. P. (1991b). Child and adolescent victims of fire: Psychological consequences. In R. W. Belter (Chair), *Short and long-term effects of trauma in children and adolescents*. Symposium conducted at the annual convention of the American Psychological Association, San Francisco.

Junn, E. N., Guerin, D. W., & Rushbrook, S. (1990). *Children's reactions to earthquake disaster*. Paper presented at the annual convention of the American Psychological Association, Boston.

Kilpatrick, D. G., Saunders, B. E., Amick-McMullen, A., Best, C. L., Veronen, L. J., & Resnick, H. S. (1989). Victim and crime factors associated with the development of crime-related posttraumatic stress disorder. *Behavior therapy, 20*, 199–214.

Lacey, G. N. (1972). Observations on Aberfan. *Journal of Psychosomatic Research, 16*, 257–260.

Lonigan, C. J., Shannon, M. P., Finch, A. J., Jr., Daugherty, T. K., & Taylor, C. M. (1991). Children's reactions to a natural disaster: Symptom severity and degree of exposure. *Advances in Behaviour Research Therapy, 13*(3), 135–154.

McFarlane, A. C. (1987). Post-traumatic phenomena in a longitudinal study of children following a natural disaster. *Journal of the American Academy of Child Psychiatry, 29*, 677–690.

McFarlane, A. C. (1988). Recent life events and psychiatric disorder in children: The interaction with preceding extreme adversity. *Journal of Child Psychology and Psychiatry, 29*, 677–690.

McFarlane, A. C., Policansky, S. K., & Irwin, C. (1987). A longitudinal study of the psychological morbidity in children due to a natural disaster. *Psychological Medicine, 17*, 727–738.

Milne, G. (1977a). Cyclone Tracy: 1. Some consequences of the evacuation for adult victims. *Australian Psychologist, 12*(1), 39–54.

Milne, G. (1977b). Cyclone Tracy: 2. The effects on Darwin children. *Australian Psychologist, 12*(1), 55–62.

Newman, C. J. (1976). Children of disaster: Clinical observation at Buffalo Creek. *American Journal of Psychiatry, 133*, 306–312.

Piotrowski, C., & Dunham, F. Y. (1983). Locus of control orientation and perception of "hurricane" in fifth graders. *Journal of General Psychology, 109*, 119–127.

Pynoos, R. S., Frederick, C., Nader, K., Arroyo, W., Steinberg, A., Eth, S., Nunez, F., & Fairbanks, L. (1987). Life threat and posttraumatic stress in school-age children. *Archives of General Psychiatry, 44*, 1057–1063.

Rangell, L. (1976). Discussion of the Buffalo Creek disaster: The course of psychic trauma. *American Journal of Psychiatry, 133*, 313–316.

Saylor, C. F., Swenson, C. C., & Powell, P. (1992). Hurricane Hugo blows down the broccoli: Preschoolers' post-disaster play and adjustment. *Child Psychiatry Human Development, 22*(3), 139–149.

Silber, E., Perry S. E., & Block, D. A. (1957). Patterns of parent-child interaction in a disaster. *Journal of Psychiatry, 21*, 159–167.

Sullivan, M. A., Saylor, C. F., & Foster, K. Y. (1991). Post hurricane adjustment of preschoolers and their families. *Advances in Behaviour Research and Therapy, 13*(3), 163–171.

Swenson, C. C., Powell, P., Foster, K. Y., & Saylor, C. F. (1991). *The long-term reactions of young children to natural disaster*. Paper presented at the annual convention of the American Psychological Association, San Francisco.

6

Technology-Related Disasters

WILLIAM YULE

INTRODUCTION

Within the literature on the effects of disasters on mental health, based mainly on studies of adults, it is widely accepted that human-made, technological disasters are associated with higher levels of later distress than are natural disasters. One year after a disaster, systematic estimates of morbidity indicate that 30%–40% of survivors may be adversely affected, with human-made disasters showing levels of over 30%–70% percent severe impairment (Raphael, 1986). The aim of this chapter is to consider what little evidence there is about the effects of technological disasters on children and adolescents.

Immediately, one confronts a problem of definition. Whereas hurricanes and tornadoes are clearly natural disasters, earthquakes are natural phenomena, but the buildings that collapse are human-made, sometimes constructed to inadequate specifications. When the dam burst at Buffalo Creek or the coal tip slid down and buried the school at Aberfan, the disasters held elements that were both natural and human-made. Accidents on all methods of mass transportation are clearly technological, although the failing that causes a crash may be human. Deliberate kidnappings, sniper attacks, war, and other personal violence are human-made, but not necessarily technological. Given the paucity of literature available, one need not be too pedantic at drawing a line as to which studies to

WILLIAM YULE • University of London Institute of Psychiatry, London, United Kingdom SE5 8AF.

Children and Disasters, edited by Conway F. Saylor. Plenum Press, New York, 1993.

review. I have chosen to cast the net fairly wide in order to examine the effects on children of a wide range of life-threatening disasters, with a view to identifying important parameters for future study.

Hodgkinson and Stewart (1991) provide a useful categorization of technological disasters:

- Mass transport: Ships, air, rail, and road/automobile
- Fire
- Building collapse
- Environmental poisoning, chemical and nuclear
- Civilian violence, terrorism, and crime

As reactions to fire and to man's deliberate inhumanity are discussed fully in other chapters, this will concentrate on the effects of transport disasters and other accidents in the technological environment.

MASS TRANSPORT DISASTERS

The 20th century has witnesses the development of many means of rapid transport. The trains and boats and planes of the popular song are, generally speaking, remarkably safe ways of getting about, but when there are collisions or crashes, then there may be many people injured or killed, and the accident may occur many miles from home.

Hodgkinson and Stewart (1991) list the following features of mass transport disasters. They occur with little warning and often in inaccessible places such that there may be a "protracted struggle for survival" (p. 49). When the accident occurs in unfamiliar territory, not only may this disorientate the survivors, it also makes it difficult for relatives to imagine what actually happened, and in turn may impede the ability of relatives to help survivors recall and come to terms with what happened.

Many airplane crashes have 100% fatalities, so that the issue for those responsible for managing the aftermath revolves around the needs of bereaved relatives, who will include children. Where a crash has occurred at high speed, this will result in multiple physical injuries in survivors and may so mutilate bodies as to make identification difficult. In turn, officials on the scene may arrange for hasty burials. It is now well established that many bereaved relatives will have greater difficulty in processing their grief if they either do not see the dead body or, worse still, if there is no body to be seen (Hodgkinson & Stewart, 1991). Again, most of this descriptive work has involved adults. Less attention has been paid to studying the best ways of helping child survivors and child relatives come to terms with their grief in similar traumatic situations.

Survivors of transport disasters often develop phobic avoidance of the type of transport and the place where the accident occurred. A common finding is that where they blame the driver/pilot/ship's captain, they develop a fear of placing responsibility for their safety in anyone else's hands. This form of generalization of phobic avoidance can lead to severe limitation on their mobility.

The experience of total helplessness in the midst of a disaster seems to be related to later feelings of depression, as expected from helplessness theory (Abramson, Seligman, & Teasdale, 1978). Survivors later develop a great deal of anger, usually directed toward those they perceive as responsible for the accident. They may also develop considerable guilt revolving around their own decision to travel on the particular trip, guilt about what they did or did not do to survive the trauma, and guilt about surviving when many others were maimed or killed.

Where the passengers involved in an accident were part of a previously established group, group cohesion may be an important aspect of how quickly they adapt. In many cases, transport disasters involve large numbers of strangers who then scatter over a wide geographical area. Given that much of the literature on the aftermath of natural disasters emphasizes the need to rebuild the community and to use that goal as a means of mobilizing mutual support within the community (Raphael, 1986), such approaches are much more difficult to implement after a transport disaster. Support groups have to be artificially constructed, and ironically, survivors with major transport phobias may have to travel long distances to participate.

Having listed the main characteristics of transport disasters as seen by Hodgkinson and Stewart (1991), let us now consider evidence from studies of children caught up in different transport disasters. Surprisingly, there appear to be no reported studies of the emotional effects on children of road traffic accidents (RTAs). Malt (1988) reported a study of the effects of RTAs on adults in Norway and concluded that posttraumatic stress disorder (PTSD) is a rare consequence. Clinically, children can show PTSD after road traffic accidents; they report intrusive memories, interference with their enjoyment of life, and various physiological symptoms, as well as specific avoidance of traveling by automobile. Thus, some children do develop PTSD following road traffic accidents, but to date, there are no published data that determine the proportion who do so nor, importantly, what distinguishes those who do from those who appear to cope and adjust well.

THE *HERALD OF FREE ENTERPRISE*

Our own studies of children who survived shipping disasters cast light on some of these issues. In March 1987, the roll-on–roll-off car ferry the *Herald of Free Enterprise*, which regularly sailed between England and Belgium, capsized in Zeebrugge harbor. Within 45 seconds, an apparently stable ship rolled over onto its side, passenger were thrown down, portholes smashed, and the cold water of the North Sea rushed in. Half those on board were killed, many be drowning. We were asked to assess the children and families who survived, and we reported on 13 of the then-known 22 surviving children under the age of 16 (Yule & Williams, 1990). At six to nine months post accident, over half the children were reported by their parents to be showing significant disturbance, whereas only 2 of the 8 children rated by teachers were said to be disturbed. We used the Rutter parent and teacher rating scales and, despite the small numbers, concluded that these screening scales were not sensitive to the subjective distress that is the hallmark of PTSD. In interviews, the children revealed much more pathology than was known to their parents or teachers.

After getting to know the children better, we were able to ask the children to complete Horowitz's Revised Impact of Events Scale (Horowitz, Wilner, & Alvarez, 1979). Children as young as 8 found the scale meaningful, and on that basis it was concluded that the children scored higher than adult patients attending Horowitz's clinic for treatment. At 12–15 months post accident, the children repeated their ratings, and it was found that the overall level had scarcely dropped.

THE *JUPITER*

On October 21, 1988, the cruise ship *Jupiter* sailed from Athens to take a party of around 400 British schoolchildren and their teachers on an educational cruise of the eastern Mediterranean. As they left harbor, it was beginning to get dark. Some of the groups were lining up for the evening meal, some were attending a briefing lecture on what they were to see on the trip. Just out of the harbor, the *Jupiter* was struck amidships by an Italian tanker and holed.

At first, no one realized the seriousness of their predicament, but very quickly, the *Jupiter* shipped water and began listing badly to the port and aft. Children were told to assemble in a lounge on an upper deck, but many were unfamiliar with the layout of the ship. As the vessel listed at 45 degrees and then worse, they found it very difficult to get around. Children became separated from friends and teachers. Many were able to jump across to tugs that had come alongside, but sadly, two seamen assisting in the transfer were fatally crushed between the ship and the tug. Many children saw their dead bodies.

Other children, some of whom were nonswimmers, clung to the

railings on the topmost deck under the lifeboats and had to jump in the water as the *Jupiter* went down, its funnel hissing and spurting out soot and smoke. Children and staff clung to wreckage in the dark, oily water until rescued. Some of those swimming in the water were terrified lest they were run down by the rescue craft. It was many hours before it was realized that all but one child and one teacher had survived. After spending a sleepless night on a sister ship moored in Piraeus harbor, the children were flown back to a barrage of publicity the next day. Although the tour company offered to arrange counseling for any of the children who requested it, schools varied enormously in how they dealt with the aftermath. Some were very sympathetic and arranged individual and group help; other discouraged children from even talking about it.

Yule and Udwin (1991) offered to help the survivors at one school. An account of the preliminary "debriefing" work is given below. All 24 survivors were screened on three scales: the Impact of Events Scale, Birleson's Depression Scale (Birleson, 1981; Birleson, Hudson, Buchanan, & Wolff, 1987), and the Revised Children's Manifest Anxiety Scale (Reynolds & Richmond, 1978). On the basis of their scores 10 days after the sinking, 10 girls aged 14 were thought to be at high risk of developing problems. When help was offered on an individual or group basis, and without saying which girls were considered to be at high risk, 8 of the 10 high-risk group came forward for help on the first day. The other 2 attended the second meeting. Only 5 others ever attended any group meeting. Thus, there was a highly significant relationship between scores on the screening scales and later help seeking, and we concluded that the battery showed considerable promise in identifying the children who most need help after a disaster.

The survivors and all other fourth-year (14- to 15-year-old) girls in that school completed the Revised Fear Survey Schedule for Children (Ollendick, Yule, & Ollier, 1991). Effectively, there were three subgroups of girls: those who went on the cruise and were traumatized, those who had wanted to go but could not get a place, and those who had shown no interest in going in the first place. However, this latter group could not be considered an unaffected control group, as the whole school was badly affected by the aftermath of the disaster. Accordingly, fourth-year girls in a nearby school also completed the fear schedule, along with the depression and anxiety scales.

Two sets of results should be noted. First, the girls who had been on the cruise were significantly more depressed and anxious than the other groups five months after the disaster. Indeed, there was a strong suggestion of an exposure–effect gradient on these two measures, reminiscent of that reported by Pynoos, Frederick, Nader, Arroyo, Steinberg, Eth,

Nunez, and Fairbanks (1987). Second, we rated the fear survey items as being either related or unrelated to the events on the cruise and agreed that 11 items were related and 33 were unrelated. We found no differences across the four exposure groups on the unrelated fears. By contrast, on the related fears, only the girls who had experienced the traumatic events showed a significant increase in reported fears. Thus, we took the opportunity of the disaster to examine the effects on children's fears and concluded that the effects are specific to the stimuli present and therefore provide more confirmatory evidence of the conditioning theory of fear acquisition (Dollinger, O'Donnell, & Staley, 1984).

Ten days after the accident, the authors met with the teachers, the pupils, and many of the parents initially in separate groups throughout an afternoon (Yule & Udwin, 1991). During this preliminary session, the pupils were encouraged to describe and share their reactions. By anticipating some of these, they were able to emphasize that their reactions were understood and were normal reactions to an abnormal experience. At the end of the afternoon, they brought the pupils and parents together and got them to share publicly some of their feelings. Hopefully, that gave permission for such discussions to take place more readily at home. Subsequently, they saw the more seriously affected girls in small groups to treat more specific fears, panic disorders, and depression.

However, it must be stressed that, whereas most professionals who have worked with recent disasters are convinced of the value of early debriefing, especially for rescue workers (Dyregrov, 1988), there is little published evidence to support this claim. There are differences about when such debriefing of victims should take place, with a consensus emerging that during the first 48 hours or so, most survivors are too numb to benefit from this intervention. Somewhere around 7–14 days after the disaster seems right, but again there have been no studies of this. Again, one must assume that there are individual differences in response to debriefing and that not all children will benefit to the same extent or to intervention at the same point in time.

Because over 20 schools were involved in the *Jupiter* disaster and not all schools welcomed outside help for the survivors, we were able to take advantage of this natural experiment. Of the young people involved, 334 completed the screening battery five months after the accident. The 24 girls in the school in which the authors worked were compared with girls from a nearby school which was known to have rejected offers of help. The data showed small, nonsignificant benefits of early intervention on measures of depression and anxiety, with significant reductions in scores on the Impact of Events Scale and the Fear Survey Schedule (Yule, 1992a). At least these results are promising and provide some evidence that early intervention does no harm.

RAIL AND AIR CRASHES

Although children and adolescents have been among the survivors of railway and air crashes, there are few published studies of their effects on children. Milgram, Toubiana, Klingman, Raviv, and Goldstein (1988) reported an accident in which a school bus was hit by a train on a level crossing; 19 children and 3 adults were killed in the bus, and other children in the following buses witnessed the accident. There were high levels of acute stress reactions during the first week. Surprisingly, the reported levels of stress reactions were higher among the children who had known the victims, no matter which buses the respondents had been on. Those who had witnessed the crash and so were regarded as a "near-miss" group did not show particularly elevated stress scores. The levels of stress reactions dropped markedly over the following nine months, although the initial levels were reasonably good predictors of later ones ($r = .51$). The findings with respect to the severity of the stressor versus personal knowledge of the victims may have been confounded by the crisis interventions undertaken immediately in the affected school.

Parry Jones and his colleagues in Glasgow (Parry Jones, Sandberg, & Puckering, 1991) studied the effects of the Pan Am Flight 103 disaster on children in the Scottish town of Lockerbie. On the December 21, 1988, the airplane was destroyed by a terrorist bomb seven miles above the town. Debris rained down on the town, which had a population of 3,500. All 259 passengers and crew were killed, as were 8 adults and 3 children living in houses that were demolished by the burning debris. Bodies and bits of bodies, together with pieces of wreckage and personal effects, remained scattered across the town for weeks as constant reminders of the tragedy.

Some time later, 54 children were individually assessed. It was found that there were no examples of delayed reactions in the group. Over half reported intrusive thoughts, and a third had traumatic dreams. Two thirds showed evidence of loss of skills, this loss being slightly commoner in younger children. Sleep disturbance was present in 80%, and half reported increased irritability and difficulties in concentration. In other words, as a group, they showed the classical signs of PTSD. Over half showed evidence of altered mood, and 61% had anxiety symptoms.

In the group as a whole, 9 children had had brief adjustment reactions, and the remaining 45 met the criteria of the *International Classification of Diseases*-9 for psychiatric diagnoses; 36 (or 66%) met the criteria for PTSD. The investigators also found that the teachers grossly underestimated the levels of psychopathology among the children. Despite the enormous publicity given to the disaster and the offers of help made, very few of the children had received postdisaster intervention of any sort.

Sugar (1989) described the seven children, aged 3–12, who were traumatized when a Pan Am airplane crashed on their community in Kenner, Louisiana, in July 1982, killing 146 on board and 6 children and 2 adults on the ground. One to three weeks after the crash, a number of posttraumatic symptoms were reported in the children, such as anxiety, insomnia, and phobias about lightning, thunder, and rain. The children talked constantly about the crash and showed posttraumatic play. They were also hostile, violent, and irritable. It was noted that the oldest boy showed the least anxiety and considerable denial. Sugar believed that the child survivors needed individualized treatment postdisaster but reported no outcome data of the treatment.

OTHER TRANSPORT ACCIDENTS

Although not strictly a transport accident, the Chowchilla bus kidnapping involved a school bus. Terr (1979, 1983) worked with the children who had been imprisoned underground for 27 hours. All the children were badly affected and, despite help, remained affected more than four year later. Terr's studies were influential in focusing on such phenomena as distortions in time perception, reenactment of the trauma in play, and the sense of a foreshortened future (see Chapter 7 in this book for further discussion).

Martini, Ryan, Nakayama, and Ramenofsky (1990) described the effects of the Pittsburgh Regatta accident on five young children A powerboat went out of control and plowed into the crowds. These five children were among those hit by the boat. On the Fredericks PTSD Reaction Index, four of the five children, aged 3–9, had scores indicating the they suffered PTSD, although only three of the children satisfied the criteria in the revised third edition of the American Psychiatric Association's *Diagnostic and Statistical Manual* (DSM-III-R; APA, 1987). This report is interesting in noting the disagreement between parents and children in the reporting of symptoms, and in illustrating that even 3-year-olds can provide detailed information on their own symptomatology following a trauma, provided that they are asked.

MUD SLIDE AND DAM DISASTERS

Just after school started on the morning of October 21, 1966, a huge coal tip slid down a mountainside in Wales and engulfed the primary school in Aberfan, killing 116 children and 28 adults; 143 primary-school children survived. Scarcely a family in the tightly knit community was unaffected by the disaster. Offers of help poured in, but plans to study the psychological effects of the disaster were strongly resisted. Lacey (1972) reported how 56 children presented at the local child guidance clinic over the following four years:

> Symptoms varied but the commonest were sleeping difficulties, nervousness, lack of friends, unwillingness to go to school or out to play, instability and enuresis. Some of the children, too, had shown some of these symptoms before the disaster, but they were said to be very much worse after it. Broadly speaking, the children who were most affected were those with other anxiety creating situations in their backgrounds.

Lacey went on to describe how some anxious parents became over-protective of their children. Fears of the dark and nightmares caused sleep problems. Bad weather upset the children as a period of bad weather had preceded the tip slide. The children rarely spoke spontaneously of their experiences. Three children played games of "burying" in the sand. Unfortunately, the villagers responded badly to the offers of help from outsiders and refused to cooperate with plans to study the effects of the disaster. Thus, an opportunity was lost to learn from the accident and so to be better prepared for the next one.

It was different in the Buffalo Creek disaster, where survivors sought help in pursuing their claims for compensation, and the professionals undertaking the assessments were able to use the systematically gathered data for research purposes. In February 1972, following several days' rain, a slag dam at the top of a valley in West Virginia collapsed, killing 125 people in the resulting flood that was unleashed.

Newman (1976) noted that, among the children who had survived, many had a precocious awareness of their own mortality and of the fragility of life. Two years after the disaster, Newman reported considerable disturbance in the children's behavior.

Fourteen years after the collapse, Green, Lindy, Grace, Gleser, Leonard, Korol, and Winget (1990) returned to reassess 120 adult survivors. The estimated rate of PTSD had dropped from 44% to 28% over the 12 years. Of interest in many of the studies are the findings of Gleser, Green, and Winget (1981) in relation to the effects of litigation on the adjustment of the Buffalo Creek survivors. The investigators had been called in by those suing for compensation, and many outsiders were critical that the survivors might exaggerate their symptoms. Since the most important symptoms of PTSD are subjective ones this is a serious charge. Gleser et al. (1981) and Green, Grace, Lindy, Gleser, Leonard, and Kramer (1989) interviewed a number of survivors who chose not to pursue legal redress. There were no significant differences in the levels of symptomatology between the litigants and the nonlitigants. Thus, it can be concluded that, in most large-scale disasters, where litigation is increasingly involved, it is unlikely that those seeking compensation are exaggerating their levels of distress, a conclusion that fits with our own observations, but clearly more studies of this question are needed.

BUILDING COLLAPSE

Despite the fact that children have been rescued from buildings that have collapsed after earthquakes and other disasters, the effects of buildings collapsing for other reasons have not been directly studied.

Blom (1986) discussed the effects of the collapse of a pedestrian skywalk on schoolchildren who were either on the walkway at the time or who witnessed the accident from the school playground. Thirteen days after the accident, questionnaire data were obtained on 156 of the 294 children (54%); 19 families indicated considerable distress. Four to six weeks after the accident, 17 children (11%) were still noticeably upset; seven months later, only three children were mildly upset. The children mainly showed anxiety about walking near walkways. The boys took longer to recover, and they showed more sleep disturbance, fighting, and fears; the girls, in contrast, showed more startle reactions and thought more frequently about the accident. In terms of age, 5- to 8-year-olds seemed less stressed than older children, showing a predominance of phobias and somatic problems; 9- to 12-year-olds showed more sleep disturbances, worry about their friends, and thoughts about the accident.

INDUSTRIAL AND CHEMICAL ACCIDENTS

As industrial society has used more and more chemicals and the output from factories has not always been closely monitored, so there have been many dramatic tragedies involving threat to life from accidents in factories in which harmful substances are widely dispersed. One has only to remember the disaster in Bhopal, India, when toxic dioxin was spread far and wide. Dioxin was again implicated in the floods that hit areas near St. Louis in December 1982 (see Smith, North, & Price, 1988, for a fuller account). Twenty-five thousand people, including children, had to be evacuated from areas like Times Beach. The floods occurred unexpectedly just as an investigation into unacceptably high levels of dioxin in the environment had begun. By chance, many of the affected people had previously been studied as part of the Epidemiological Catchment Area studies. Thus, fortuitously, predisaster data were available but, sadly, only on adults.

The investigators attempted to tease out whether exposure to the floods produced more psychopathology than knowledge that the subjects had been exposed long term to low levels of a toxic substance. They concluded that the effects of the two types of disaster happening simultaneously were additive. Depressions increased, but mainly among those with previous histories of depression. In contrast, PTSD did occur in direct relation to the severity of exposure. Although symptoms of PTSD were very frequent, only 5% of those studied met the DSM-III-R criteria for PTSD.

Lopez-Ibor, Soria, Canas, and Rodriguez-Gamazo, (1985) reported data on the Spanish toxic oil catastrophe that came to light in 1981. Cooking oil, widely used in Spanish cooking, was somehow contaminated, and over 20,000 people, of whom 349 died, were affected. Of those affected 20%–30% presented with mood changes and loss of concentration, and many more showed anxiety and depression. Because the most seriously affected developed paralyses and wasting disorders before death, the anxiety was understandable. Unfortunately, to date, no data have been published on the children involved.

These studies are mentioned in this section for two reasons. First, because children must have been exposed, it is unfortunate that their reactions and needs were not separately studied. Second, studies such as these highlight another set of methodological problems for anyone venturing into this area. In the case of the Spanish cooking-oil disaster, there is still considerable disagreement about the source of the toxin. Indeed, some have argued that the poisoning resulted from an organophosphate fertilizer rather than from adulterated oil.

Either way, such toxins may have direct effects on the central nervous system, and one has the additional problem of separating direct toxic effects from psychological effects—a problem almost the reverse of the one encountered by those of us who had studied the effects of lead on children's development (Lansdown & Yule, 1986).

NUCLEAR PLANT DISASTERS

The accident at Chernobyl in 1986 released a cloud of radioactive pollution that silently blew across Europe, contaminating wide areas for many years. Anxieties have been expressed about effects on the food chain, with sheep in Wales still, in some cases five years later, being regarded as unfit for human consumption. Anxieties remain, too, about the effects on increasing leukemia and other cancers. To date, there have been no published studies about the psychological effects of this disaster on children.

A similar disaster was only just averted at the Three Mile Island Nuclear Power Plant near Middletown, Pennsylvania, some seven years earlier. A series of mishaps resulted in a partial meltdown of the reactor core which in turn led to a plume of radioactive material a half-mile wide being released in to the atmosphere (Handford, Mayes, Mattison, Humphrey, Bagnato, Bixler, & Kales, 1986). It was not until two days later that women and children under 5 years of age living within a five-mile radius were evacuated. Fortunately, there were no direct injuries or deaths outside the plant.

Handford et al. (1986) carried out a detailed study of 35 children aged 5–19 one-and-a-half years after the Three Mile Island (TMI) nuclear accident. This study is important in establishing that parents underreport the extent and severity of their children's reactions and in demonstrating that the widely used Quay and Peterson (1979) Behavior Problem Checklist completed by parents is insensitive to the children's reactions. However, it must be seriously questioned whether this is really a study of the effects of a major disaster in that, as the authors put it, Three Mile Island was a silent disaster with no apparent physical damage to people or property, and the children were not separated from their parents during the time of the evacuation that some of them experienced.

Further studies related to Three Mile Island are reviewed by Bromet (1989). More than three years after the accident, no significant differences were found on a range of standardized measures of adjustment between TMI children and a comparison group. However, where families were less supportive, children who experienced most stress at the time of the accident remained more symptomatic at follow-up. Contrary to the earliest short-term studies, the later follow-up studies did find some residual effects on the survivors' mental health. Both prior psychiatric history and level of exposure were found to be predictive of later adjustment.

CONCLUSIONS

It is clear from this review that studies of PTSD in children and adolescents are rapidly progressing from simple, clinical-descriptive studies to ones using more sophisticated methodology that incorporates standard measures and semistandard interviews, together with clearer criteria for diagnosis. Moreover, recent studies are avoiding many of the methodological weaknesses identified by Garmezy (1986) and incorporate more appropriate control groups. Some studies, such as those of Pynoos et al. (1987), Pynoos and Nader (1988), Nader, Pynoos, Fairbanks, and Frederick (1990), and Yule, Udwin, and Murdoch (1990), have investigated additional measures and have been able to test out more general hypotheses related to developmental psychopathology.

It is now reasonably well established that in children, as in adults, the severity of the disaster is related to the overall level of subsequent morbidity. Within a particular disaster, there is an exposure response gradient: The greater the threat perceived by the individual, the greater the risk of developing PTSD. Individual differences and risk and protective factors have been reviewed elsewhere (Yule, 1992b), but in summary, there is a trend toward finding that girls report more psychopathology following a disaster than boys.

There are clearly differences in the pattern of symptomatology with differences in age, but insufficient numbers of preschool children have been studied to allow firm conclusions. Under age 6, children are more likely to show repetitive play and repetitive drawings of the trauma (Sullivan, Saylor, & Foster, 1991; Terr, 1988). There are isolated reports of preverbal children's being able to recall details of the trauma years later when they have developed language. Such developmental factors merit closer study.

Tsui, Dagwell, and Yule (1992) reported that children who survived the *Jupiter* sinking showed adverse effects on their academic attainment compared with their predisaster levels. In particular, the less able children showed the greatest fall off in achievement, and it appeared to last longer. These effects may have been mediated by the well-documented difficulties with concentration and memory shown in PTSD, but apart from one study of the effects of a tornado that did not incorporate measures of the children's emotional adjustment (Martin & Little, 1986), this has not previously been studied.

As children spend a great deal of their lives in school, and as some disasters involve schools directly, it is important that school personnel be better advised and supported in dealing with child victims. It is understandable that many teachers wish to underplay the effects of disasters on children (Earls, Smith, Reich, & Jung, 1988), but such denial often adds to the children's burdens. It is clear that many postdisaster problems manifest themselves at school, and teachers need support from mental health professionals to ensure that they will be able to cope with these problems.

Earlier, we (Yule & Udwin, 1991) argued that it is possible to identify high-risk groups at an early posttrauma stage. Our own data and those of Nader, Pynoos, Fairbanks, and Frederick (1990) show that the scores of high-risk groups on measures of distress remain remarkably stable over a one-year period. We conclude from this that even in these early stages, it is possible to do some screening and ensure that services are delivered to the most needy. However, it must be emphasized that the screening and assessment batteries should be specially selected to enquire about symptoms of PTSD, rather than merely try to obtain data from general screening check lists. It is always necessary to interview the child survivors themselves.

The evidence on the specificity of fears fairly clearly indicates that children do suffer direct effects from disaster. Some writers (Bloch, Silber, & Perry, 1956; McFarlane, 1987) have stressed the indirect effects of disasters and have argued that such children's reactions as there are are mediated by effects on parents. Clearly, where parents are themselves adversely affected, this will impair their ability to cope with the children's reactions. Parents may convey some of their own anxieties to their children. Thus, in trying to understand what factors make some children more vulnerable than others, and, conversely, what factors act as protection against the effects of the disaster, family functioning needs to be considered.

Unfortunately, little is written about treating child survivors from major disasters. In many cases of natural disasters—flooding, fires, tornadoes, earthquakes—people emphasize the need to facilitate the rebuilding of the community, to treat people in groups in which children can participate. In the case of mass transport disasters, there is no natural group and with survivors scattered over thousands of square miles, it is difficult to get useful groups established. In the case of school journey disasters, there are clear groups to work with.

So, what work needs to be done? In the immediate aftermath, children usually need to be reunited with their parents and family. Even teenagers may go back to sleeping in their parents' bed. Tolerance and understanding are called for. Survivors need to talk over what happened so as get the sequence of events clear in their minds as well as to master the feelings that recall engenders. Repetitive retelling is not enough alone. Professionals can help by creating a relatively safe environment in which such recounting can take place. Experiencing that the world does not come to an end when feelings are shared between parent and child can be very facilitating. Learning that other survivors share similar, irrational guilt about surviving can help to get things in perspective. Learning how to deal with anxiety attacks, how to identify trigger stimuli, how to take each day as it comes—all are important therapeutic tasks.

However, these things should not be left to chance. Mental health professionals are rapidly learning that formal psychological debriefing can help adult victims of disaster (Dyregrov, 1988). Yule and Udwin (1991) describe their experience with girls who survived the sinking of the *Jupiter* suggests that this can also be helpful with teenagers. Working with groups of children and parents who survived the *Herald of Free Enterprise* disaster is described elsewhere (Yule & Williams, 1990).

Rachman's (1980) paper on emotional processing is very helpful in formulating what to do with child survivors. He lists a number of factors that promote emotional processing after it has got stuck following a disaster. Relaxation figures prominently, as does a low level of arousal. The presentation of distressing scenes should be both vivid and long, the very characteristics that most adults in the child's everyday surroundings shy away from. Agitated rehearsals which stress a lack of coping skills only make things worse. Where distressing scenes are badly organized or presented too briefly, as may happen when a child spontaneously tells an adult what happened, this is likely to be associated with poor recovery. There are promising cognitive-behavioral therapies in which prolonged exposure is a key element (e.g., Saigh 1987a,b, 1989).

Technological disasters will continue to occur and will involve children both directly and indirectly. This chapter has demonstrated that child and adolescent survivors of such technology-related disasters are likely to develop many problems, including PTSD. Emergency service planners should bear this in mind when developing contingency plans for disaster management. Mental health professionals and researchers should agree on a minimum protocol to be used in evaluating survivors and their needs.

REFERENCES

Abramson, L. Y., Seligman, M. E. P., & Teasdale, J. D. (1978). Learned helplessness in humans: Critique and reformulation. *Journal of Abnormal Psychology, 87*, 49–74.

American Psychiatric Association. (1987). *Diagnostic and statistical manual of mental disorders* (3rd ed., rev.). Washington, DC: Author.

Birleson, P. (1981). The validity of depressive disorder in childhood and the development of a self-rating scale: A research report. *Journal of Child Psychology and Psychiatry, 21*, 83–88.

Birleson, P., Hudson, I., Buchanan, D. G., & Wolff, S. (1987). Clinical evaluation of a self-rating scale for depressive disorder in childhood (Depression Self-Rating Scale). *Journal of Child Psychology and Psychiatry, 28*, 43–60.

Bloch, D. A., Silber, E., & Perry, S. E. (1956). Some factors in the emotional reactions of children to disaster. *American Journal of Psychiatry, 133*, 416–422.

Blom, G. E. (1986). A school disaster—Intervention and research aspects. *Journal of American Academy of Child Psychiatry, 25*, 336–345.

Bromet, E. J. (1989). The nature and effects of technological failures. In R. Gist & B. Lubin (Eds.) *Psychosocial aspects of disaster* (pp. 120–139). New York: Wiley.

Dollinger, S. J., O'Donnell, J. P., & Staley, A. A. (1984). Lightning-strike disaster: Effects on children's fears and worries. *Journal of Consulting and Clinical Psychology, 52*, 1028–1038.

Dyregrov, A. (1988). *Critical incident stress debriefings.* Unpublished manuscript, Research Center for Occupational Health and Safety, University of Bergen, Norway.

Earls, F., Smith, E., Reich, W., & Jung, K. G. (1988). Investigating psychopathological consequences of a disaster in children: A pilot study incorporating a structured diagnostic approach. *Journal of the American Academy of Child and Adolescent Psychiatry, 27*, 90–95.

Garmezy, N. (1986). Children under severe stress: Critique and comments. *Journal of the American Academy of Child Psychiatry, 25,* 384–392.

Gleser, G., Green, B. L., & Winget, C. (1981). *Prolonged psychosocial effects of disaster: A study of Buffalo Creek.* New York: Plenum Press.

Green, B. L., Grace, M. C., Lindy, J. D., Gleser, G. C., Leonard, A. C., & Kramer, T. L. (1989). *Buffalo Creek survivors in the second decade: Comparison with unexposed and non-litigant groups.* Manuscript submitted for publication; cited in Green et al, 1990).

Green, B. L., Lindy, J. D., Grace, M. C., Gleser, G. C., Leonard, A. C., Korol, M., & Winget, C. (1990). Buffalo Creek survivors in the second decade: Stability of stress symptoms. *American Journal of Orthopsychiatry, 60,* 43–54.

Handford, H. A., Mayes, S. O., Mattison, R. E., Humphrey, F. J., Bagnato, S., Bixler, E. O., & Kales, J. D. (1986). Child and parent reaction to the TMI nuclear accident. *Journal of the American Academy of Child and Adolescent Psychiatry, 25,* 346–355.

Hodgkinson, P. E., & Stewart, M. (1991). *Coping with catastrophe: A handbook of disaster management.* London: Routledge.

Horowitz, M. J., Wilner, N., & Alvarez, W. (1979). Impact of event scale: A measure of subjective stress. *Psychosomatic Medicine, 41,* 209–218.

Lacey, G. N. (1972). Observations on Aberfan. *Journal of Psychosomatic Research, 6,* 257–260.

Lansdown, R., & Yule, W. (Eds.). (1986). *The lead debate: The environment, toxicology and child health.* London: Croom Helm.

Lopez-Ibor, J. J, Soria, J., Canas, F., & Rodriguez-Gamazo, M. (1985). Psychopathological aspects of the toxic oil syndrome catastrophe. *British Journal of Psychiatry, 147,* 352–365.

Malt, U. (1988). The long-term psychiatric consequences of accidental injury: A longitudinal study of 107 adults. *British Journal of Psychiatry, 153,* 810–818.

Martin, S., & Little, B. (1986). The effects of a natural disaster on academic abilities and social behavior of school children. *British Columbia Journal of Special Education, 10,* 167–182.

Martini, D. R., Ryan, C., Nakayama, D., & Ramenofsky, M. (1990). Psychiatric sequelae after traumatic injury: The Pittsburgh Regatta accident. *Journal of the American Academy of Child and Adolescent Psychiatry, 29,* 70–75.

McFarlane, A. C. (1987). Family functioning and overprotection following a natural disaster: The longitudinal effects of post-traumatic morbidity. *Australian and New Zealand Journal of Psychiatry, 21,* 210–218.

Milgram, N. A., Toubiana, Y. H., Klingman, A., Raviv, A., & Goldstein, I. (1988). Situational exposure and personal loss in children's acute and chronic stress reactions to a school bus disaster. *Journal of Traumatic Stress, 1,* 339–352.

Nader, K., Pynoos, R. S., Fairbanks, L., & Frederick, C., (1990). Childhood PTSD reactions one year after a sniper attack. *American Journal of Psychiatry, 146,* 1526–1530.

Newman, C. J. (1976). Children of disaster: Clinical observation at Buffalo Creek. *American Journal of Psychiatry, 133,* 306–312.

Ollendick, T. H., Yule, W., & Ollier, K. (1991). Fears in British children and their relationship to Manifest Anxiety and Depression. *Journal of Child Psychology and Psychiatry, 32,* 321–331.

Parry Jones, W., Sandberg, S., & Puckering, C. (1991). *Children of Lockerbie.* Paper presented to meeting at Guys Hospital, London (Publication in preparation).

Pynoos, R. S., & Nader, K. (1988). Psychological first aid and treatment approach for children exposed to community violence: Research implications. *Journal of Traumatic Stress, 1,* 243–267.

Pynoos, R. S., Frederick, C., Nader, K., Arroyo, W., Steinberg, A., Eth, S., Nunez, F., & Fairbanks, L. (1987). Life threat and posttraumatic stress in school-age children. *Archives of General Psychiatry, 44,* 1057–1063.

Quay, H. C., & Peterson, D. R. (1979). *Manual of the Behavior Problem Checklist* (unpublished).

Rachman, S. (1980). Emotional processing. *Behaviour Research and Therapy, 18,* 51–60.

Raphael, B. (1986). *When disaster strikes: A handbook for the caring professions.* London, Hutchinson.

Reynolds, C. R., & Richmond, B. O. (1978). What I think and feel: A revised measure of children's manifest anxiety. *Journal of Abnormal Child Psychology, 6,* 271–280.

Saigh, P. A. (1987a). *In vitro* flooding of a childhood post-traumatic stress disorder. *School Psychology Review, 16,* 203–211.

Saigh, P. A. (1987b). *In vitro* flooding of an adolescent's post-traumatic stress disorder. *Journal of Clinical Child Psychology, 16,* 147–150.

Saigh, P. A. (1989). The use of *in vitro* flooding in the treatment of traumatized adolescents. *Journal of Behavioural and Developmental Pediatrics, 10,* 17–21.

Smith, E. M., North, C. S., & Price, P. C. (1988). Response to technological accidents. In M. Lystad (Ed.), *Mental health response to mass emergencies* (pp. 52–95). New York: Brunner/Mazel.

Sugar, M. (1989). Children in disaster: An overview. *Child Psychiatry and Human Development, 19,* 163–179.

Sullivan, M. A., Saylor, C. F., & Foster, K. Y. (1991). Post-hurricane adjustment of preschoolers and their families. *Advances in Behaviour Research and Therapy, 13,* 163–171.

Terr, L. C. (1979). The children of Chowchilla. *Psychoanalytic Study of the Child, 34,* 547–623.

Terr, L. C. (1983). Chowchilla revisited: The effects of psychic trauma four years after a schoolbus kidnapping. *American Journal of Psychiatry, 140,* 1543–1550.

Terr, L. C. (1988). What happens to early memories of trauma? A study of twenty children under five at the time of the documented traumatic events. *Journal of the American Academy of Child and Adolescent Psychiatry, 27,* 96–104.

Tsui, E., Dagwell, K., & Yule, W. (1992). Effects of a disaster on children's academic attainment (in preparation).

World Health Organization (1978) International Classification of Diseases: 9th Edition (ICD-9). WHO: Geneva.

Yule, W. (1992a). Post traumatic stress disorders in child survivors of shipping disasters: The sinking of the "Jupiter." *Journal of Psychotherapy and Psychosomatics, 57,* 200–205.

Yule, W. (1992b). Resilience and vulnerability in child survivors of disasters. In B. Tizard & V. Varma (Eds.). *Vulnerability and resilience: A Festschrift for Ann and Alan Clarke* (pp. 182–198). London: Jessica Kingsley.

Yule, W., & Udwin, O. (1991). Screening child survivors for post-traumatic stress disorders: Experiences from the "Jupiter" sinking. *British Journal of Clinical Psychology, 30,* 131–138.

Yule, W., & Williams, R. (1990). Post traumatic stress reactions in children. *Journal of Traumatic Stress, 3*(2), 279–295.

Yule, W., Udwin, O., & Murdoch, K. (1990). The "Jupiter" sinking: Effects on children's fears, depression and anxiety. *Journal of Child Psychology and Psychiatry, 31,* 1051–1061.

7

Psychological Response of Children to Shootings and Hostage Situations

RONALD H. ROZENSKY, IRA H. SLOAN, EITAN D. SCHWARZ, and JANICE M. KOWALSKI

INTRODUCTION: CHILDREN AND CRIME STATISTICS

Despite the seemingly endless news coverage of sensationalized stories of children as victims of shooting, kidnapping, and hostage situations, it has been noted that the empirical literature on the psychological sequelae of these experiences is rather meager (Forehand, Long, Zogg, & Parrish, 1989), and few longitudinal studies exist (Nader, Pynoos, Fairbanks, & Frederick, 1990). National crime statistics in the United States point out that between 25,000 and 100,000 children a year are the victims of parental kidnapping (Shetky & Haller, 1983), and in 1988 alone, between 200 and 300 children were kidnapped or held hostage by assailants unknown to them (Finkelhor, Hotaling, & Sedlak, 1990). Estimates suggest that over 3 million children annually witness violence in the home (Silvern & Kaersvang, 1989).

With the increasing number of children and adolescents in this country becoming both victims of and witnesses to "an epidemic of

RONALD H. ROZENSKY, IRA H. SLOAN, EITAN D. SCHWARZ, and JANICE M. KOWALSKI • Department of Psychiatry, Evanston Hospital and Northwestern University and Medical School, Evanston, Illinois 60201.

Children and Disasters, edited by Conway F. Saylor. Plenum Press, New York, 1993.

violence" (West, 1984), children's exposure to human-made violence is becoming a significant public health concern (Garmezy, 1986; Pynoos & Nader, 1990). To illustrate, approximately 16% of the 19,000 homicides and nonnegligent manslaughters that occurred in 1989 involved as victims young people under the age of 19 (U.S. Department of Justice, 1989). Pynoos and Eth (1986) estimated that 20% of the direct witnesses of homicides are children, and Dyson (1990) cited a survey from an inner-city Chicago elementary school reporting that 4% of all the fifth- through eighth-grade students (ages 11–15) had seen someone shot; 31% had seen a stabbing; and 22% had seen someone murdered. Such data highlight the extent of children's exposure, both indirectly and indirectly, to human violence.

The purpose of this chapter is to review the available literature pertaining to the kidnapping of children and shooting incidents involving children. Clinical descriptions of the effects of these experiences will be offered along with the available empirical data collected from victims. Issues surrounding research and treatment of victims of these types of crimes will be discussed along lines of self-psychology and the formation of the trauma membrane.

KIDNAPPING AND HOSTAGE SITUATIONS

In a series of reports, Terr (1979, 1981, 1983b, 1990), documented her longitudinal clinical findings concerning 26 children, ranging in age from 5 to 14, kidnapped by unknown assailants from their school bus in Chowchilla, California. Following approximately 11 hours of being driven around in two vans, the children were transferred to a buried truck-trailer. They were buried for 16 hours until two of the oldest and strongest boys dug them out.

Between 5 and 13 months after the event, Terr interviewed all of the 23 children and their parents who remained in Chowchilla after the incident. Terr (1979) stated that this population offered a unique opportunity to study traumatized children who were normal psychologically, not physically harmed, selected at random (by the kidnappers), and representing a group mixed in age, gender, and ethnic origin. Each of these children was subjected to the same (traumatic) external situation. Terr (1979) uses rich clinical descriptions and the children's own subjective experiences to illustrate their trauma. During the abduction, children reported fear of separation from parents and siblings, fear of death, and fear of further trauma. Some children reported a sense of premonition, becoming obsessed with perceived "omens" of the event. "Misperceptions and hallucinations were dramatic evidence of ego malfunction at the instant of the trauma" (Terr, 1979, p. 563).

During examination, nearly all of the children reported both kidnap-related fears and an increase in nonspecific fears. Eight suffered panic attacks. Personality and behavioral changes were observed. Terr (1979) reported that the children did not experience the type of intrusive visions reported in the adult trauma literature. However, the majority of the children played out the trauma in a repetitive manner and all reported dreams related to the kidnapping. Terr (1981) reported that no period of amnesia or haziness took place in the children, although distortions in perception and time were noted. Terr (1979) concluded that "there appears also to be a correlation [positive] between prior major physical or emotional vulnerability of the child and posttraumatic symptoms" (p. 605).

Terr (1983b) conducted a four-year follow-up of all but one of the Chowchilla kidnap victims and included a child let off the bus immediately before the abduction. She reported that, at follow-up, the children "felt naked, humiliated, or totally exposed when anyone knew how vulnerable they had been" (p. 1544) during the abduction and that, more often than not, they avoided discussion of their kidnapping experience in social situations. Everyone of the children reported a continuation of kidnap-related or nonspecific fears. Spontaneous resolution of some fears was reported by 19 children. Eighteen children had used a conscious suppression of thoughts of the kidnapping. Only four children exhibited school-related problems. Misperceptions of the incident, disruptions in a sense of time duration and sequencing, omen formation, and a sense of a foreshortened future were revealed by many of the children.

Although the overall frequency of nightmares had decreased, a number of the children reported continued kidnap-related dreams. Evidence of repetitive play themes related to the incident was reported by 18 victims. None of the families had sought trauma-related counseling, and there was a general tendency toward minimization of the impact of the kidnapping on both child and family. Terr stated that, although she found no correlation between symptom severity and family problems one year after the abduction, at four to five years there was a positive relationship. She concluded that "*every* child was found to suffer from a posttraumatic stress response syndrome as late as 4 to 5 years after the incident" (Terr, 1983b, p. 1550).

Terr's writings present extensive, detailed clinical descriptions of a unique population of kidnapped children who were held hostage. They appeared relatively willing to be interviewed and open to discuss their experiences. This material provides a heuristic base for further longitudinal study of children traumatized by abduction by an unknown assailant.

Although there is little doubt that children are deeply affected by such experiences, of interest would be quantitative data, as well as qualitative data, on such a population so that comparisons can be made with nontraumatized children over time.

In contrast to kidnapping carried out by a stranger, upward of 100,000 children are "snatched" yearly ("snatching" is defined as "the removal of a child by one parent from the custody of the other without legal approval"; Senior, Gladstone, & Nurcome, 1982, p. 579). Motives for this type of kidnapping range from perceived benevolence toward the child to punitive retribution against the custodial parent. According to Senior *et al.* (1982), the psychological sequelae of child snatching differ qualitatively from abduction by a stranger due to the emotional bond between victim and abductor and an unconscious or real threat that the noncustodial parent will again abduct the child. Nonetheless, this type of trauma to a child may shed some light on the experiences of child hostages held in situations more likely to fit the definition of disaster.

Terr (1983a) described her findings following the clinical examination of 18 children who were snatched or who experienced abortive attempts. She lists the following symptoms upon clinical exam: "post-traumatic stress response syndrome or after-effects of severe fright, 11 children; the effects of mental indoctrination (brainwashing), 7; grief for or rage about the absent parent, 7; extrusions (rejections) by the child of an offending parent or wish-fulfillment about a parent, 2" (p. 153). Only 2 of the 18 children showed no direct clinical effects from the snatching.

Using a randomly selected sample of names chosen from a national organization that helps families find missing children, Forehand *et al.* (1989) reported on 17 families from whom a child had been abducted (only 22 of 48 families responded and 5 provided insufficient data). Standardized self-report instruments were administered to the custodial parent, on the average, 10.8 months after the child's return. Children were found to be more symptomatic immediately following abduction than prior to abduction, and improved, but not back to, preabduction functioning "at present". Pre- and postabduction ratings were retrospective. Significant increases in conduct problems, learning problems, psychosomatic complaints, and anxiety were found. However, such increases were seen as transient and not as severe as previous clinical studies on psychiatrically referred children have suggested. Correlational findings suggested that the negative effects of the abductions were not related to the length of abduction, the age of the child, the time since the child's return, or the adjustment of the custodial parent. Self-reported data on their own adjustment suggested that the parents had coped with the abduction by using problem-focused rather than emotionally focused coping strategies. Despite the small sample size, the small return rate, and the retrospective character of the data, the Forehand *et al.* study was an attempt to investigate a difficult topic empirically.

SHOOTINGS

In the first systematic and large-scale study of children's psychological responses to violence, Pynoos, Frederick, Nader, Arroyo, Steinberg, Eth, Nunez, and Fairbanks (1987) examined children following the fatal sniper shooting of a child on the grounds of an elementary school. The authors sampled 159 children (14.5% of the school's children) one month after the event. Crisis teams conducted consultations in nearly all of the school's classrooms; five teachers, including one from a classroom directly exposed to the shooting, did not participate. All of the children from the participating 33 classrooms were involved in drawing and storytelling exercises. Five to eight children were then randomly selected from each classroom and interviewed more extensively with a semistructured clinical interview, which included administration of the Reaction Index (RI).

Children participating in the clinical interviews ranged in age from 5 through 13, with a mean age of 9.2. The study group represented the ethnic diversity of the school. Of the group, 28% were in grades K–2, 32% were in grades 3–4, and 40% were in grades 4–5; 59% were black and 50% were Hispanic. Of the children interviewed, 35 had been on the school playground where the shooting occurred, 18 had been in the school, 43 had not been in school, and 63 had been on vacation (Pynoos *et al.*, 1987).

Pynoos *et al.*, (1987) reported a significant relationship between degree of exposure and reports posttraumatic stress disorder (PTSD) symptomatology. In this sample, 77% of the children on the playground reported moderate to severe PTSD symptomatology, and 88% of the children on vacation reported no symptoms to mild PTSD symptoms. A significant relationship between knowledge of the victim and the severity of the symptoms across exposure levels was reported. Guilt was also positively related to the severity of the symptoms. There were no significant differences by age, sex, or ethnicity and no interactions of these variables with degree of exposure. No significant relationship was reported between previous trauma and the degree of symptomatology. However, the children who had experience recent traumatic events reported increased memories and thoughts about it.

An analysis of the RI items revealed three factors—reexperiencing and numbing, postevent fear and anxiety, and concentration difficulties and sleep disturbance—that accounted for 50% of the variance among the children's responses. These factors were useful in differentiating symptom severity. Although postevent fear and anxiety were generally reported by the majority of the children, regardless of symptom severity, the other two factors were commonly associated with moderate to severe degrees of symptomatology. Nader et al. (1990) reported a 14-month follow-up after the shooting. Of the original 159 children, 100 were reinterviewed. The methodology closely resembled that used in the initial study. The degree of posttraumatic stress symptomatology was significantly associated with exposure. At follow-up, 74% (n = 14) of the children on the playground continued to report PTSD symptoms, whereas 81% of the nonexposed children reported no symptoms. Acquaintanceship with the deceased was associated with the severity of the symptomatology in the less exposed children. In general, the percentage of PTSD symptom reports decreased over time. Exposure did not seem to be associated with such symptoms as omen formation, development of new fears, or changes in eating habits.

As a part of this follow-up study, Pynoos, Nader, Frederick, Gonda, and Stuber (1987) examined grief reactions in a stratified sample of 251 students from the elementary school. Chosen from all grade levels, these children ranged in age from 6 through 13, with a mean age of 10.2. Sex and ethnic composition were comparable to that of the school population. The degree of reported grief was positively related to both the degree of acquaintanceship with the deceased child and exposure to the incident. The authors concluded that the grief process in children is similar to that in adults and, for this sample, was ongoing one year after the event. They also suggested that, although grief and posttraumatic stress reaction may interact in children, the phenomena may be independent and should be addressed as such.

To examine the relationship between proximity to the shooting and memory, Pynoos and Nader (1989) administered a semistructured clinical interview to 10% of the student body (n = 113) 6 and 16 weeks after the event. Each child was asked to freely recall his or her own experience of the shooting and then to recall the incident by using various aids (reviewing the events in slow motion; drawing or dramatizing the events; walking through the sequence of events; or being given affective prompts). Proximity to the trauma was found to impact on memory. In initial free recall, children who had been directly exposed tended to diminish their degree of life threat while those less exposed tended to increase life threat. Other findings included: variation in recall associated with differential memory markers; temporal distortions; and the importance of contextual cues in the assistance in recall.

Ornitz and Pynoos (1989) examined startle-response mechanisms in six children who had been on the school playground (two boys and four girls, aged 8–13) and six matched controls. All six of the clinical group had been preselected on the basis of meeting the criteria in the third edition of the American Psychiatric Association's *Diagnostic and Statistical Manual* (DSM-III; APA, 1980) for PTSD and exhibition of exaggerated posttraumatic startle response. Startle responses were recorded for each child 17–21 months after the event. Observations of physiological processes (tonic electromyographic activity, vertex EEG activity, eyelid position, and heart rate) were made. The authors reported that the children with PTSD experienced a significant loss of normal inhibitory modulation of the startle response and suggested that this acquired function may be adversely affected by severe stress.

This series of reports offered extensive descriptions of the types of responses and reactions children may exhibit after exposure to violence. The authors had a unique opportunity to study the group quickly and to reenter the community for follow-up. However, as with most such efforts, there were problems with the selection of a representative sample, because five teachers refused to participate, and it is unclear what proportion of the population was thus made inaccessible. Within this limitation, random sampling was attempted. The use of the RI, although probably clinically valid, was based on the magnitude and number of the symptoms and may not have reflected the DSM-III criteria as specified by clusters. The premorbid characteristics of the subjects, as well as of the larger community, may have affected the clinical picture and need to be considered when generalizations are made.

Schwarz and Kowalski (1991a,b) studied the impact of the fatal school shooting of one child and the wounding of five others on students, parents, and school personnel in an upper-middle-class suburban elementary school. This incident was described in detail by Eggington (1991). Schwarz and Kowalski used the term "malignant memory" to organize their understanding of posttraumatic reaction, conceptualizing it as both a neurophysiological and a psychosocial phenomenon. Within this framework, they suggested that the formation of a malignant memory, initiated by a severe stressor, represents a stable, persistent biopsychological configuration that serves to link arousal, cognition, affect, and behavior.

As part of a larger study group, 64 children, representing 21% of the student body, were assessed for PTSD and associated psychological sequelae 8–14 months after the event. The clinical screening, consisting of a standardized clinical interview and standardized self-report measures, was administered by school social service personnel. The PTSD assessment was based on a children's version of the RI expanded to reflect the criteria in the revised third edition of the *Diagnostic and Statistical Manual* (DSM-III-R; APA, 1987) and specifically tailored to this shooting (K. Nader, personal communication, December 1989).

Of the 64 children, 16% (n = 10) had been in the classroom where the children had been wounded and the child had been murdered; 14% (n = 9) had been in the same wing; 50% (n = 32) had been in the school that day; and 20% (n = 13) had been off the school grounds. Fifty percent of the children were female. The children ranged in age from 5 to 14, with a mean of 8.6 years. All of the children were Caucasian.

The authors reported that 27% of the children met the DSM-III-R criteria for PTSD. Unlike in the work of Pynoos and his colleagues, Schwarz and Kowalski did not report a significant relationship between proximity and the severity of PTSD symptoms across the entire study group. Of the 17 children meeting the DSM-III-R criteria for PTSD, 2 had been in the classroom, 3 in the school wing, 11 elsewhere in the school, and 1 off-campus. The authors suggested that the concept of exposure be broadened to include not only physical nearness, but emotional states as well, because affective reactions during the disaster may link the event and the formation of malignant memories.

In this study group, the children reported reexperiencing symptoms regardless of the diagnosis; however, reports of avoidant and arousal symptoms were most associated with a PTSD diagnosis. In terms of the DSM-III-R criteria for the entire sample, 88% reported reexperiencing the event through repetitive play; 67% reported exaggerated startle response; 52% reported an inability to remember aspects of the shooting; 48% reported a restricted range of affect; and 41% reported a loss of recently developed skills or regressive behaviors (e.g., thumb sucking or sleeping in their parents' bed). An additional 19% reported omen formation and 12% future foreshortening. Older children tended to report more anger than younger children. Of the symptoms described as specific to childhood and included in the DSM-III-R, only the loss of recently acquired developmental skills was associated with PTSD. Guilt, included in the DSM-III but eliminated from the DSM-III-R, appears to merit reconsideration as a PTSD symptom because it was associated with PTSD diagnosis.

Schwarz and Kowalski (1991b) speculated that developmental factors make a significant contribution to the formation and/or perpetuation of malignant memories. Greater frequencies of startle response, recurrent distressing dreams, and physiological reactivity indicate the persistence of arousal states and may reflect central-nervous-system-based immaturity. These are consistent with children's as yet poorly developed abilities to use neurophysiological mechanisms, cognitive reappraisal, or intervening positive affective experiences to "downregulate" or otherwise modify arousal and their subjective experience of it. Children may continue to respond in a more intense but less integrated way, simultaneously reexperiencing, avoiding, and remaining aroused.

The limitations of this study derived from self-selection and self-reporting. A one-time screening by self-report or interview may not adequately pick up certain symptoms. This may be especially true in PTSD, where avoidance symptomatology, central to the nature of the disorder itself, may interfere with self-reporting and may be best assessed in a clinical interview. Additionally, reports of experiences during the event relied on recall after a period of time when retrospective distortion, contagion, and intervention may have diluted the proximity effects. The differences in exposure and in the methods used to collect data make conclusions about developmental influences tentative. As in the Pynoos *et al.* reports, the unique characteristics of the subjects and the community, as well as the methodology, pose difficulties for generalization.

Gillis (1991) examined the effects of a sniper shooting on a school's grounds during a morning recess when over 400 children were at play; 5 children were murdered, and 30 others, including 1 teacher, were wounded. The school was attended by a large number of Southeast Asian children, many of whom had had refugee and resettlement experiences and were considered "high-risk" because of these previous traumatic experiences.

Working closely with school personnel, Gillis obtained clinical assessments of the exposed children, grades 1–6, at two points in time, allowing for a preliminary examination of the course of posttraumatic reactions in the children. At Time 1, approximately three months after the shooting, classroom teachers were asked to complete a brief symptom checklist on a study group of 321 children, all of whom had been referred to the school counseling staff for psychosocial and/or behavioral difficulties. The symptom checklist, developed by school psychologists, included both internalizing (excessive fears and clinginess) and externalizing (oppositional) behavior. Of this study group, approximately 53% were Southeast Asian. A total of 108 boys and 127 girls were included, with 160 in grades 1–3 and the remaining 105 in grades 4–6. Information on the gender of 86 children was not available. The children from grades 1–3 had been on the playground during the shooting, whereas the children from grades 4–6 had been in their respective classrooms.

At Time 2, approximately 27 months after the shooting, the symptom checklist was again completed by classroom teachers for the children in the original study group. A total of 151 children, 64 boys and 79 girls, were included; 95 of the children were Southeast Asian. Gillis noted that the school population was transient and that a number of the original study group had moved out of the area. In addition, the parents of 27 students still remaining in group treatment, offered through the school, completed the behavior checklist and survey of posttraumatic stress symptoms with their child's therapist.

Gillis (1991) reported a similar symptom picture for girls and boys in terms of overall symptom numbers at both Time 1 and Time 2. Both groups exhibited more total symptoms at Time 1 than at Time 2, with more internalizing behaviors reported at Time 1. No such differences were reported for externalizing behaviors. The boys exhibited more externalizing behaviors than the girls at both Time 1 and Time 2, and the girls exhibited a tendency toward more internalizing behaviors at Time 2. Gillis suggested that the observed decrease in overall symptomatology was consistent with discrete trauma, in which time may have an ameliorating effect. Additionally, he suggested that the presence of more internalizing symptoms may reflect the initial internalizing nature of the posttraumatic response. Looking at ethnicity, Gillis reported no significant differences between the Asian and non-Asian children in overall degree of symptomatology. Both groups exhibited more overall symptoms at Time 1 than Time 2. Interestingly, although both groups exhibited significantly more internalizing behavior than externalizing behavior at Time 1, the non-Asian children exhibited more externalizing symptoms at Time 2. Gillis concluded that the initial impact of a traumatic event may lead to internalizing types of posttraumatic reaction in all children. However, he also hypothesized that, with time, there may be a resumption of more long-standing (familial or cultural) types of reaction.

Looking at the effects of proximity and symptom development, Gillis reported no significant differences in overall symptom number between the children directly exposed on the playground and those in the school. However, the results indicated that the children on the playground exhibited significantly more internalizing symptoms than those in the school, whereas those in the school exhibited more externalizing behaviors. Gillis cautioned careful interpretation of these results, as proximity may have been confounded by developmental factors (grades 1–3 on the playground vs. grades 4–6 in the school building).

In looking at the effects of group treatment on the children, Gillis reported that the children who had participated in group treatment exhibited fewer internalizing symptoms than those who had not. Although this decrease was observed as a general phenomenon, the decrease was seen as significant.

Gillis had the unique opportunity to study the impact of the shooting on a number of the direct victims. Unlike the nonwounded children, those wounded were not observed to exhibit a significant decrease in symptom number from Time 1 to Time 2. Interestingly, some symptoms appeared to increase (a change in ability to concentrate), whereas others appeared to decrease (excessive fears).

Like the work of Schwarz and Kowalski (1991b) Gillis's study evolved out of initial efforts to provide clinical services for the children and adults affected by the shooting. Thus, similar difficulties related to self-selection and bias in reporting, as well as the effects of clinical intervention, need to be highlighted when interpreting the results. However, in spite of these methodological issues, which are often inherent in the disaster literature, Gillis's work provides an additional understanding of the longitudinal course of posttraumatic symptoms and offers as well insights into cultural factors that may contribute to important group differences in presentation and course. Gillis framed his conclusions carefully, mindful of the methodological issues and the small numbers in some cases.

Hough, Vega, Valle, Kolody, del Castillo, and Tarke (1989) reported anecdotally about children's responses to a shooting at a fast-food restaurant that resulted in 21 deaths and 15 injuries. A total of 303 Mexican-American women, aged 35–50, with household incomes below the county median and representing 35% of the households in the community, were interviewed about their reactions to the shooting six months after the event. None of the women had been direct witnesses of the violence.

The survey participants were questioned about whether they felt their children needed any additional help in dealing with the shooting: 89.8% reported their children needed no more help than usual; 5% said their children needed a little more help than usual; 1.1% said their children needed considerably more help; and 3.2% said their children needed very much more help. No specific age range was specified for those children most in need of help. Although most of the participants viewed themselves as effective in dealing with the needs of their children, 16.2% said they did not feel very or at all effective, and 19% reported seeking out professional assistance for their problems in helping their children cope. These findings stand in contrast to those reported by other investigators. The relatively mild range of posttraumatic reactions observed by these mothers may reflect minimization of the impact. These findings, lacking independent validation, need to be interpreted with caution.

Only one report has specifically attempted to examine the impact of direct exposure to a life threat within the familial context. Malmquist (1986) interviewed 16 children, all of whom had witnessed the murder of a parent. Six of the children were between the ages of 5 and 10 and each had witnessed incidents of the parental murder. Two of these children had been directly threatened; one had been shot. The remaining 10 children were all members of the same family who had witnessed the murder of a parent by a family member. One of the children had been directly shot at; the others had successfully run away and/or hid.

As part of the interview, Malmquist administered the Impact of Event Scale (IES). He concluded that all of the children met the DSM-III criteria for PTSD. All of the children reported intrusive distressing recollections of the event, and 14 of the 16 reported nightmares. Malmquist noted an increased number of arousal (rather than avoidance or numbing) responses: anxiety, restlessness, hypervigilance, jumpiness, and difficulty with concentration. School declines were reported. In addition, symptoms of affective disorder were present, and many of the children exhibited persistent mood disturbance. Ten of the children developed psychophysiological complaints for the first time.

On the IES, all items were checked off by 50%–100% of the children. Two items—"I had waves of strong feelings about it" and "Things I saw or heard suddenly reminded me of it"—were checked by all of the respondents. In general, the avoidance items were less often checked than the intrusive items. However, Malmquist author did not differentiate between the symptom pictures of the children who had witnessed the violence and of those who had been directly threatened or injured.

Although clinically relevant, the Malmquist study included children not randomly selected and participating in mental health services. Additionally, there was no control for preexisting and coexisting personality, family, and social factors. It is likely that the dynamics of such violence compounded symptom presentation in the child. Generalizations from these data should be made with caution.

TRAUMA MEMBRANE AND FUTURE STUDY

Mental health professionals might expect that more than those individuals visible to them are affected in a trauma. In addition, even aggressive outreach may well fail to reach those in need. Lindy, Grace, and Green (1981) formulated the concept of the trauma membrane that surrounds and protects those affected by trauma when, after a supper club fire, only 5% of those they felt were touched by the trauma stepped forward for evaluation. Those trusted individuals who surround the victims can often "interpret" the trauma and can serve either an insulating function or, conversely, a helpful opening function. As noted, Pynoos *et al.* (1987) evaluated only 14.5% of the children in a school shooting, and Schwarz and Kowalski (1991b) saw only 23.5% of the available population. In the Pynoos work, some teachers would not permit an evaluation of the children in their classroom, and in the Schwarz and Kowalski study (1991a,b), the parents were the referral agents.

In the clinical work discussed by Schwarz and Kowalski (1991a), because of the early intervention and continued work in the community, our screening may well reflect the clinical picture within the membrane. Future research and clinical intervention should be directed toward discovering ways of piercing that membrane or positioning professionals inside the membrane for the best clinical interventions. Epidemiological data, PTSD diagnostic criteria, and even clinical follow-up data are useful but are limited by the validity of the sample assessed. Clinical care may not be available to those in need unless this protective membrane is studied, understood, respected, and somehow circumvented (Sloan, 1989).

REFERENCES

American Psychiatric Association. (1980). *Diagnostic and statistical manual of mental disorders* (3rd ed.; DSM-III). Washington, DC: Author.

American Psychiatric Association. (1987). *Diagnostic and statistical manual of mental disorders* (3rd ed., rev.; DSM-III-R). Washington, DC: Author.

Dyson, J. L. (1990). The effect of family violence on children's academic performance and behavior. *Journal of the National Medical Association, 82,* 17–22.

Eggington, J. (1991). *Day of fury.* New York: Morrow.

Finkelhor, D., Hotaling, G., & Sedlak, A. (1990). *Missing, abducted, runaway, and thrown away children in America: First report, numbers and characteristics, national incidence studies.* Washington, DC: U.S. Department of Justice, Office of Juvenile Justice and Delinquency Prevention.

Forehand, R., Long, N., Zogg, C., & Parrish, E. (1989). Parent and child functioning following return. *Clinical Pediatrics, 28,* 311–316.

Garmezy, N. (1986). Children under severe stress: Critique and commentary. *Journal of the American Academy of Child Psychiatry, 25,* 384–392.

Gillis, H. M. (1991, Aug.). *Children's responses and symptomatology following the Stockton, California school-yard shooting.* Paper presented the American Psychological Association Convention, San Francisco.

Hough, R. L., Vega, W., Valle, R., Kolody, B., del Castillo, R. G., & Tarke, H. (1989). Mental health consequences of the San Ysidro McDonald's massacre: A community study. *Journal of Traumatic Stress, 3,* 71–92.

Lindy, J. D., Grace, M. C., & Green, B. L. (1981). Survivors: Outreach to a reluctant population. *American Journal of Orthopsychiatry, 51,* 468–478.

Malmquist, C. P. (1986). Children who witness parental murder: posttraumatic aspects. *Journal of the American Academy of Child Psychiatry, 25,* 320–325.

Nader, K., Pynoos, R., Fairbanks, L., & Frederick, C. (1990). Children's PTSD reactions one year after a sniper attack at their school. *American Journal of Psychiatry, 147,* 1526–1530.

Ornitz, E. D., & Pynoos, R. S. (1989). Startle modulation in children with posttraumatic stress disorder. *American Journal of Psychiatry, 146,* 866–870.

Pynoos, R. S., & Eth, S. (1986). Witness to violence: The child interview. *Journal of the American Academy of Child Psychiatry, 25,* 306–319.

Pynoos, R. S., & Nader, K. (1989). Children's memory and proximity to violence. *Journal of the American Academy of Child and Adolescent Psychiatry, 28,* 236–241.

Pynoos, R. S., & Nader, K. (1990). Children's exposure to violence and traumatic death. *Psychiatric Annals, 20,* 334–344.

Pynoos, R. S., Frederick, C., Nader, K., Arroyo, W., Steinberg, A., Eth, S., Nunez, F., & Fairbanks, L. (1987). Life threat and posttraumatic stress disorder in school-age children. *Archives of General Psychiatry, 44,* 1057–1063.

Pynoos, R. S., Nader, K., Frederick, C., Gonda, L., & Stuber, M., (1987). Grief reactions in school age children following a sniper attack at school. *Israeli Journal of Psychiatry and Related Sciences, 24,* 53–63.

Schwarz, E. D., & Kowalski, J. M. (1991a). Posttraumatic stress disorder after a school shooting: Effects of symptom threshold selection and diagnosis by DSM-III, DSM-III-R, or Proposed DSM-IV. *American Journal of Psychiatry, 148,* 592–597.

Schwarz, E. D., & Kowalski, J. M. (1991b). Malignant memories: Posttraumatic stress disorder in children following a school shooting. *Journal of the American Academy of Child and Adolescent Psychiatry,*

Senior, N., Gladstone, T., & Nurcome, B. (1982). Child snatching: A case report. *Journal of the American Academy of Child Psychiatry, 21,* 579–583.

Shetky, D. H., & Haller, L. H. (1983). Parental kidnapping, *American Academy of Child Psychiatry, 22,* 279–285.

Silvern, L., & Kaersvang, L. (1989). The traumatized children of violent marriages. *Child Welfare, 68,* 421–436.

Sloan, I. H. (1989, Oct.). *Multiple shootings in an elementary school.* Symposium chaired at the Illinois Psychiatric Society Annual Meeting, Chicago.

Terr, L. C. (1979). Children of Chowchilla: A study of psychic trauma. *Psychoanalytic Study of the Child, 34,* 547–623.

Terr, L. C. (1981). Psychic trauma in children: Observations following the Chowchilla school-bus kidnapping. *The American Journal of Psychiatry, 138,* 14–19.

Terr, L. C. (1983a). Child snatching: A new epidemic of an ancient malady. *Journal of Pediatrics, 103,* 151–156.

Terr, L. C. (1983b). Chowchilla revisited: The effects of psychic trauma four years after a school-bus kidnapping. *American Journal of Psychiatry, 140,* 1543–1550.

Terr, L. C. (1990). *Too scared to cry.* New York: Harper & Row.

U.S. Department of Justice, Federal Bureau of Investigation. (1989). *Uniform crime reports for the United States.* Washington, DC: U.S. Government Printing Office.

West, L. J. (1984, May). *The epidemic of violence.* Presented at the annual meeting of the American Psychiatric Association, Los Angeles.

8

Children and War

CYNTHIA CUPIT SWENSON and AVIGDOR KLINGMAN

Although many people hope for world peace, war continues to be a part of daily life. Over 20 wars are currently occurring throughout the world (Macksoud, 1991). As a result, millions of children are faced with the experience of war. Exposure to traumatic events, such as the death of a loved one, displacement, or witnessing violence are common occurrences, as are children's direct military participation and the difficulties of family or community members who are or have been involved in military action.

This chapter explores the effects of war on children. First, we discuss the direct effects of conventional war and political violence on children. Second, we will present the long-term effects of war on adult survivors of childhood war experiences. Third, we address how war affects children via their parents' experiences, and finally, we explore interventions that assist individuals in coping with the stress of war.

THE DIRECT EFFECTS OF WAR ON CHILDREN

Conventional Warfare

The initial studies of the effects of war on children were conducted during World War II. The results varied; some studies indicated limited

CYNTHIA CUPIT SWENSON • Charleston–Dorchester Community Mental Health Center—Division of Children, Adolescents and Families, 4 Carriage Lane, Suite 40S, Charleston, South Carolina 29407.   AVIGDOR KLINGMAN • Chair, Department of Counseling, School of Education, University of Haifa, Mt. Carmel, Haifa 31905, Israel.
Children and Disasters, edited by Conway F. Saylor. Plenum Press, New York, 1993.

psychological effects (Freud & Burlingame, 1942), and others found psychiatric disturbances (Dunsdon, 1941). Several studies noting emotional difficulties in children experiencing war attributed these problems to the parents' anxiety (Burt, 1943) or to the child's emotional adjustment or personality characteristics before the war (Carey-Trefzer, 1949; Mercier & Despert, 1942). Although the literature is sparse, researchers from several countries have further addressed the effects of war on children.

The Yom Kippur War in Israel. The Yom Kippur war (the Arab–Israeli war in 1973) is set apart from other wars in that it happened quickly, lasting only three weeks. Yet, a large number of casualties were incurred. Therefore, in addition to the anxiety of war, bereavement became a focal issue (Palgi, 1973). Following the Yom Kippur war, Milgram and Milgram (1976) found that the children showing the lowest anxiety levels during peacetime experienced the largest increases in anxiety during the war. The increase in anxiety was greater for males than for females, and greater for children from upper-middle than from lower socioeconomic status. Surprisingly, personal stress factors were not significantly related to an increase in wartime anxiety.

One-and-one-half years following the Yom Kippur war, Ziv, Kruglanski, and Shulman (1974) assessed 818 elementary-school-aged children. Of these children, 521 lived in areas that had been exposed to frequent shelling, and 297 came from settlements that had never been exposed to shelling. Ziv *et al.* found that children who had experienced shelling showed a more positive attitude toward their place of residence, which may have been an indication of increased group cohesiveness. These children also exhibited a significantly greater degree of externally oriented aggressiveness and showed a predominance of aggressive dreams with themes of defeat of the enemy.

Kaffman (1977) treated children living on kibbutzim during the same war. Kibbutzim are described as settlements characterized by highly educated members, a high degree of community organization, self-sufficiency, and the communal rearing of children (Milgram, 1982). Although near the front lines, few of the kibbutz members were referred for treatment due to war-related psychological impairment. In two years of follow-up care, no increases in psychological difficulties were noted. However, those children on the kibbutzim whose fathers had been killed in the war (approximately one half of the children studied) did demonstrate excessive mourning reactions. The mourning of these kibbutz children lasted from six months to three years, and the intensity of the difficulty was not significantly different from that experienced by nonkibbutz children (Kaffman & Elizur, 1983). The factors related to long-term pathological bereavement were low impulse control, emotional lability, a tendency to react with explosive rage to frustrations, withdrawal, pretraumatic long-term separation from the father, pretraumatic family conflict, the mother's anxiety, and the absence of a substitute father figure (Elizur & Kaffman, 1983).

War in Lebanon.   Many individuals living in Lebanon are described as experiencing continual warfare, violence and death being a daily occurrence (Bryce, Walker, & Peterson, 1989). Macksoud (1991) reported on the war experiences of Lebanese children. She indicated that, of those children exposed to war, 96% had been exposed to at least one traumatic event and that most children had been exposed to more than five traumatic events. Children from lower socioeconomic status and children from certain regions had been exposed to more trauma than other children. The most common event that the children were reported to have experienced was shelling or combat (94%), followed by displacement (68%), bereavement over the death of a parent or of a close relative (70%), witnessing violence (45%), extreme deprivation (20%), and direct involvement in combat (3%). Further, Macksoud stated that most of the children studied had long-term symptoms of posttraumatic stress disorder (PTSD), as well as feelings of betrayal that altered their sense of safety and trust.

Through self-report measures that they had developed, Chimienti, Nasr, and Khalifeh (1989) evaluated 1,039 three- to nine-year-olds living in Lebanon during wartime. Their parents reported behavioral symptoms including overdependence; crying easily; physical complaints; possessiveness; shouting, screaming, and defiance with other children; hyperactivity; and nagging. Consistent with some of the Israeli studies (Elizur & Kaffman, 1983), the children who had experienced personal stressors, such as the death of a family member, were significantly more likely to show anxiety, fears, and behavioral difficulties than those who had not experienced such stressors.

Saigh (1989) assessed 840 Lebanese children, aged 9–12, who were exhibiting emotional problems following exposure to war stressors. These children had been referred by physicians, mental health workers, educators, and Red Cross workers because of their development of emotional problems following war-related stressors. Of the children assessed, 273 warranted a diagnosis of chronic PTSD. The children diagnosed with PTSD showed higher levels of anxiety, depression, and behavioral difficulties than did their nonclinical peers and children with phobias.

The Gulf War.   In January 1991, the U.S. Congress declared war in the Middle East. Several countries joined together to launch a war campaign like no other that had occurred in the past. Operation Desert Storm, also termed the Gulf War, was initiated to reclaim independence for Kuwait, which had been captured by Iraq on August 2, 1990. This war was different from previous wars because of the high level of technology and around-the-clock television news coverage. Aerial bombing was constant for a period of three weeks. From the United States, 540,000 troops were deployed. Of those troops, 35,000 were women, 16,300 were single parents, and 60% were married. Bloch (1991) estimated that 750,000–1 million children in the United States were affected in some way by the war, facing separation from one or both parents. Worries about loved ones were continually reinforced by almost constant news coverage. Rubenstein (1991), who worked closely with one school system, described the feelings of children and adolescents experiencing deployment stress. She found that these children had a variety of symptoms, including anger, sadness, abandonment, loss, irritation, confusion, depression, anxiety, fears for the deployed person, fears about their own physical safety, feelings of being out of balance and out of control, and feelings of isolation and loneliness. In addition to the children's difficulties with the deployment, Rubenstein (1991) noted homecoming adjustment difficulties in the families of deployed individuals.

A clinical description of children's acute sensitivity was provided by the American Psychological Association's report of the telephone hotline established in the United States during the war. American children expressed fear that Iraqi missiles would land in the United States; one child asked if he should go to the Rocky Mountains to escape the Iraqi bombing (DeAngeles, 1991).

The Israeli experience during the Persian Gulf War of 1991 presented a new war-related phenomenon. For the first time in human history, advanced technology created a situation in which a distant country, not involved in the warfare, was attacked. Furthermore, the uncertainty about which weapon type (conventional or unconventional warhead) would be used made this war beyond conventional and closer to a nuclear disaster threat.

Over a period of six weeks, the Israeli civilian population was subjected to 18 different attacks in which 39 Scud missiles fell. Most of the attacks occurred in densely populated areas, causing considerable damage to property, bodily injury, and loss of life. Schools remained closed for long periods during the war; initially, only essential employees went to work. In each home, a room was set aside in which all windows and doors were sealed. When the air-raid alarm sounded, the family immediately entered the sealed room, put on gas masks, completed sealing the door from the inside, and then waited for the area of explosion and nature of the missile to be determined (in certain areas this took several hours). Children soon became irritable due to being awakened by sirens night after night, often more than once in a single night. The gas masks caused additional problems owing to the complicated nature of fastening the mask and the tendency of the mask to fog up. Many children had to be convinced, or even forced, to don the masks (Klingman, 1992a). Children under the age of 3 were placed in gasproof cots that physically isolated them from the rest of the family.

During and immediately following the war, several attempts were made to gather data on the response of children and adolescents. No well-controlled studies are available because of the difficulties of conducting research at the time: technical problems (e.g., transportation limitations and school suspension), the pressures on and overinvolvement of the researchers, a resistance to empirical studies (perceived as nonfunctional by the population), the lack of time for a thorough formulation of the research questions and goals, budget problems, and methodological difficulties (e.g., population sampling). Nevertheless, a few studies were conducted with children during the war.

Klingman (1992c) administered a Post-Traumatic Stress Reaction Scale to 7th-, 10th-, and 12th-graders during the first and fourth weeks of the war. This questionnaire consisted of 14 items derived from the clinical literature on acute stress reactions in children and was modified from a previously used scale (Milgram, Toubiana, Klingman, Raviv, & Goldstein, 1988) so that it would assess the current stressor (i.e., missile attacks). The results indicated that the intensity of stress reactions was significantly greater during the first week than in the fourth week of the war (a mean of 5.8 in contrast to 3.0 in the fourth week). Of the 14 items, those most frequently identified were fear of missiles hitting me (69%), frightening images of falling missiles (65%), refraining from enjoyable activities (59%), and difficulty in falling asleep following a siren (58%). Other responses included overeating (49%), a sense of physical weakness (48%), difficulties with concentration (48%), sleep disturbances (43%), restlessness (35%), and physical pains (31%). Situational exposure (the intensity of the attack and the scope of the destruction) was found to be an important factor in influencing stress reactions. Subjects from the most intensely attacked area reported a significantly greater frequency of the following symptoms: avoiding pleasant activities, physical weakness, physical pains, and restlessness. As for gender differences, females reported a higher frequency of stress reactions than did males.

During the fifth week of the war. Rosenbaum and Ronen (1991) assessed fifth- and sixth-grade students and their parents, using a 0-to-10 anxiety-rating scale. The subjects were living in shelled areas, but none were in areas that had been directly hit by the missiles. The results showed an increase in anxiety as evening grew near. Anxiety was noted to be lower during the fifth week than during the first week of the war, and females were more anxious than males. The mothers were the most anxious in the family, and the fathers were the least anxious. A significant positive correlation was shown between the children's perception of their own anxiety and the parents' perception of their children's anxiety.

Studies conducted one week following the cease-fire revealed similar data. Using Spielberger's State and Trait Anxiety questionnaires, Mintz (1991) found that children aged 12 and 16 who lived closer to the attacked area were more anxious than children living farther away from the attacked area. Females were more anxious than males, and younger children were more anxious than older children (on the state questionnaire only). Physiological symptoms were highly correlated with anxiety level.

In a study with 5th-, 7th-, and 10th-grade children conducted three weeks after the war ended, Schwarzwald, Weisenberg, Waysman, Solomon, and Klingman (1991) revealed that stress reactions were related to age and level of objective stress (i.e., the proximity to missile explosions and damage as well as the child's relationship to victims who where injured and subjective stress (i.e., the perceived threat to oneself, to relatives, and to acquaintances). The younger children and those who reported higher levels of objective and subjective stress indicated a higher level of stress reaction. Posttraumatic rates ranged from 33.5% for the youngest group to 9.1% for the oldest group, with an overall rate of 20.4%. The overall emotional reaction of the majority of these children who reported how they felt when they were in the sealed room was found to be optimistic. Their behavior typically reflected an interest in seeking information, in checking safety measures, and in calming others. Once the minimal available safety measures had been taken, emotion-focused coping (such as avoidance and distraction strategies) was associated with fewer postwar stress reactions than persistence in direct problem-focused actions (Weisenberg, Schwartzwald, Waysman, Solomon, & Klingman, 1991). This pattern of results is consistent with the stress and coping theory of Lazarus and Folkman (1984).

A semiprojective assessment (Zeidner, Klingman, & Itzkovitz, 1992) was conducted with fourth- and fifth-grade pupils approximately one week following the cease-fire. Open-ended questionnaires were designed to assess children's attitudes, perceptions, fears, and anxieties about various facets of life in the classroom, in the social network, and at home. Pictures representing images of significant others were used to elicit children's preconscious thematic contents and issues. One notable finding was related to the role of the family as a support system. Children who perceived their parents as anxious tended to display higher anxiety levels and greater emotionality. The children perceived the anxiety of the mother to be significantly higher than that of the father. Children who viewed their families as being more communicative and supportive also tended to be more aware of their feelings, showed more congruent emotional expression, and expressed more empathy toward others in their environs. These children also showed greater perceived responsibility for the situation and had more effective defenses.

A telephone survey of 273 adults approximately three weeks after the beginning of the war (Klingman, Sagi, & Raviv, in press) revealed that the interviewees perceived the adult population as being the most fearful (males 41.4%; females 54.7%), followed by elderly males (24.3%; females 18.4%) and children (males 24.3%; females 17.3%). In contrast, young adults (males 7.1%; females 4.5%) and teenagers (males 2.9%; females 5%) were seen as the least fearful. A telephone survey conducted in June 1991 addressing parents' observations of the fears of their children (aged 14–18) during the war and at the time of the survey revealed that the parents noted greater fears among younger children (under age 14) than among older children. They also reported a near absence of fears among adolescents and a substantial decrease in fears at the time of the survey compared with during the war. However, some of the younger children (1.5%) were still exhibiting signs of fear at the time of the survey. Finally, it was noted that those young children reporting fears during the war were the most likely to be experiencing fear at the time of the survey (Spearman rank $r = .33$, $p < .01$).

Sleep habits and sleep disturbances of toddlers were studied (Lavie, Amit, Epstein, & Tzischinsky, 1992) by means of a questionnaire completed by parents and recordings on an actigraph (a monitor worn on the wrist in bed). No noticeable effects of the emergency situation (during the war) on sleep were detected. Overall sleep quality was minimally affected.

The data from the Israeli Gulf War studies reviewed in this section reveal that the child population studied appeared to adjust to the situation over time. This phenomenon is similar to the reported reactions of children in England during the blitz (Rachman, 1990) and to children's reactions to shelling in border towns in Israel (Raviv & Klingman, 1983). These data seem to support further the notion of habituation as suggested by Rachman (1990). It should be emphasized, however, that the child population investigated in these studies was not from an area directly hit by Scud missiles. It is plausible that, although initially uncontrollability and unpredictability were extremely high, as time passed the prediction of the use of chemical or bacteriological warheads (i.e., a general catastrophe) had not been supported. Therefore, the probability of personal harm seemed less acute; and a reevaluation took place permitting a decrease in fear. It is also likely that the strength of the natural coping processes and the familial natural support systems available (i.e., a sense of "togetherness") grew. Also, many children, particularly adolescents, found active roles for themselves within the family (i.e., some self-efficacy). Denial, a very commonly used coping mechanism, is another possible explanation. It is known that denial is quite effective when used by young children, at least during a short-term exposure to crises when there is little to do to cope directly with the source of threat (Pynoos & Eth, 1985).

Many examples were observed of children who became support figures, essentially turning into "parental children." These youths took responsibility for their parents, grandparents, and younger siblings, making sure that they entered the sealed room quickly, donned their masks properly, and received essential information (via radio, TV, and telephone calls to other members of the family). In addition, they helped seal the door from the inside and entertained their younger siblings. Much in evidence were the families in which previously existing problems had been intensified by the war experience. For example, communication difficulties worsened the stress phenomena. These cases likely reflect populations at-risk for more acute posttraumatic reactions (Arazi, 1991; Raviv, in press).

The content and characteristics of crisis hotline calls are another source of information of a clinical nature. Raviv (in press) summarized surveys of telephone crisis-hotline services in Israel during the Gulf War. Although the data collected do not allow a precise estimation of the number of calls received by the hotline services, it seems that although most calls were from adults, children made a higher percentage of the calls to the hotlines geared specifically to them: One such hotline service reported over 6,000 calls, one third from adults and two thirds from children. Moreover, children were well represented by parents who called concerning their children's problems. Most calls expressed helplessness, anxiety, and fear and complained about somatic symptoms. Parents called for advice concerning their children who expressed fears, had trouble sleeping, were eating less, refused to put on gas masks, vomited, and became aggressive. The most frequent reactions of children reported by the parents at the beginning of the war were their children's refusal to put on the gas masks and physiological symptoms such as pain and vomiting.

The reader should note that most of the data summarized here are from self-reports and are retrospective. Thus, they are subject to the error of memory, distortion, social desirability, and so on. However, for all their limitations, these data appear to offer the most feasible approach under the circumstances (see Folkman, Lazarus, Gruen, & DeLongis, 1986). The studies reported here permitted a unique data collection from relatively large and representative samples, close to the event and in a relatively short time (Weisenberg *et al.*, 1991). Such data are indeed scarce concerning children's responses and coping in large-scale disasters and traumatic situations.

Political Violence

Political violence differs from conventional warfare in that political violence may be more long-term and often is random, therefore creating a need to be constantly hypervigilant to the possibility of violence. In political violence, civilians are personally involved in violence and children are often combatants. The distinction between enemies and nonenemies or civilians and combatants is unclear (Ronstrom, 1989). The enemy territory is also poorly defined. In fact, schools, homes, and neighborhoods are often the site of combat (Fraser, 1974). In political warfare, children are subjected to the bombing and massacre of villages, as well as the destruction of homes and crops. Many hide out in the mountains or in refugee camps. These children have to hide their identities for survival purposes and therefore are unable to talk about the trauma they are experiencing (Ronstrom, 1989). Because the trauma continues to be imminent, children are unable to work through these experiences. Thus, political violence has been referred to as producing a continuous traumatic stress syndrome (Straker & The Sanctuaries Team, 1987).

Political violence occurs in different forms in different countries. It may occur in various contexts and may include a variety of methods of violence. Therefore, the effect on individual children may differ. The effects of political violence may have some commonalities with the effects of conventional warfare. There is the trauma of losing a loved one who is detained, fears for one's own safety as well as that of family members, and the difficulty of reintegration of the detainee into the family.

Palestinian Population. Punamaki (1989) compared children living in the Israeli-occupied West Bank and the Gaza Strip to Palestinian children living within the 1948 borders of Israel. Exposure to political hardships increased psychological symptoms. Like children in conventional war, girls were noted to be significantly more fearful than boys. The anxiety level among children exposed to hardships was reported to increase only in children whose mothers showed an external locus of control. The mothers' psychological symptoms were related to high levels of psychological symptoms among their children.

Ireland.   Since 1968, Northern Ireland has experienced long periods of political violence (Cairns & Wilson, 1989). Many studies conducted in Northern Ireland indicate that a small percentage of the population has experienced psychiatric difficulties due to political violence (Lyons, 1972; Lyons & Bindall, 1977). In a study assessing the impact of political violence on adults, Fraser (1971) found that neither psychiatric inpatient admissions nor psychiatric referrals had increased in areas of considerable violence. However, in areas of intermediate violence, referrals of male psychotics and male neurotics had increased significantly. Fraser concluded that psychiatric difficulties were maximal in areas under the threat of attack compared to areas in which the risk was more obvious. Despite the lack of increase in adult referrals in areas of violence, Fraser (1974) reported 10 case studies of children who had experienced violent events due to political disturbances. The symptoms of these children included sleep disturbances and somatic complaints. In two separate studies using teacher ratings, Fee (1980; 1983) noted decreases in behavioral problems among children that coincided with a decrease in political violence.

South Africa.   The high level of political violence in South Africa may particularly effect children growing up in the black townships. Dawes, Tredoux, and Feinstein (1989) interviewed children and parents who were part of four communities burned to the ground in South Africa. Thousands of people were left homeless, and 53 were killed. Families in this study had rebuilt their shacks three months after eviction. There was a constant threat of future attacks. Approximately 63% of the mothers were diagnosed as having PTSD. Among the younger children, boys showed a higher frequency of stress symptoms than girls; boys and girls were similar in middle childhood; and among adolescents, more girls than boys showed stress symptoms. Overall, 40% of the children showed symptoms of stress. Nine percent of the children were diagnosed as having PTSD, a higher percentage of girls than boys receiving this diagnosis. Children whose mothers were diagnosed as having PTSD were more likely to show multiple symptoms of stress.

Mozambique.   Boothby (1991) reported anecdotal information from his work with children in Mozambique. He stated that 70% of the children in war zones in Mozambique witness many deaths, and that approximately 50,000 children have watched loved ones being murdered. In addition to the trauma of viewing violence, Boothby estimated that one half of these children have been tortured and 75% have been abducted. In fact, 200,000 have reportedly been separated from their families. Children who have been abducted (the average age is 11) have been taken to training camps and forced to kill. This training is reported to occur in three steps: (1) Children watch others being abused and are made to not show any concern; (2) children participate in violence, and those who do best get higher positions; and (3) rituals are conducted in which children drink the blood of those they kill.

Central America. In El Salvador, civil wars have gone on over eight years. Violence has been committed against military combatants and civilians suspected of sympathizing with the insurgents. The social polarization of groups toward opposite extremes has created an atmosphere of tension (Martin-Baro, 1989). According to Gottlieb (1985), women and children have been especially vulnerable in Central American civil wars, sex crimes being common methods of torture. Rape has reportedly been used to torture an individual or to break the resistance of family members undergoing interrogation.

Problems noted among children in Central America include emotional as well as physical effects. Ronstrom (1989) anecdotally described children who had experienced political violence in Central America as showing behaviors such as hysteria on hearing loud noises, sleep disturbances, sadness, and malnutrition. Although no specific percentages were cited, Ronstrom (1989) reported that many of these children exhibited enuresis, encopresis, fears, somatic complaints, and excessive demands for affection and security. Arroyo and Eth (1985) examined 30 children (aged preschool to adolescence) who were in the United States from 3 weeks to 34 months following warfare in Central America. Ten were diagnosed as having PTSD. The young children's symptoms were regression and separation anxiety. The latency-aged children showed learning and conduct problems. The adolescents tended to act out with aggression and delinquency. Although a third of these children were diagnosed as having PTSD, it is unclear if there were any characteristic differences between these children and those who did not have PTSD. Of the children described, many had witnessed atrocities. Their difficulties had been compounded by separation from (or abandonment by) their parents, who had emigrated to the United States before or without them.

Martin-Baro (1989) reviewed a study that found that classical conditioning can occur during political violence. People in a small village in El Salvador reported that the presence of the army elicited fears and increased their physiological arousal (e.g., pulse increase and body trembling).

Children of Latin American Refugees. Consistent with studies on the effects of conventional warfare, the role of social support in assisting children who have experienced political violence has been shown to be important. Although adult Latin American refugees and torture victims have shown psychological distress and social maladaptation up to 10 years following the trauma, adult refugees assessed in Canada have reported no significant differences in their children from immigrant children who have not experienced trauma. It should be noted that all of these children had remained with at least one parent or an adequate substitute at all times. Therefore, these parents may have sheltered their children and may have dealt with their experiences in a way that protected them against anxiety. Thus, the lack of reported symptomatology in the children may have been due to these children not being separated from the parents (Allodi, 1989).

Cambodian Children in a Concentration Camp. In semistructured interviews two years after their release, over half of the Cambodian children studied who had been in concentration camps reported PTSD symptoms of avoidance and hyperarousal, as well as depressive symptomatology. The current living situation was significantly related to the psychiatric diagnosis; children living in foster care were more likely to have a psychiatric diagnosis than children living with their family (Kinzie, Sack, Angell, Manson, & Rath, 1986).

THE LONG-TERM EFFECTS OF WAR ON CHILDREN: ADULT SURVIVORS OF CHILDHOOD WAR EXPERIENCES

Research has consistently documented stress reactions in adults who have been exposed to war (Bloch, 1969; Goldsmith & Cretokos, 1969; Modlin, 1960, 1967; Strange & Brown, 1970). In addition, a number of studies have documented the long-term effects on adults who experienced war as children. During World War II, the events whose aim was the destruction of the Jews of Europe (the Holocaust) represented a severe, lengthy trauma for many children. Over 40 years later, many survivors continued to experience daily difficulties as a result of living through the Holocaust. Gampel (1988) obtained anecdotal information from adults who were child victims of the Holocaust. The survivors reported that, during the time of war, death was a daily occurrence. They became so accustomed to death that they generally felt apathy when it occurred. The one factor that gave them the drive to survive was the desire for revenge. As adults, they reported that they continued not to experience the death of others on a deep level. However, they acknowledged somatic complaints, difficulty with aggression, and anxiety in regard to themselves and their own children.

Twenty-five years after captivity, 42 Israeli citizens who were survivors of the Nazi concentration camps during World War II were compared with 20 individuals who had not been in concentration camps. The age at which the survivors had been interned was not reported. The survivors indicated that they were less accessible to others, had poorer emotional control, and were more conservative, careful, conventional, and practical (Dor-Shav, 1978). Robinson (1979) reported that children who were younger during Nazi persecution experienced more psychological damage than did older children.

According to Hogman (1983), who administered an unstructured interview to child survivors immediately after the war, Holocaust survivors felt cheated out of their childhood and were angry, anxious, and frequently delinquent. In adulthood, the effects of their childhood war experience appeared to be associated with family survival and prewar family adjustment. Individuals with parents who survived or who had had a positive family life before the war showed the best adjustment. Other child survivors showed difficulty in trusting others, which was reflected in their difficulties with relationships.

Mazor, Gampel, Enright, and Orenstein (1990) interviewed adult survivors of the Holocaust who had been ages 6–16 at the beginning of World War II. They reported that, immediately after the war, survivors tended to avoid war memories, instead busying themselves with tasks related to reentry into the postwar period. However, 45 years after the war, many survivors were making an effort to remember their war experiences. Some memories had been triggered by external cues that were reminders of the war. As memories were brought out, the survivors described themselves as feeling helpless, feeling a sense of loss, and feeling as if they were strangers in society. Interestingly, they also felt relief. Some of the survivors had attempted to talk with their own children about the war experiences. Those who had not, remained silent in an attempt to protect their children or because of feelings of humiliation or inferiority.

The long-term effects of war are also documented among survivors of the Japanese concentration camps. Through case studies, Krell (1990) described two childhood survivors of Japanese concentration camps in Indonesia. One of these individuals experienced memory loss, anxiety attacks, insomnia, and loss of sexual desire many years after release. These symptoms seemed to be elicited by a return to the sites of the camps, which were gone. In a second case, a woman who had survived internment in a Japanese camp functioned adaptively until she experienced the stress of the loss of a family servant.

Doreleijers and Donovan (1990) gave an anecdotal account of their general observations of adults referred to their clinic for psychiatric problems who, as children, had been prisoners of Japanese internment camps in the Dutch West Indies. These authors reported that both males and females showed a tendency to choose partners with psychiatric problems. The males showed difficulties in modulating aggressive feelings. Psychosomatic and passive-aggressive behavior were reported to be frequent. Of particular interest to these observers was that only 9 of 53 couples had divorced.

After the bombing of Pearl Harbor during World War II, many second-generation Japanese-Americans were ordered into internment camps. Although they were American citizens, these Japanese-Americans remained in concentration camps for two to three years. According to Nagata (1990), the trauma due to internment varied, though the tendency to avoid communication regarding the internment was common to the survivors. This paucity of communication continued between second-generation Japanese-Americans and their children. Third-generation Japanese-Americans having two parents who had been interned spoke more frequently with their parents about this experience than did those children having only one parent who had been interned. Despite the limited communication regarding the internment, third-generation Japanese-Americans showed a strong interest in obtaining information about the internment.

THE INDIRECT EFFECTS OF WAR ON CHILDREN: CHILDREN OF SURVIVORS

Because war has such strong, long-term effects on individuals who have experienced war as children, the question of long-term transgenerational influences has arisen. Rosenheck and Nathan (1985) termed the relationship between the fathers' difficulties in war and their children's problems "secondary traumatization." In a case study, they reported a child experiencing guilt, anxiety, aggressiveness, and preoccupation with those events traumatic to the father. There are approximately a quarter of a million children of Holocaust survivors in the United States alone. The children of these survivors have been described as experiencing a unique syndrome or feeling scarred, special, of different (Fogelman & Savran, 1979).

Freyberg (1980) gave an anecdotal report of children of Nazi Holocaust survivors. Many have sought treatment for sexual dysfunction, depression, phobias, anxiety, relationship difficulties, and somatic complaints. In addition to their own difficulties, they reportedly had relationship problems with their parents (the Holocaust survivors) as well, describing them as cold, controlling, and overprotective. Freyberg (1980) speculated that the parents viewed separation as loss, and thus, the children grew up feeling responsible for their parents' happiness.

Nadler, Kav-Venaki, and Gleitman (1985) compared children of Holocaust survivors with children of parents from a similar ethnic background with no Holocaust experience. The subjects of this study were from a nonclinical population. Nadler *et al.* found that, when presented with a frustrating situation, Holocaust survivors' children were more likely to internalize aggressive tendencies and admit their own guilt. The authors explained that children of Holocaust survivors have a strong sense of responsibility for their parents and may repress aggression to prevent their parents from experiencing further suffering. Solomon, Kotler, and Mikulincer (1988) found a higher rate of PTSD among soldiers in the Lebanon war whose parents were Holocaust survivors than among those whose parents had not been involved in the Holocaust.

Leon, Butcher, Kleinman, Goldberg, and Almagor (1981) assessed World War II concentration-camp survivors and their children, 33 years after the parents' liberation. The subjects of this study were from the general community rather than from a group of individuals referred for psychological difficulties. Neither the parents nor the children exhibited serious psychological impairment. There were no significant differences in psychological adjustment between the children of survivors and the control subjects. These results were inconsistent with those of other studies addressing long-term consequences. The differences may have been due to the measures used or the influence of other variables not measured (such as social support), and perhaps the degree to which the children of the survivors had been affected by their parents' Holocaust experience varied from person to person.

Doreleijers and Donovan (1990) anecdotally reported on 53 children of survivors of Japanese concentration camps. Seventy-five percent of the children showing second-generation problems were boys, with the presenting problems of aggression, psychosomatic complaints, depression, and learning and identity problems. These authors argued against a second-generation syndrome, although they acknowledged problems in the children that appeared to be related to the difficulty that the parents had had in resolving their past.

Sigal, DiNicola, and Buonvino (1988) looked at grandchildren of survivors of Nazi persecution and found, based on parental report, that these grandchildren of survivors did not differ significantly from control subjects. There were methodological problems in this study, including an overrepresentation of grandchildren of survivors in the population studied and the use of a nonstandardized measure of child problems.

Via semistructured interviews, Rosenheck (1986) assessed the adult children of five World War II veterans who had chronic PTSD. Although none of the veterans had discussed their war experiences directly with their children, 9 of the 12 children were aware, before they were 6 years old, that their fathers had had combat experiences. The children reported that they had not connected their fathers' problems with the war experience until their late teens to early 20s. One fourth of the children were categorized as having experienced secondary traumatization in that they had been exposed to their fathers' depression and rage and then, in turn, had experienced depression and distress themselves.

For many Vietnam veterans, PTSD symptoms are disruptive to marriages and parent–child relationships. Some veterans isolate themselves to deal with their problems, bringing about an emotional emptiness in the family. As a result, their spouses and children may feel a sense of responsibility for the problem (Rosenheck & Thomson, 1986).

Parsons, Kehle, and Owen (1990) examined the social and emotional effects of Vietnam veteran fathers' PTSD on children. Fathers with the diagnosis of PTSD rated their children as showing significantly more externalizing behavior problems. There appeared to be some developmental and sex differences in the children's difficulties. Younger females (aged 6–11) of PTSD fathers were described as showing significantly more aggression and somatic complaints. Older females (aged 12–16) were described as significantly more depressed and withdrawn than female children of non-PTSD fathers. Younger males (aged 6–11) of PTSD fathers were described as significantly more anxious; older males (aged 12–16) were described as significantly more hyperactive, immature, and inattentive.

Davidson, Smith, and Kudler (1989) compared World War II, Korean War, and Vietnam war veterans with nonpsychiatric controls on family history of psychiatric illness. They found no differences in the morbidity risk for psychiatric disorders between the PTSD group and any control groups. However, more children of the PTSD patients had received psychiatric treatment than had the children of the control subjects. The children of the Vietnam veterans showed a higher frequency of chronic psychiatric disorders and psychiatric treatment than did the children of World War II veterans. Further, when World War II and Vietnam veterans were compared, the relatives of Vietnam veterans showed more alcoholism and drug abuse.

INTERVENTION FOLLOWING CONVENTIONAL WAR

War not only induces psychic trauma in individuals but also brings about social trauma to entire populations (Martin-Baro, 1989). Therefore, psychotherapy alone is often inadequate to deal with the effects of war. Although social change must also occur, individual intervention is often needed to assist children in coping with grief and fears associated with separation and other war experiences. When intervention is provided, the developmental level of the child should be considered. Although the literature on war stress and adults includes numerous studies on dealing with PTSD, the literature on children and war stress is limited. These studies present interventions that have been helpful to the individual child and groups of children, representing a first step in resolving trauma due to war.

Individualized training in skills for coping with specific stressors has proved helpful to children in war. Day and Sadek (1982) used Benson's relaxation response with fifth-graders in Lebanon. Before and during the study, combat was taking place in the city where these children lived. Teachers led the children in relaxation one time daily for six weeks. After that period, the students who had participated in the relaxation showed significantly lower anxiety levels than a similar control group. In a three-week follow-up, during which combat had escalated and relaxation was not practiced, the children's anxiety had returned to prestudy levels.

Saigh (1986) reported a case study of a 6-year-old Lebanese boy who had exhibited symptoms of PTSD 25 months following a bomb blast. Through the use of relaxation training and *in vitro* flooding, decreases in anxiety and depressive symptomatology and increases in test scores measuring short-term memory and concentration were noted. These changes were maintained over 25 months. A case study of an Israeli preschool child who rejected the use of a gas mask was also reported. A parent-implemented cognitive-behavioral modification intervention using a combination of story reading, play, and behavioral modification on the targeted noncompliance behavior was used and found effective (Klingman, 1992a).

In addition to individual treatments of children, assisting the community, schools, and families provides help for many children. Kaffman (1977) reported that children living in kibbutzim were aided in coping with the war by adults who engaged them in asking questions, talking, playing games, drawing, and telling stories related to war. The children also carried on their regular daily program and practiced air-raid drills with plane noises.

Through case studies, Baider and Rosenfeld (1974) stressed the importance of parents' talking openly with young children about their fathers' going away to war and about the children's feelings. These authors argued that talking with children even as young as 2 may prevent their feeling responsible for their fathers' absence and their mothers' stress. The importance of expressing thoughts and affect regarding stressful experiences has also been demonstrated empirically. Klingman (1985) administered a free writing workshop (eight sessions of 50 minutes each) to fifth- and sixth-grade children living on the northern border of Israel, a high probability area for war-related crises. Free writing was described as a way of eliciting the direct expression of thoughts and feelings. The children who participated in the free writing wrote more statements expressing their feelings, clarifying their feelings, and expressing their stress than did the children in a control group both after the workshop and following a stressful event (the shelling of the town). Klingman stressed that expressing feelings through activities such as free writing may be used as an intervention tool with children under stress and as preventive skills training for the promotion of coping skills.

According to Lystad (1984), the family is a major resource for a child experiencing trauma. A supportive, caring parent is important. Tsoi, Yu, and Lieh-Mak (1986) interviewed Vietnamese children who were refugees in Hong Kong following the fall of the South Vietnam regime in 1975. Like Lystad (1984), they found that remaining with their families and receiving emotional support from their families seemed to buffer some children from the adverse psychological affects of the war. In addition to staying with the children, the parents may provide support by telling stories through drawing or using puppets and by providing basic, accurate information.

Klingman (1982) introduced to an elementary-school faculty a simulation of a crisis situation focusing on dealing with children under stress. The teachers who were involved in the simulation reported that they had attempted more behavioral activities related to anticipatory preparation for potential crises in their classrooms than had teachers who attended a lecture–discussion group. Klingman concluded that using role simulation may be effective in counteracting defensive avoidance, which he initially found to occur when teachers were provided with traditional intervention methods for preparatory guidance.

A novel phenomenon, countrywide intervention, took place in Israel during the Gulf War. Telephone hotlines were set up in psychoeducational service centers. One center reported that 25% of the callers were under age 15. Children were reported to talk about their fears of going crazy, their anxiety related to the war, and their concerns about their families. Many children sought information about the effects of chemical weapons and how to deal with alarms sounding while they were on their way to school (Noy, 1991). In addition to the hotline, numerous self-help materials were provided for children, teachers, and parents (for a review, see Klingman 1992b), and mass communication was used by psychologists to provide oral and visual information regarding the mental health aspects of stress and to provide guidelines for coping with war stress (Klingman, 1992b).

During the Gulf War, Bloch (1991) found that, for families in the United States, normalizing the experience of anxiety and sadness was vital to adjustment. Similarly, Perez (1991) suggested three steps for dealing with a traumatic event such as war. The first step involves normalizing the experience to distinguish healthy from unhealthy responses and giving information about the event and what to expect. The second step is education about emotional responses, and the third is free-form counseling focusing on what each individual can do externally for the troops. These three steps seem to help people cope with anxiety, although no data are available. An example of the third step is performing a physical act, such as sending care packages to help decrease one's own anxiety. According to Perez (1991), these three steps help people cope in time of war, but one can start to work through a traumatic event only after the event has ended.

Rubenstein (1991) worked with school systems to assist in the adjustment of children in the United States during the Gulf War. Regularly scheduled group meetings were held. The children were given time to talk about the feelings they were experiencing, after which they participated in an activity to figure out how to handle those feelings. The activities included group letter writing to a deployed parent and putting together a care package for a deployed person. In addition, pamphlets were developed for children and teachers to assist in adjustment (Embry, 1990a). The teacher's pamphlet consisted of suggestions for assisting children, including teaching lessons on the Middle East and information on how to start support groups. Suggestions for dealing with grief were also provided. Other pamphlets were also developed to assist in homecoming difficulties (Embry, 1990b, 1991; Rubenstein & Embry, 1990a,b, 1991).

SUMMARY AND FUTURE DIRECTIONS

Although the literature on the effects of war on children is sparse, six important points have emerged. First, many children show anxiety and fears when faced with the stressors of war. Females tend to show higher anxiety levels than males, and younger children show higher anxiety levels than older children. Anxiety decreases over time, possibly because of habituation to the stress (Klingman, 1992c). At first, uncontrollability and unpredictability are high in wartime. Increases in predictability over time appear to be associated with a decrease in anxiety level, at least during conventional warfare. For children who are experiencing political violence, the predictability of incidents may not increase over time. Therefore, the children are left with the prediction that violence may occur at any time.

Children whose loved ones are directly involved in combat may not show a decrease in anxiety over time and may require intervention to deal with the anxiety (Perez, 1991).

Second, despite a child's adjustment, additional personal stressors or reminders of the trauma may lead to the development of psychological symptoms (Chimienti et al., 1989; Elizur & Kaffman, 1983). These problems may occur years after the trauma has ended (Mazor et al., 1990). This finding was especially noted in research on Holocaust survivors.

Third, studies on war and children indicate that mothers' psychological symptoms are related to high levels of psychological symptoms in children. This finding is consistent with the literature in several areas of childhood disorders (Fendrich, Warner, & Weissman, 1990; Hammen et al., 1987; Hammen, Burge, & Stansbury, 1990; Orvaschel, Weissman, & Kidd, 1980; Rutter & Quinton, 1984), as well as with the literature on natural disasters and children (Crawshaw, 1963; Swenson, Powell, Foster, & Saylor, 1991). Parents may avoid discussing traumatic events in an effort to protect their children (Mazor et al., 1990). This lack of communication about war events may leave children to create their own reality, which may lead to unnecessary anxiety. Also, parents may be so overwhelmed by their own tasks that their children may be left to cope on their own. Young children in particular may rely on the actions of adults in their lives to guide their understanding of situations. Therefore, they may respond with those behaviors and coping strategies that they observe in their parents.

A fourth important finding relates to support. Several studies indicated that social support, particularly by family members, serves as a buffer against the psychological difficulties of war in general (Kaffman, 1977; Kaffman & Elizur, 1983; Tsoi et al., 1986). Social support by a cohesive community also appears to shield children from the negative effects of war (Ziv & Israeli, 1973). Children who perceived their family as supportive tend to have more effective defenses. When war occurs and one or both parents are involved in combat, a child's major support system is severed. For children who experience political violence, long-term separation from parents is common. Therefore, some researchers are using support by community members as an intervention to assist children in areas of political violence (Boothby, 1991). In conventional warfare, peer support groups and mobilizing community and family resources to provide support for children and other family members seem vital.

The fifth point regards the transgenerational effects of war. Just as children's psychological responses to stress have been shown to be related to their parents' (particularly their mothers') responses to stress, some children of adult survivors show psychological difficulties similar to those of their parents. Much of the literature is indicative of transgenerational effects. However, at least one study of individuals from a nonclinical population did not support the existence of transgenerational effects. The degree to which the children of survivors are affected by their parents' war experiences varies from person to person and may depend on a number of factors. These factors may include the effectiveness of the parents' coping, the second-generation person's own coping skills, and the level of social support by extended family, peers, or community. Although transgenerational effects of war are documented in some cases, additional research is needed to assess the factors that determine whether the parents' psychological problems will be taken on by the child.

Sixth, although interventions that alleviate war stress among children have not been researched extensively, the existing empirical and anecdotal data suggest that any intervention should be a multifaceted. Interventions for war stress should be implemented according to the developmental level of the child and may involve individual skills training to help the child manage anxiety, as well as a systemwide approach. An education component that helps to normalize one's feelings and that helps one to express worries related to war by writing, talking, or playing appears essential to children for managing war-related issues.

Studying children who are currently involved in a trauma or children who have experienced trauma in the past is often very difficult. Many researchers place their own safety at risk. Others meet resistance from authority figures in the child's life. McFarlane, Policansky, and Irwin (1987) attempted to study the effects on children of experiencing a bushfire. The schools were hesitant to participate because of a belief that past emotions should be left in the past. This belief is not restricted to schools or parents. According to Kestenberg (1985), researchers and survivors may fear adverse effects from an interview. Yet, other researchers report that discouraging children from talking about war-related stressors prevents them from making informed cognitive appraisals of the war, from ventilating their concerns, and from receiving reassurance (Baider & Rosenfeld, 1974; Koubovi, 1987).

Research consistently indicates that parents and teachers report less psychopathology among children than do the children themselves (Earls, Smith, Reich, & Jung, 1988; Kashani, Orvaschel, Burk, & Reid, 1985; McFarlane et al., 1987). Yule and Williams (1990) found that teachers did not note the behavioral or emotional difficulties that were occurring among their students who had survived a ferry disaster. Often, parents and teachers minimize the difficulties a child may have encountered because of the trauma; thus, the psychological effects of war may be underreported.

In addition, many parents are unable to participate in research studies because of their own difficulties in dealing with extreme stress, as well as the day-to-day demands of their lives. For individuals experiencing a community disaster such as war, the daily demands of life are greatly intensified, placing participation in research low on the priority list.

Children in some countries are not studied because of governmental opposition. Wars are often viewed as necessary to meet a certain goal. Therefore, viewing the war as a positive experience rather than as one that brings about emotional difficulties for children or adults may be seen as a way to boost the country's morale.

Partly because of some of the above-noted difficulties, the existing literature on children and war is full with methodological difficulties. Many studies have access to only a small sample of subjects. There is a lack of controlled, systematic studies and a tendency to rely on anecdotal accounts of children's experiences. In areas of political violence, the violence is not experienced at a consistent level over time. This variation in intensity makes a comparison of data over time difficult. Also, people tend to habituate to violence over time. In many areas, there are other community problems that may lead to psychiatric difficulties (Cairns & Wilson, 1989), thus confounding the interpretation of the data. Many studies use self-report measures that are affected by difficulties with memory and social desirability. Surveys may miss consequences if they are not asked about specifically. Yet, open-ended questions are subject to rater bias.

All in all, studying the effects of war on children is a formidable task. Despite the methodological difficulties, the existing data represent a valid attempt to meet the needs of children. Some children and families have evidently benefited from the work of researchers. Future research should focus on well-controlled studies that use standardized measures, including an assessment of coping. Children would benefit from the cooperation and participation of schools, communities, and government in assessments of and interventions for children who have experienced war. Much of our knowledge of how best to treat children and families who suffer a stressor as extreme as war lies in future research.

ACKNOWLEDGMENTS. We would like to thank Renae Duncan for her editorial comments, Marshall Swenson for his ardent support, and Donna Lubcker for sharing her Gulf War experiences.

REFERENCES

Allodi, F. (1989). The children of victims of political persecution and torture: A psychological study of a Latin American refugee community. *International Journal of Mental Health, 18,* 3–15.

Arazi, S. (1991). *A summary of the activities of a national hotline*. Unpublished manuscript. Ramat-Hen: Mental Health Center (in Hebrew).

Arroyo, W., & Eth, S. (1985). Children traumatized by Central American warfare. In S. Eth & R. Pynoos (Eds.), *Post-traumatic stress disorder in children*. Washington DC: American Psychiatric Press.

Baider, L, & Rosenfeld, E. (1974). Effect of parental fears on children in wartime. *Social Casework, 55*, 497–503.

Bloch, E. (1991, Aug.). *Approaching war, abating street: Psychology in action in the community.* Paper presented at the annual meeting of the American Psychological Association. San Francisco.

Bloch, H. S. (1969). Army clinical psychiatry in the combat zone—1967–1968. *American Journal of Psychiatry, 126*, 289–298.

Boothby, N. (1991, Aug.). *War zones: Psychological theory and practice in the field..* Paper presented at the annual meeting of the American Psychological Association. San Francisco.

Bryce, J. W., Walker, N., & Peterson, C. (1989). Predicting symptoms of depression among women in Beirut: The importance of daily life. *International Journal of Mental Health, 18*, 57–70.

Burt, C. (1943). War neuroses in British children. *Nervous Child, 2*, 324–337.

Cairns, E., & Wilson, R. (1989). Mental health aspects of political violence in Northern Ireland. *International Journal of Mental Health, 18*, 38–56.

Carey-Trefzer, C. (1949). The results of a clinical study of war-damaged children who attended the child guidance clinic, the Hospital for Sick Children, Great Ormand Street, London. *The Journal of Mental Science, 95*, 535–559.

Chimienti, G., Nasr, J. A., & Khalifeh, I. (1989). Children's reactions to war-related stress. *Social Psychiatry and Psychiatric Epidemiology, 24*, 282–287.

Crawshaw, R. (1963). Reaction to disaster. *Archives of General Psychiatry, 9*, 157–162.

Davidson, J., Smith, R., & Kudler, H. (1989). Familial psychiatric illness in chronic post-traumatic stress disorder. *Comprehensive Psychiatry, 30*, 339–345.

Dawes, A., Tredoux, C., & Feinstein, A. (1989). Political violence in South Africa: Some effects on children of the violent destruction of their community. *International Journal of Mental Health, 18*, 16–43.

Day, R. C., & Sadek, S. N. (1982). The effect of Benson's relaxation response on the anxiety levels of Lebanese children under stress. *Journal of Experimental Child Psychology, 34*, 350–356.

DeAngelis, T. (1991, March). Psychologists take calls from kids. *American Psychological Association Monitor, 22*, 8.

Doreleijers, T. A. H., & Donovan, D. M (1990). Transgenerational traumatization in children of parents interned in Japanese civil internment camps in the Dutch East Indies during world war II. *The Journal of Psychohistory, 17*, 435–447.

Dor-Shav, N. K. (1978). On the long-range effects of concentration camp internment on Nazi victims: 25 years later. *Journal of Consulting and Clinical Psychology, 46*, 1–11.

Dunsdon, M. I. (1941). A psychologist's contribution to air-raid problems. *Mental Health, 2*, 37–41.

Earls, F, Smith, E., Reich, W., & Jung, K. G. (1988). Investigating psychopathological consequences of a disaster in children: A pilot study incorporating a structured diagnosis approach. *Journal of the American Academy of Child and Adolescent Psychiatry, 27*, 90–95.

Elizur, E., & Kaffman, M. (1983). Factors influencing the severity of childhood bereavement reactions. *American Journal of Orthopsychiatry, 53*, 668–676.

Embry, D. D. (1990a). *I get support from friends. A story/workbook to help young people of active duty, reserve & national guard families affected by Desert Storm*. Tucson, AZ: Project Me.

Embry, D. D. (1990b). *They're coming home: This story/workbook stars your child, and helps your child cope with problems that might arise when a loved one returns from deployment*. Tucson, AZ: Project Me.

Embry, D. D. (1991). *They're coming home. A guide for parents of infants and toddlers affected by deployment*. Tucson, AZ: Project Me.

Fee, F. (1980). Responses to a behavioural questionnaire of a group of Belfast children. In J. Harbison & J. Harbison (Eds.), *A society under stress: Children and young people in Northern Ireland*. Somerset, NJ: Open Books.

Fee, F. (1983). Educational change in Belfast school children 1975–81. In J. Harbison (Ed.), *Children of the troubles: Children in Northern Ireland*. Belfast: Stranmillis College Learning Resources Unit.

Fendrich, M., Warner, V., & Weissman, M. (1990). Family risk factors, parental depression, and psychopathology in offspring. *Developmental Psychology, 26*, 40–50.

Fogelman, E., & Savran, B. (1979). Therapeutic groups for children of Holocaust survivors. *International Journal of Group Psychotherapy, 29*, 211–235.

Folkman, S., Lazarus, R. S., Gruen, R. J., & DeLongis, A. (1986). Appraisal, coping, health status, and psychological symptoms. *Journal of Personality and Social Psychology, 50*, 571–579.

Fraser, M. (1971). The cost of commotion—Analysis of psychiatric sequelae of 1969 Belfast riots. *British Journal of Psychiatry, 118*, 257.

Fraser, M. (1974). *Children in conflict*. Harmondsworth, England: Penguin.

Freud, A., & Burlingame, D. (1942). *Young children in wartime*. London: George Allen & Unwin.

Freyberg, J. T. (1980). Difficulties in separation-individuation as experienced by offspring of Nazi Holocaust survivors. *American Journal of Orthopsychiatry, 50*, 87–95.

Gampel, Y. (1988). Facing war, murder, torture, and death in latency. *Psychoanalytic Review, 75*, 499–509.

Goldsmith, W., & Cretokos, C. (1969). Unhappy odysseys: Psychiatric hospitalization among Viet Nam returnees. *American Journal of Psychiatry, 20*, 78–83.

Gottlieb, B. (1985, Spring). Women and children as victims of war. *Response*, 19–21.

Hammen, C., Adrian, C., Gordon, D., Burge, D., Jaenicke, C., & Hiroto, D. (1987). Children of depressed mothers: Maternal strain and symptom predictors of dysfunction. *Journal of Abnormal Psychology, 96*, 190–198.

Hammen, C., Burge, D., & Stansbury, K. (1990). Relationship of mother and child variables to child outcomes in a high-risk sample: A causal modeling analysis. *Developmental Psychology, 26*, 24–30.

Hogman, F. (1983). Displaced Jewish children during World War II: How they coped. *Journal of Humanistic Psychology, 23*, 51–66.

Kaffman, M. (1977). Kibbutz civilian population under war stress. *British Journal of Psychiatry, 130*, 489–494.

Kaffman, M., & Elizur, E. (1983). Bereavement responses of kibbutz and nonkibbutz children following the death of the father. *Journal of Child Psychology and Psychiatry, 24*, 290–299.

Kashani, J. H., Orvaschel, H., Burk, J. P., & Reid, J. C. (1985). Informant variance: The issue of parent-child disagreement. *Journal of the American Academy of Child Psychiatry, 24*, 437–441.

Kestenberg, J. (1985). Child survivors of the Holocaust—40 years later: Reflections and commentary. *The American Academy of Child Psychiatry, 24*, 408–412.

Kinzie, J. D., Sack, W. H., Angell, R. H., Manson, S., & Rath, B. (1986). The psychiatric effects of massive trauma on Cambodian children: 1. the children. *Journal of The American Academy of Child Psychiatry, 25*, 370–376.

Klingman, A. (1985). Free writing: Evaluation of a preventive program with elementary school children. *Journal of School Psychology, 23*, 167–175.

Klingman, A. (1982). Persuasive communication in avoidance behavior: Using role simulation as a strategy. *Simulation and Games, 13*, 37–50.

Klingman, A. (1992a). The effects of parent-implemented crisis-intervention: A real-life emergency involving a child's refusal to use a gas-mask. *Journal of Clinical Child Psychology, 21*, 70–75.

Klingman, A. (1992b). School psychology services: Community-based, first-order crisis intervention during the Gulf War. *Psychology in the Schools, 29*, 376–384.

Klingman, A. (1992c). Stress reactions of Israeli youth during the Gulf War: A quantitative study. *Professional Psychology: Research and Practice, 23*, 521–527.

Klingman, A., Sagi, A., & Raviv, A. (in press). Effects of war on Israeli children. In L. A. Leavitt, & N. A. Fox (Eds.), *Psychological effects of war and violence on children.* New York: Lawrence Erlbaum.

Koubovi, D. (1987). Therapeutic teaching of literature during the war and its aftermath. In C. D. Spielberger, I. G. Sarason, & N. A. Milgram (Eds.), *Stress and Anxiety* (Vol. 8, pp. 345–349). Washington, DC: Hemisphere.

Krell, R. (1990). Children who survived Japanese concentration camps: Clinical observations and therapy. *Canadian Journal of Psychiatry, 35*, 149–152.

Lavie, P., Amit, Y., Epstein, R., & Tzischinsky, O. (1992, June). *Children's sleep under the threat of the Scud missiles.* Paper presented at the Annual Meeting of the Association of Sleep Research, Phoenix, AZ.

Lazarus, R. S., & Folkman, S. (1984). *Stress, appraisal and coping.* New York: Lawrence Erlbaum.

Leon, G. R., Butcher, J. N., Kleinman, M. Goldberg, A., & Almagor, M. (1981). Survivors of the Holocaust and their children: Current status and adjustment. *Journal of Personality and Social Psychology, 41*, 503–516.

Lyons, H. A. (1972). Depressive illness and aggression in Belfast. *British Medical Journal, 1*, 342.

Lyons, H. A., & Bindall, K. K. (1977). Attempted suicide in Belfast: A continuation of a study in a district general hospital. *Irish Medical Journal, 70*, 322.

Lystad, M. (1984). Children's responses to disaster: Family implications. *International Journal of Family Psychiatry, 5*, 41–60.

Macksoud, M. (1991, Aug.). *The war experiences of Lebanese children.* Paper presented at the annual meeting of the American Psychological Association. San Francisco, California.

Martin-Baro, I. (1989). Political violence and war as causes of psychosocial trauma in El Salvador. *International Journal of Mental Health, 18*, 3–20.

Mazor, A., Gampel, Y., Enright, R. D., & Orenstein, R. (1990). Holocaust survivors: Coping with post-traumatic memories in childhood and 40 years later. *Journal of Traumatic Stress, 3*, 1–14.

McFarlane, A. C., Policansky, S., & Irwin, C. P. (1987). A longitudinal study of the psychological morbidity in children due to natural disaster. *Psychological Medicine, 17*, 727–738.

Mercier, M. H., & Despert, J. L. (1942). Psychological effects of the war on French children. *Psychosomatic Medicine, 5*, 266–272.

Milgram, N. A. (1982). War related stress in Israeli children and youth. In L. Goldberger & S. Breznitz (Eds.), *Handbook of stress: Theoretical and clinical aspects.* New York: Free Press.

Milgram, N. A., Toubiana, Y., Klingman, A., Raviv, A., & Goldstein, I. (1988). Situational exposure and personal loss in children's acute and chronic stress reactions to a school disaster. *Journal of Traumatic Stress, 1,* 339–352.

Milgram, R. M., & Milgram, N. A. (1976). The effect of the Yom Kippur war on anxiety level in Israeli children. *The Journal of Psychology, 94,* 107–113.

Mintz, M. (1991). *A comparison between children in two areas following the Gulf War.* Unpublished manuscript, Department of Psychology, Tel Aviv University (in Hebrew).

Modlin, H. C. (1960). The trauma in "trauma neurosis." *Bulletin of the Menninger Clinic, 24,* 40–56.

Modlin, H. C. (1967). The postaccident anxiety syndrome: Psychosocial aspects. *American Journal of Psychiatry, 123,* 1008–1021.

Nadler, A., Kav-Venaki, S., & Gleitman, B. (1985). Transgenerational effects of the Holocaust: Externalization of aggression in second generation of Holocaust survivors. *Journal of Consulting and Clinical Psychology, 53,* 365–369.

Nagata, D. (1990). The Japanese American internment: Exploring the transgenerational consequences of traumatic stress. *Journal of Traumatic Stress, 3,* 47–69.

Noy, B. (1991). *Pupils' calls to the Open Line during the emergency period of the Gulf War.* Jerusalem: Ministry of Education and Culture.

Orvaschel, H., Weissman, M., & Kidd, K. (1980). Children and depression. *Journal of Affective Disorders, 2,* 1–16.

Palgi, P. (1973). The socio-cultural expressions and implications of death, mourning and bereavement arising out of the war situation in Israel. *The Israel Annals of Psychiatry and Related Disciplines, 11,* 301–329.

Parsons, J., Kehle, T. J., & Owen, S. V. (1990). Incidence of behavior problems among children of Vietnam war veterans. *School Psychology International, 11,* 253–259.

Perez, J. (1991, Aug.). *Operational homefront: Psychology's response to the Mideast crisis.* Paper presented at the annual meeting of the American Psychological Association, San Francisco.

Punamaki, R. (1989). Factors affecting the mental health of Palestinian children exposed to political violence. *International Journal of Mental Health, 18,* 63–79.

Pynoos, R. S., & Eth, S. (1985). Developmental perspective on psychic trauma in child-hood. In C. R. Figley (Ed.), *Trauma and its wake* (Vol. 2, pp. 36–52). New York: Brunner/Mazel.

Rachman, S. J. (1990). *Fear and courage.* New York: W. H. Freeman.

Raviv, A. (in press). The use of hotline and media interventions in Israel during the Gulf War. In L. A. Leavitt & N. A. Fox (Eds.), *Psychological effects of war and violence on children.* New York: Lawrence Erlbaum.

Raviv, A., & Klingman, A. (1983). Children under stress. In S. Breznitz (Ed.), *Stress in Israel* (pp. 138–162). New York: Van Nostrand Reinhold.

Robinson, S. (1979). Late effects of persecution in persons who—as children or young adolescents—survived Nazi occupation in Europe. *Israel Annals of Psychiatry and Related Disciplines, 17,* 209–214.

Ronstrom, A. (1989). Children in Central America: Victims of war. *Child Welfare, 68,* 145–153.

Rosenbaum, M., & Ronen, T. (1991, Nov.). *How did Israeli children and their parents cope with being daily attacked by Scud missiles during the Gulf War?* Paper presented at the 25th Annual Convention for the Advancement of Behavior Therapy, New York City.

Rosenheck, R. (1986). Impact of posttraumatic stress disorder of World War II on the next generation. *The Journal of Nervous and Mental Disease, 174,* 319–327.

Rosenheck, R., & Nathan, P. (1985). Secondary traumatization in children of Vietnam veterans. *Hospital and Community Psychiatry, 36,* 538–539.

Rosenheck, R., & Thomson, J. (1986). "Detoxification" of Vietnam war trauma: A combined family-individual approach. *Family Process, 25,* 559–570.

Rubenstein, A. (1991, Aug.). *The children left behind: Preventive interventions in the school system.* Paper presented at the annual meeting of the American Psychological Association, San Francisco.

Rubenstein, A., & Embry, D. D. (1990a). *How to support our children during Operation Desert Storm.* Tucson, AZ: Project Me.

Rubenstein, A., & Embry, D. D. (1990b). *They're coming home: This story/workbook stars you and is about having a good homecoming when someone you love returns from deployment.* Tucson, AZ: Project Me.

Rubenstein, A., & Embry, D. D. (1991). *They're coming home: A guide for friends and relatives, schools, employers, coworkers, and the community.* Tucson, AZ: Project Me.

Rutter, M., & Quinton, D. (1984). Parental psychiatric disorder: Effects on children. *Psychological Medicine, 14,* 853–880.

Saigh, P. (1986). In vitro flooding in the treatment of a 6-yr.-old boy's posttraumatic stress disorder. *Behavior Research and Therapy, 24,* 685–688.

Saigh, P. (1989). The validity of the DSM-III posttraumatic stress disorder classification as applied to children. *Journal of Abnormal Psychology, 98,* 189–192.

Schwarzwald, J., Weisenberg, M., Waysman, M., Solomon, Z., & Klingman, A. (1991). *Stress reaction of school-age children to the bombardment by Scud missiles.* Unpublished manuscript. Department of Mental Health, Medical Corps, Israel Defense Forces (in Hebrew).

Sigal, J. J., DiNicola, V. F., & Buonvino, M. (1988). Grandchildren of survivors: Can negative effects of prolonged exposure to excessive stress be observed two generations later? *Canadian Journal of Psychiatry, 33,* 207–212.

Solomon, Z., Kotler, M., & Mikulincer, M. (1988). Combat-related posttraumatic stress disorder among second-generation Holocaust survivors: Preliminary findings. *American Journal of Psychiatry, 145,* 865–868.

Straker, G., & the Sanctuaries Team. (1987). The continuous traumatic stress syndrome: The single therapeutic interview. *Psychology in Society, 8,* 48.

Strange, R. E., & Brown, D. E. (1970). Home from the wars. *American Journal of Psychiatry, 127,* 488–492.

Swenson, C. C., Powell, M. P., Foster, K. Y., & Saylor, C. F. (1991, Aug.). *Long-term reactions of young children to natural disaster.* Paper presented at the annual meeting of the American Psychological Association, San Francisco.

Tsoi, M. M., Yu, G. K. K., & Lieh-Mak, F. (1986). Vietnamese refugee children in camps in Hong Kong. *Social Science Medicine, 23,* 1147–1150.

Weisenberg, M., Schwartzwald, J., Waysman, M., Solomon, Z., & Klingman, A. (1991). *Coping of school-age children in the sealed room during scud missile bombardment and postwar stress reactions.* Unpublished manuscript, Department of Mental Health, Medical Corps, Israel Defense Forces (in Hebrew).

Yule, W., & Williams, R. M. (1990). Post-traumatic stress reactions in children. *Journal of Traumatic Stress, 3,* 279–295.

Zeidner, M., Klingman, A., & Itzkovitz, R. (in press). Children's affective reactions and coping under missile attack: A semi-projective assessment procedure. *Journal of Personality Assessment.*

Ziv, A., & Israeli, R. (1973). Effects of bombardment on the manifest anxiety levels of children living in the kibbutz. *Journal of Consulting and Clinical Psychology, 40,* 287–291.

Ziv, A., Kruglanski, A. W., & Shulman, S. (1974). Children's psychological reactions to wartime stress. *Journal of Personality and Social Psychology, 30,* 24–30.

9

Individual and Small-Group Psychotherapy for Children Involved in Trauma and Disaster

HOWARD M. GILLIS

INTRODUCTION

A young girl has lost both of her parents, killed in an earthquake. Each afternoon she expectantly awaits their return home, somehow knowing, too, that they never will return. A young boy limps when others run on his school playground, where a few months ago a lone sniper seriously wounded him. He recalls his terror on that day and wonders why he had to be one of the injured. Loss, overwhelming panic and helplessness, and significant and long-lasting bodily injury—these experiences and feelings are part and parcel of disaster and trauma. How as psychotherapists do we address such tragedies and their effects? This chapter delineates approaches to the treatment of children who have experienced a variety of traumatic events.

HOWARD M. GILLIS • Assistant Clinical Professor, Division of Behavioral and Developmental Pediatrics, University of California, San Francisco Medical Center, 1736 Divisadero Street, San Francisco, California 94115.
Children and Disasters, edited by Conway F. Saylor. Plenum Press, New York, 1993.

Other chapters in this book outline the short- and long-term effects on children who have been exposed to disaster and trauma. We know that such exposure has a potentially significant impact on a child's personality development (Gislason & Call, 1982; Terr, 1990, 1991). Raphael (1986) stated, "As with community disasters, those personal disasters that occur with little warning (unpredictable), that cannot be prevented or controlled, and contain highly stressful elements are more likely to lead to prolonged dysfunction and morbidity" (p. 11). Lingering fears of vulnerability, anticipation of future harm, guilt over some action performed or not performed, an ongoing sense of loss, and "concern with the randomness of life events, sense of helplessness, distrust in the future, and ongoing perceptual and cognitive distortion" (Terr, 1989, p. 15)—all can lead to personality changes. The overwhelming nature of traumatic experience taxes children's usual coping mechanisms and places unusual stresses on the family. These demands can lead to short- or long-term maladaptive resolutions and adjustments.

Thus, traumatic events, by virtue of the severe demands they impose, can hamper children's development. A central goal in child psychotherapy is the removal or attenuation of disruptions in children's personality development in order to help them resume its normal course. We are growing in our knowledge of the treatment of traumatized children; effective work on disaster or trauma involves a multidimensional plan involving psychotherapeutic as well as community-based interventions (Raphael, 1986). This chapter focuses on group and individual psychotherapy.

Although each traumatic event must be treated individually, certain common principles arise in the psychotherapy of traumatized children. These principles are common to the work with children who have suffered through all types of disaster, whether natural or human-made. These principles serve as guiding, basic assumptions and are first-level organizers for conceptualizing an approach to treatment. It is suggested that these principles are essential to all psychotherapeutic work with psychically traumatized children, either in individual treatment or in group therapy. After a discussion of these overall principles, I provide more specific information about individual and group therapy.

This chapter focuses primarily on preschool and latency-age children, as adolescent responses more closely resemble those of adults. However, much stated here is also relevant to work with adolescents. Also, although the focus of this chapter is on discrete traumatic events and disaster, much of the material presented is relevant to chronic or ongoing traumatic situations (e.g., physical or sexual abuse).

UNDERLYING PRINCIPLES OF TREATING CHILDREN
WHO HAVE EXPERIENCED DISASTER OR TRAUMA

Representation of the Trauma in Treatment

In order for children to work through a traumatic event, they must be able to symbolically represent or reexperience the event in tolerable doses within a safe and supportive context. This task does not only pose a special challenge for the child, but also for the therapist. As traumatic material is by its very nature highly emotionally charged, and as children's responses are often colored by their rather graphic memories based upon direct sensory impressions, the clinician must be willing to discuss these matters without avoiding material that may be anxiety-provoking for either the child or the therapist. The clinician's gentle perseverance and steadfastness in the face of pain is required in order to help the child come to terms with his experience.

Thus, the clinician must provide the context in which such material can be explored safely without, of course, retraumatizing the child through confronting him with more trauma-based material than he can integrate or process at the moment. Too much confrontation is often borne of the therapists' own difficulty in containing highly emotionally charged traumatic material. Some therapists may feel a sense of therapeutic urgency related to their own sense of helplessness and rage in the face of the trauma. This may lead to prematurely confronting the child with anxiety-provoking material in the misguided notion that it is best for the child to cathart and "get out all his feelings." As with any child therapy, it is crucial to respect the child's defenses and coping styles with regard to the pacing of highly charged emotional material. Other clinicians may sense the tendency to shield the child from further pain and avoid confrontation with anxiety-provoking material. In these situations, it is important to remember that helping the child to reexperience or at least re-present the trauma is essential to effective treatment. In returning psychologically to the traumatic events, children are allowed to more fully understand what happened to them, to master the overwhelming aspects of the experience, and to establish greater control over their memories.

Often, by virtue of the strong press of the traumatic material on the child's psyche, one can count on its entering into the treatment situation, either directly or indirectly, in the child's verbalizations, play, drawings, or overall attitude (Peterson, Prout, & Schwarz, 1991; Scurfield, 1985; Pynoos & Eth, 1986). It is in the responses to these cues that the therapist can most artfully begin the process of reexposing the child to the various aspects of the traumatic event. For example, during an initial play session, a 5-year-old girl who had been sexually abused began to play with a toy baby and its pacifier. The child was soon jabbing the pacifier in the doll's vaginal area. This highly idiosyncratic play presented the therapist with the opportunity to begin exploring with this young girl her one-time sexual trauma.

Some children, however, may not allude to the trauma either directly or indirectly. Indeed, the avoidance of thoughts and feelings associated with a traumatic event is a common response of traumatized children (Gillis, 1991). In these situations, the therapist's main task is to discover ways to bring up the traumatic material. A strong alliance, reassurance regarding the safety of the therapeutic setting, and gentle interpretation of the child's avoidance are important in helping children to express themselves more readily. Workbooks related to the trauma can be used to facilitate the elaboration of feelings (Deaton, 1989; Frederick, 1985). Play materials with special relevance to the trauma are often particularly helpful (Levy, 1939; Shapiro, 1973), for example, toy planes for plane crash victims or trees, houses, and telephone poles for tornado victims. Semi-structured art activities may help to stimulate associations to and memories of the traumatic event. Relaxation, desensitization, and other stress reduction techniques may also be taught to children to help them feel calmer while expressing their thoughts and memories.

Most clinicians agree that, if children are to gain mastery over their overwhelming feelings and thoughts after a trauma, they need help to remember and reexperience the traumatic event in therapy. However, reports vary about whether a child needs to discuss the traumatic events explicitly with the therapist, or if traumatic resolution may occur simply within the confines of the play, without direct reference to the child's experience. Accounts of successful treatments exist in which the clinician has remained within the metaphor of the child's play without directly interpreting the child's experience (MacLean, 1977; Terr, 1989). In these instances the clinician established play situations in which the child was able to represent aspects of the traumatic experience and intervened within the symbol system of the child's play. There are other accounts which suggest that children are able to tolerate direct interventions which explicitly link their experience with their symbolic play and in fact benefit from such direct interventions (Gillis, 1991; Terr, 1989). More will be said about this subject later. At this time, we know little of the precise factors that may dictate a more metaphoric mode or a more direct personal approach. It may be that developmental factors play a key role; younger children (i.e., of preschool age) may be less able to tolerate direct approaches and may benefit more from metaphoric modes of intervention, whereas older children (of latency age and adolescence) may tolerate both approaches, yet benefit especially from direct interventions.

Early Intervention

The hours and days after a traumatic event are a key time for mental health intervention (Figley, 1985; Johnson, 1989; Klingman, 1987). Immediately after a traumatic event, the affected individuals are likely to be in crisis, and intervention at this point may enhance effective coping strategies and prevent longer term maladaptive resolutions. The longer children go unattended, the more likely is the case that maladaptive responses will become more ingrained (Epstein, 1990; Peterson et al., 1991).

From a psychotherapeutic standpoint, early intervention involves (1) discussing the facts around the event; (2) clarifying misconceptions about the events surrounding the traumatic incident; (3) encouraging expression if the child is avoiding recognition of the trauma; and (4) allowing the child to tell and retell or play and replay the experience. It is also important to realize that, after a traumatic experience, children are often quite concerned about being separated from their families. Where possible, the family should be reunified as soon as possible.

At this early stage, debriefings may fulfill numerous therapeutic functions (Gillis, 1991; Mitchell, 1983). Usually carried out in groups, and lasting for one to several sessions, debriefings provide an opportunity for children to talk about their trauma-based feelings and experiences, to clarify misconceptions, and to feel a sense of commonality and support with others who have had similar experiences. In addition, the participants learn of the kinds of posttraumatic stress responses that most people face after a trauma. Ideally, children feel comforted in the fact that they are not alone in their reactions and that their feelings are understandable. When debriefing occurs within the days following a traumatic event, it can do much to enhance children's sense of mastery and to help them regain a sense of inner control.

Parental and Other Significant Adult Involvement

In all phases of the intervention process with traumatized children, it is crucial that their parents be closely involved. Optimally, the basic treatment unit is the family, even when the child is seen individually. There is some difference of opinion about how parental factors affect children's responses. Whereas some reports suggest that parental anxiety is an important factor in the development of symptomatology in children exposed to traumatic situations (Freud & Burlingham, 1943; Ziv & Israeli,

1973), other reports suggest that children experience posttraumatic symptoms irrespective of their parents' responses (Sugar, 1989). It is likely that children's responses after a traumatic event exist independently of a parent's reaction, with the exception, perhaps, of very young children. At the same time, however, the degree to which the important adults in a child's life (e.g., parents and teachers) can effectively deal with the traumatic event seems to be an important predictor of adjustment after a traumatic event (Lyons, 1987).

Whereas parents can do much to facilitate their children's coming to terms with traumatic events, their desire to shield their children from pain may lead to an initial resistance to intervention. Traumatic events evoke not only protective responses from parents, but also feelings of vulnerability, guilt, and sometimes memories of prior traumas. A common reaction of parents is to want to avoid discussion of the trauma with their children. This is the opposite of what is helpful to the child. Therefore, it is crucial to attend to the emotional needs of the parents and to overcome their resistance. If the parents explore the meaning and other aspects of the trauma and are helped to experience a measure of relief themselves, they may come to see how useful such an opportunity will be to their children (Gillis, 1991). In addition, family-oriented sessions may help family members overcome their avoidance of their own trauma-related feelings (Figley, 1988).

In school- or community-based disasters, the school is an especially useful setting for intervention (for detailed review, see Chapter 10 in this book). Teachers can play a key role in helping children talk about and deal with their trauma-based responses. A major goal for the clinician or consultant is to educate teachers about the effects of traumatic events on children and to help teachers feel comfortable in discussing them (Johnson, 1989). We have found that, in our debriefings of students, the presence of teachers as well as mental health professionals was invaluable. Teachers gave essential information regarding their students, facilitated an easy transition to talking about emotionally charged material, and provided continuity and follow-up (Gillis, Armstrong, Busher, Landman, & Ruggles, 1990).

Education about Typical Posttraumatic Stress Responses

Knowledge of the usual and expectable posttraumatic responses is helpful in reducing anxiety following a traumatic event. As children learn that, indeed, many others like them have had similar reactions, their anxiety is lessened. Through a better understanding of their reactions, children can achieve a greater sense of inner control and equilibrium. Thus, traumatized children are likely to be helped by learning about some of the more typical posttraumatic responses, such as nightmares, startle reactions, increased anxiety with exposure to traumatic reminders, and intrusive imagery. For example, one young victim of a school sniper attack was visibly relieved when he was told that loud noises might remind him of the shooting incident. The child said that he had indeed been feeling "jumpy" a lot and was worried that he was "going crazy."

In addition to anxiety-related responses, many children are confronted with feelings related to loss and death after a trauma or disaster. The dual demands of overwhelming anxiety and profound grief make trauma resolution particularly challenging for children (Eth & Pynoos, 1985b). The clinician must be aware of both of these aspects of responses to trauma. Children's reactions to loss vary from anger and denial to sadness and grief. They can misinterpret the circumstances of the death and may create their own idiosyncratic meanings regarding the death. Egocentric responses such as self-blame may complicate the grieving process. Increased aggression and/or regression are also common. Some children, however, block or hide their grief, either because of uncertainty about the response of their environment, or out of a desire to avoid pain themselves, or both. The clinician must be particularly aware of hidden grief or misconceptions about the circumstances of the death. Children may be reticent in sharing their feelings of grief, and clinicians may miss important reactions unless they make a point of asking about them.

Clearing Up Cognitive Distortions

It is not uncommon for children to misunderstand how traumatic events have unfolded. Such distortions impede trauma resolution and may leave children with unresolved thoughts and feelings that may affect their future adjustment. For example, after a school sniper attack during which the sniper committed suicide, many students believed that there had been two snipers. They continued to experience feelings of threat and impending danger that made their posttrauma adjustment difficult. Only after a discussion of these fears was it discovered that the children had confused a SWAT team member who was on the roof of a building with the feared "second shooter."

Because children are highly susceptible to cognitive distortions, it is quite important that clinicians find out as much about the traumatic event as possible from collateral sources, preferably before seeing the children, so that, in discussing the trauma, any misunderstandings or misperceptions can be clarified. Any treatment of traumatized children, then, must include opportunities to clear up misperceptions about the event and whatever rumors may have become established.

Exploring Personal Meanings of the Trauma and Altering Dysfunctional Meanings

Children may attribute special, personalized meanings to traumatic events as a result of both their own life histories and the nature of the traumatic event itself. The traumatic event may, in addition, reevoke memories of prior traumas or may exacerbate certain other preexisting difficulties in the child. The clinician would do well to be aware of these more idiosyncratic manifestations of the traumatic experience. In fact, a common goal of the psychotherapy of posttraumatic stress disorder (PTSD) is to modify or alter such dysfunctional meanings (Peterson *et al.*, 1991). For example, one 10-year-old boy who had been a victim of a school sniper attack had been raised by a father who was quite critical of his behavior and who frequently pointed out instances in which the boy appeared inept. His mother, although pained by the father's behavior, felt helpless to deal with her husband's harshness and sought primarily to appease and placate him. This boy was plagued by self-doubt and a sense of failure in not having helped his friend during the sniper attack. He had construed the traumatic event as yet another occasion that demonstrated his ineptitude. His unrealistic fantasies of heroism, which, of course, he had failed to live up to, tormented him as his father did. His own helplessness and self-criticism, as well as his idealization of his father and his rage at him, played important roles in his interpretation of the traumatic event. An important goal of the psychotherapy with this boy was to help him understand and appreciate his realistic and appropriate fears and to help him understand that, if he had acted differently, he would have placed his own life in greater jeopardy.

The therapeutic goal of altering the meaning of the trauma has often been referred to as *trauma mastery, resolving the trauma,* or *working through the trauma.* The objective is for children to learn that the event was not so overwhelming that they cannot stand the painful memories associated with it. Children can emerge from victims to survivors and experience the sense of self-efficacy and action that this emergence implies. Children thus gain and learn something from the experience, if only to overcome it, and to move forward from it toward the enjoyment of relationships, work, and play.

The Therapist's Reactions and Countertransference

Working with children who have experienced a disaster or other traumatic situations can, of course, evoke a variety of strong reactions and feelings in the therapist, including avoidance, anger, hopelessness, helplessness, and denial. A wish to protect the child from further pain may lead to a reluctance to fully pursue painful memories and to an avoidance of setting limits. Anger directed at a perpetrator may lead to prematurely encouraging the child's anger and thereby raising his or her anxiety. As James (1989) noted, insofar as some children are convinced that the traumatic event was their fault, they may feel that the therapist's anger is really directed at them, not at the perpetrator. Anger directed at a parent may make it more difficult for the therapist to foster more effective communication between parent and child. A therapist's sense of hopelessness, resignation, and dejection after a disaster may lead to a feeling of helplessness and a lack of vitality in the therapeutic relationship with the child. Finally, a therapist's denial may foreclose full exploration of material related to the trauma.

Few therapeutic encounters are more likely to evoke strong countertransference reactions than working with a child who has been traumatized. Such feelings are part and parcel of the work; consultation with colleagues and opportunities for one's own debriefing are important components of the treatment of traumatized children.

So far, this chapter has discussed underlying principles that are applicable to all forms of intervention with traumatized children. All children exposed to a disaster or a traumatic event should be debriefed (Johnson, 1989). More intensive intervention should be made available to those whose traumatic reactions (e.g., intrusive images, hyperarousal, a marked change in behavior, and overall high levels of anxiety) last longer than several weeks or are of such magnitude that they interfere with the child's functioning. The remainder of this chapter discusses group and individual therapy.

ISSUES IN GROUP PSYCHOTHERAPY

An abundance of evidence suggests that healing after a trauma is facilitated when children feel supported by their peers, and when they can talk with others who have had similar experiences (Galante & Foa, 1986; Lystad, 1985; Terr, 1989; Weinberg, 1990; Yule & Williams, 1990). In groups, children can be reassured that others feel as they do. They can learn different coping skills and problem-solving techniques from others. They can get a sense of validation from others' responses and can vicariously work through issues as a result of others' expressed feelings. They can experience the satisfaction of helping others. They can see others at different stages of trauma resolution, and ideally, they will see that their difficulties can be dealt with and overcome. Yule and Williams (1990) suggested that an important part of group work following a disaster is that the children simply have time together without the pressure of having to talk about the trauma. That sense of community and of having simply been through something together is in itself healing. Space does not allow for an exhaustive discussion of group therapy with traumatized children, but key elements, such as the frequency of meetings, and the size, makeup, and structure of groups, are covered in the following paragraphs.

As reported in the literature, group sessions range from being held weekly to occurring approximately every four to six weeks (Galante & Foa, 1986; Yule & Williams, 1990). The frequency of meetings often seems to be determined more by the logistics of getting to the group sessions than by the nature of the trauma. Often, children who have to travel greater distances to a group meet less frequently. In the literature, the size of posttrauma groups ranges from 4 to 12 children. In general, about 6–8 children appears to be the optimal size. Although some differences of opinion exist about the makeup of groups (Zimmerman, 1983), it is generally accepted that groups should be composed of children of roughly the same age and level of maturity. In addition, in our work with children exposed to a school sniper attack (Gillis et al., 1990), because of the generally different behavioral responses of boys and girls (boys being more externalizing in their behavior and girls being more internalizing), we found it helpful to arrange groups by gender as well. In this way, the girls' anxiety level was not unduly raised by the boys' aggression, and the boys felt less inhibited in expressing their aggressive impulses. This particular grouping may not be necessary in other traumatic situations. In keeping with the idea of the family as the basic treatment unit, some clinicians suggest that a parallel group with parents be held (Yule & Williams, 1990). In such a group, the parents can discuss their own concerns as well as those of their children, and they can learn how best to support their children.

Generally speaking, early in the group (typically in the first session), the children, each in turn, are asked about where they were at the time of the incident, what they saw and experienced, and how, from their perspective, the events unfolded. Typically, the group atmosphere is very supportive at this stage, and until all have had a chance to speak and greater trust is established, it is wise to gently divert strong expressions of emotion. Doing so prevents the group from being monopolized by one member and guards against other members' becoming more upset by the sharing of strong emotions. The group leader(s) explains that there will be much time to talk about and express feelings during later meetings. This early collective retelling of the traumatic experience is an important first step in safely reexperiencing the traumatic episode within the group context.

Clinicians vary in the degree of structure they impose on the group. Frederick (1987) recommended incident-specific treatment, which includes "sharing and support from other members, a simulation of the event, and where applicable, returning to the actual scene of the trauma" (p. 99). Galante and Foa (1986) used a relatively structured format in their treatment of young children (grades 1–4) after an earthquake. They held monthly group meetings for a year. Each session had a clearly stated objective and an accompanying activity. For example, for one meeting, the objective was "to involve the children in an active discharge of feelings about the earthquake and place the earthquake in the past." (Galante & Foa, 1986, p. 360). The accompanying activity consisted of making a large drawing of an earthquake-stricken village and furnishing it with toys. This image spontaneously elicited a reenactment of the earthquake. A discussion followed about what the children had done after the earthquake to return to a normal life. Other objectives involved discussing fears, myths, and misconceptions about earthquakes; releasing the power of the image of death; and talking about how one can take an active part in one's own survival. The activities involved drawing, listening to stories, structured play, role playing, discussion, and the use of rituals.

In treating young victims of a ferryboat disaster, Yule and Williams (1990) developed a less structured approach that involved addressing important themes as they emerged from the group process. During the first group meeting, for instance, one boy, quite upset, told of his having been "teased at school by another child who said such things as, 'I wish you had died on the ferry.'" The group then together attempted to solve this problem, and it was agreed that the group leader would approach the boy's parents and ask them to talk to the head teacher about the incident. Though the group meetings were less structured (they even involved time alone for the children without the leader present) and tended to impose less direct discussion of the traumatic event (perhaps because the first meeting occurred nine months after the incident), several important issues emerged and were addressed. Among them were discussions of typical symptoms, coping strategies, and the impact of anniversary reactions.

Our group work with children following a school sniper attack (Gillis et al., 1990) involved both structured and more open-ended elements. Role plays and re-creations of the shooting incident were conducted in small groups to assist the children in reexperiencing the traumatic event. At the same time, opportunities were provided for the group to define its own activity in free play. Often, this free play revealed important aspects of the children's traumatic experience. For example, in one group, the children introduced into their play the theme of helicopters with their accompanying noise and their function of taking away the wounded. This theme provided the opportunity to talk with the wounded children about their specific fears of loud noises, and to help them remember their helicopter ride to the hospital, their fear of being removed from familiar surroundings, and their confusion about what was happening.

It is important to note that, when groups are less structured and allow for more free play, the implementation of clear limits is very important. As a response to traumatic events, children may act out in aggressive, violent, or otherwise undercontrolled ways. These outlets should be controlled, for they may heighten the children's anxiety. Clearly, aggression, threats toward others, and roughhousing should be limited. Although setting limits on the expression of aggression is sometimes necessary, it is also important to use aggressive behavior therapeutically and to link such actions to the children's particular feelings surrounding the traumatic events. For example, in response to the high level of aggression in a boys' group dealing with a shooting, the therapist commented that perhaps the boys wished that at the time of the shooting they had felt as strong and tough as they were acting now.

In their evaluation and treatment of children exposed to violence, Pynoos and Nader (1988) focused on four symptom groupings: posttraumatic stress disorder, grief reactions, separation anxiety symptoms, and exacerbation or renewal of symptomatology. They suggested that the small group is an especially useful setting in which to establish and maintain ongoing support in the early phase of grief. The group experience provides needed emotional support, a structured time in which to come to terms with the loss, and opportunities to reminisce together.

Given the commonality of profound experience, children develop strong ties in a group, and termination may become an especially important part of the group experience. The way in which a series of group meetings comes to a close is an important part of the group experience. Aside from the usual termination process (i.e., dealing with feelings of loss and sadness, reviewing the ground that has been covered, and saying good-bye), various rituals or ceremonies may be useful in groups of traumatized children. Ceremonies that deal with moving from victim to survivor, with the giving of the group's emblem to each member, with noting what each member likes about the others, and so on may all have a powerful affirming effect on the members.

There is substantial evidence to suggest that a group experience for traumatized children may be powerful and useful (Frederick, 1985; Galante & Foa, 1986; James, 1985; Terr, 1987; Weinberg, 1990; Yule & Williams, 1990). It can help them deal with a wide range of symptoms and responses and can serve as an important learning experience for finding ways to deal with one's own pain and for developing new resources for coping. In addition, in group settings, large numbers of children can be effectively served after a disaster. However, there are also limitations to group work. Group approaches may not provide as in-depth an experience as some children need (Terr, 1989). Children's fantasies and inner life regarding the trauma (e.g., concealed feelings of shame, self-blame, or violent-revenge fantasies) may not be as fully explored as is necessary. Also, group leaders must be aware of the possible spread of trauma-related symptoms from one member to another (Terr, 1990). Children may also mimic others and label another's experience as their own, thus preventing exploration of their own thoughts and feelings. Some particularly withdrawn children may never feel truly comfortable in a group.

Groups may also be helpful in screening for those children who need more individualized attention. In working with traumatized adolescents in a school, Weinberg (1990) identified six indicators for identifying students who may be at risk of more serious disturbance and who need more in-depth evaluation:

a) The absence of emotional reactions in a student who either was close to the victim or witnessed the incident; b) An inability to bring emotion under control; c) Excessive self blame or intro-punitive anger; d) Allusions to or admissions of suicidal thoughts or intentions; e) Evidence of loose associations or bizarre behavior; and f) Preoccupation with personal, family, or relationship problems. (p. 275)

In addition, consistent with the views of others (Pynoos, 1990), we have found (Gillis *et al.*, 1990) the following factors to be helpful in identifying those children who may require individual treatment: direct proximity to the traumatic event, physical injury, personal loss as a result of the event, preexisting psychological problems, and significant family dysfunction or a lack of social support.

ISSUES IN INDIVIDUAL PSYCHOTHERAPY

Any psychotherapy for traumatized children must have at its center the establishment of a safe and encouraging atmosphere in which to explore traumatic memories. Basic to any dynamically oriented therapy is helping children to understand the meaning of their posttraumatic responses, whether these are rooted in the trauma itself or have reevoked memories of earlier difficulties. Though there are only beginning reports in the literature, it appears that a number of trauma-specific responses can be addressed effectively by individual intervention (Pynoos & Nader, 1988; Terr, 1989). In the remainder of the chapter, I discuss important trauma-related issues that are relevant to the individual treatment of children: avoidance; exacerbation of symptomatology; posttraumatic play and other reexperiencing phenomena; fantasies of revenge; self-blame, guilt, and underlying helplessness; concerns about future safety, the unpredictability of life events, and distrust in the future; concern about significant others; and sadness and grief.

Avoidance

In many ways, traumatized children are quite able and willing to report on their experience. Terr (1989), for example, stated that, in contrast to children with more ingrained neurotic difficulties, traumatized children need little encouragement to talk. This does not necessarily mean that children will discuss freely all aspects of their experience. Often, they avoid certain painful parts of the traumatic incident for fear of being once again overwhelmed with anxiety. Sometimes, children's concerns about being blamed or judged, which are rooted in misconceptions about the event, prevent the free flow of trauma-related material.

As mentioned earlier, the pacing of the emergence of trauma-related material is important. Yet it is helpful sometimes to focus away from the trauma—that is, to talk more generally about feelings that are unrelated to the traumatic events—so that painful material can emerge more easily without force or imposition. Workbooks and other creative modes (drawings, collages, role playing, and free writing) facilitate the emergence of painful material and at the same time allow the child to feel in control (Klingman, 1987). In addition, it may be important to comment on the child's reluctance to discuss her or his memories because of how painful they are. The child can then be reassured that the therapist is the person who can help her or him with those upsetting and difficult feelings.

Exacerbation of Symptomatology

As new traumatic memories are discussed, played out, or otherwise reexperienced in therapy, it is not unusual for children to show temporary exacerbations of their symptoms (Lyons, 1987). One must evaluate the situation carefully. An exacerbation of symptoms may be due to exposure to traumatic reminders or memories of a prior trauma. Alternatively, increases in symptomatology may mean that children are allowing themselves to experience a wider range of feelings associated with the trauma. In these situations, rather than indicating problems in the treatment, these increases in symptomatology may mean that the therapy is proceeding well. When children start to show more symptoms, parents are understandably alarmed, so it is important to forewarn the parents at the beginning of treatment that such exacerbations are possible and perhaps even likely.

Posttraumatic Play and Other Reexperiencing Phenomena

In an attempt to modify the overwhelming nature of traumatic events, children often reenact the trauma in their play. It is well known that play helps children release suppressed emotions. When children are dealing with stressful situations, play allows them to regulate facing aspects of their experience in tolerable enough doses to help them integrate their experiences. In play, children can reenact the situation with a happier and more successful outcome, thereby, at least temporarily, reducing anxiety (e.g., Saylor, Swenson, & Powell, 1992).

Yet, for many severely traumatized children, play does not effectively reduce anxiety. Posttraumatic play is typically quite literal in its reenactment of traumatic events, and traumatic themes are compulsively repeated (Terr, 1981). Instead of alleviating the tension of traumatic events, posttraumatic play may increase the child's anxiety by unconsciously exposing the child to traumatic cues. It is striking that the connection between the posttraumatic play and the traumatic event remains unconscious (Terr, 1981); that is, when children are asked about their posttraumatic play, they do not see its connection with the original traumatic event.

Posttraumatic play can, however, be used effectively within the treatment to reduce children's anxiety and to help them achieve a greater sense of mastery. When children are unaware of the connection between their play and the traumatic event, it may be helpful to interpret this link to them, together with the affects associated with the event. This approach allows the children not only to explore such feelings as terror, rage, sadness, and helplessness as they emerge in the play, but also to experience a greater measure of internal control as they more fully understand their feelings and actions.

For example, after a schoolyard sniper attack, one young boy vehemently sought out other children to repeatedly play "machine gun." In this play, he inevitably took the other children's guns away and shot them all dead. Early interventions pointed to the fact that this boy must feel strong and in charge when he played this role. Soon, after talking with him about his play over several sessions, the therapist commented, "When you were feeling so scared on that day of the shooting, you must have wished that you could be that strong." A painful sigh of recognition followed. As the therapy progressed, this child's feelings of helplessness and rage were also discussed in connection with his play. Over time, the driven quality of this boy's posttraumatic play gradually declined. Thus, his play itself was quite useful in helping him explore the variety of his feelings that were associated with the shooting.

In addition to posttraumatic play, other phenomena may evoke a reexperiencing of the trauma and may serve to renew children's sense of life threat (Pynoos & Nader, 1988). It is therefore quite important to reduce the intensity of such phenomena as intrusive images and traumatic reminders. As in group therapy, letting children know that these reactions are common can relieve their anxiety. It may be especially useful to help children identify and recognize those aspects of their environment that may remind them of the trauma. When children are helped to anticipate potential reactions, a feeling of greater inner control is established. It is important also to alert parents and teachers to these potentially anxiety-evoking stimuli, so that they can comfort their children more effectively.

For example, one 7-year-old boy in ongoing psychotherapy, who had experienced a school sniper attack, refused to wear newly washed pants each day to school. In discussion with his parents, it was learned that he had worn newly washed pants to school on the day of the shooting. His clothing thus served as a traumatic reminder. He feared in addition that wearing these pants might evoke another attack or otherwise place him in danger. When his fears were highlighted and connected with the traumatic incident, they were eased (Gillis, 1991).

Fantasies of Revenge

Particularly in response to human-made disasters, children may develop powerful revenge fantasies. For example, the children who experienced a shooting at their school shared such fantasies as wishing to "take him (the sniper) to a garbage dump and bury him with a ton of garbage," or wanting to "take him to the jungle and tie him down and pour killer ants over him" (Gillis, 1991). It is important to elicit such fantasies within psychotherapy. These expressions not only provide a degree of cathartic release but also allow for the creative expression of aggression within the context of a safe and protected relationship. As fantasies of revenge are discussed and accepted, obsessive preoccupation with them is diminished. It is important to recognize that, as children explore their revenge fantasies, fears of the assailant's retaliation may be evoked. These fears must also be discussed with the child with the goal of reinforcing the child's sense of safety.

Self-Blame, Guilt, and Underlying Helplessness

It is not unusual for children to experience feelings of self-blame or guilt after a disaster or other traumatic event. Such worries may take the form of concern about having done something that they should not have, or about not having done something that they believe they should have.

These concerns may be alleviated by a sensitive explanation of the reality of the situation, for example, as explaining to a preschool child that earthquakes are not started by stomping on the ground. Alternatively, one can reframe children's guilt by suggesting that they are very brave to accept responsibility and that this indicates their kindness and thoughtfulness regarding others (Figley, 1988). However, children's sense of self-blame or guilt is often impervious to such reassurances, because their guilt is essential in protecting them from a more terrifying feeling: helplessness. In these cases, children compensate for feeling inadequate and helpless, as they had during the event, by imagining a sense of grandiose responsibility or power. This fantasy of increased responsibility makes them more vulnerable to feelings of self-blame. In particular, traumatized latency-aged children may develop inner plans of action that involve unrealistic ideas about their own roles and actions during traumatic events (Eth & Pynoos, 1985a). For example, one young boy who was especially upset about a friend who had been hurt during a school sniper attack stated later, with much regret, that he missed the opportunity to run up to the assailant, kick him in the shin, and take his gun.

In dealing with self-blame and guilt, it is important first to elicit the details of the context in which the feelings of guilt have arisen. One can remind children of just how afraid they were at the time, and how helpless they must have felt. They can be told that they used good judgment in not attempting to attack the assailant, for they would surely have endangered themselves by undertaking this action. Although these interventions are sometimes helpful, children may nevertheless continue to experience guilt and self-blame to help them compensate for feelings of helplessness. Because guilt has a protective function, longer term treatment is sometimes necessary.

Concern about Future Safety, the Unpredictability of Life Events, and Distrust in the Future

During traumatic events, children may see adults who are themselves rendered helpless or paralyzed with fear, for example, rescue personnel who arrive on the scene too late or who are otherwise inadequate in dealing with the immensity of the task at hand, as well as other adults who flee in panic and abandon the scene. Traumatic events can shake the foundations of trust that children have in the ability of important adults to protect and care for them. In traumatic situations, children are seriously hindered in their capacity to identify with helpful and protective figures (Terr, 1981) and thus in maintaining an inner sense of safety and security.

A major goal of psychotherapy with traumatized children is to help them regain this sense of inner security, safety, and trust in the world. The clinician seeks to help children symbolically represent aspects of their traumatic experience through play, drawing, verbalization, and so on. In this way, the child gradually experiences a greater sense of psychological distance from the event and a greater measure of internal control. In the play, the therapist symbolically introduces themes of protection and safety, as well as alternative resolutions to the traumatic experience. For example, one 6-year-old earthquake victim repeatedly reenacted scenes of dishes being knocked off shaking tables, houses falling over, and children being separated from their parents. The therapist commented on how upsetting and unsafe all this seemed and how frightening it must be for those involved. Initially, these comments were met with denial. This girl would have no part of these feelings. However, when the therapist introduced Scotch tape to hold the dishes in place, the young patient gleefully shook the table, seeing that the dishes stayed just where they were. Gradually, the therapist and the child designed "supports" to keep the house from falling over. Toy children were given special "communicators" to remain in contact with those important to them. In a short while, this child was incorporating these elements into her play and was devising her own safety-enhancing features for protection against another earthquake. In this way, the introduction of helping elements gradually paved the way for the child to reestablish her own safety-enhancing identifications.

Other variations on this theme include one suggested by Lenore Terr (1983). Rather than working symbolically within the child's metaphor, her approach involves helping children find a real solution that might have avoided, stopped, or attenuated the trauma. The children are helped to see that they did not know what to do during the trauma and so could not have avoided it. They are assisted in developing means of dealing with the traumatic event, should it ever happen again. These coping skills presumably enhance children's sense of self-efficacy and help relieve their guilt and fear. Of course, this approach is useful only with traumatic situations in which such solutions would have been effective. Terr noted that large-scale natural disasters or unprovoked random attacks cannot be dealt with in this way (Terr, 1983).

Concern about Significant Others

During traumatic situations, children are often confronted with considerable worry about significant others (Pynoos & Nader, 1988). Sudden separations, thwarted reunions, and fears of harm befalling another all impose significant stress and intense fear. These occurrences may lead to insecurity about important relationships that manifests itself in several ways. Some children show intense separation anxiety after a traumatic event and become panicked when significant others leave. Other children evidence avoidance of or ambivalence about important others because of highly conflicting feelings: strong feelings of love, fears of loss, and anger about unavailability.

Pynoos and Nader (1988) suggested that an important goal in individual psychotherapy with children is "to thoroughly explore the event-based etiology of this worry" (p. 468), and they outlined useful guidelines for working with this anxiety. They suggested that it is important to talk with children in as much detail as possible about their experience of worry regarding another during the event. In particular, a discussion of the child's safe reunion with loved ones may enhance the child's sense of inner security and safety. Any continued worry may be linked to the traumatic event. A child may be reassured that the significant other is fine by a reviewing of the everyday things that they do together. One can also support children in discussing their feelings directly with the significant other (Pynoos & Nader, 1988).

Sadness and Grief

As mentioned earlier, traumatic events confront children not only with anxiety-related responses, but also with experiences of loss. Clinicians must help children distinguish their trauma-related responses from those related to grief (Pynoos & Nader, 1988). It is important to address the trauma first in order to decrease the likelihood that violent images will interfere with the work of grief (Pynoos & Nader, 1988). The clinician can help the child restore a more intact image of the deceased, especially in cases where the child witnessed the violence or harm, by together looking at pictures of the deceased, by talking about non-trauma-related memories, or by repairing wounds in play. Through reminiscing together and role-playing conversations with the deceased, unresolved feelings due to the suddenness of the event may be addressed.

If the child has ambivalent feelings regarding the deceased, such as anger and love, the natural mourning process will be more complicated. It then becomes more important to deal with the child's anger, whether it originated either before the trauma or as a result of it. This must be done in the context of acknowledging the child's loving feelings. The experience of grief is ongoing, and significant others in the child's world should be prepared for this fact. Also, it may be important to discuss the various ways in which the child will be reminded of the deceased during the course of daily events.

SUMMARY AND FUTURE DIRECTIONS

This chapter seeks to elucidate key issues in the group and individual therapy of traumatized children. The importance of such underlying principles as helping the child to reexperience or symbolically represent the traumatic event within the treatment, the need for early intervention, and the crucial role that parents and other significant adults play were discussed. A central goal of psychotherapy with traumatized children is helping them to more fully experience the thoughts and feelings associated with a traumatic event without being flooded with emotion or using excessive avoidance. This goal is achieved through a number of different processes. Through establishing the link between play and the traumatic event, children can more fully understand the nature of their experience and thereby achieve a measure of control over it. Through utilizing the creative alternatives of trauma-linked play, children can be assisted in reestablishing positive, safety-enhancing identifications that reinforce their sense of inner security. Through discovering ways to deal with traumatic events should they occur in the future, children can experience a greater sense of personal efficacy and mastery. Through symbolically representing the trauma in play or words, children are assisted in creating a greater measure of psychological distance from the event. All of these processes facilitate a reworking of the disaster or traumatic experience.

Though our expertise grows in treating traumatized children, many challenges and unanswered questions lie ahead. Much more research is needed on the utility of different kinds of procedures with different kinds of traumatized children. Some adult intervention procedures have been adapted for children and show promise, especially with adolescents. For example, Saigh has carefully demonstrated the effectiveness of flooding procedures with adolescents (Saigh, 1987b, 1989) and children (Saigh, 1986, 1987a,c). More of this kind of work, with systematic replication across populations, is needed before we can safely and confidently recommend specific interventions for children after a disaster. Other questions also need to be addressed through quality clinical research. For example, what are the factors that seem to buffer some children against the adverse effects of trauma? In what ways are children's social support systems crucial to their healing? What are the factors that determine rate of recovery? How will effective treatment strategies vary according to different developmental stages?

Truly creative techniques must be used if we are to effectively serve the potentially large numbers of children who will experience disaster. It is hoped that this chapter provides some useful guidelines.

REFERENCES

Deaton, W. (1989). *I survived an earthquake*. Claremont, CA: Hunter House.

Epstein, S. (1990). Beliefs and symptoms in maladaptive resolutions of the traumatic neurosis. In D. Ozer, J. M. Healy, & A. J. Stewart (Eds.), *Perspectives on personality* (Vol. 3). London: Jessica Kingsley.

Eth, S., & Pynoos, R. S. (1985a). Developmental perspective on psychic trauma in childhood. In C. Figley (Ed.), *Trauma and its wake* (pp. 36–52). New York: Brunner/Mazel.

Eth, S., & Pynoos, R. (Eds.). (1985b). *Post-traumatic stress disorder in children*. Washington, DC: American Psychiatric Press.

Figley, C. R. (Ed.). (1985). *Trauma and its wake: The study and treatment of post-traumatic stress disorder*. New York: Brunner/Mazel.

Figley, C. R. (1988). Post-traumatic family therapy. In F. Ochberg (Ed.). *Post-traumatic therapy and victims of violence*. New York: Brunner/Mazel.

Frederick, C. J. (1985). Children traumatized by catastrophic situations. In S. Eth & R. S. Pynoos (Eds.), *Post-traumatic stress disorder in children* (pp. 71–100). Washington, DC: American Psychiatric Press.

Frederick, C. J. (1987). Psychic trauma in victims of crime and terrorism. In G. R. Vanden Bos and B. K. Bryant (Eds.), *Cataclysms, crises, and catastrophes: Psychology in action* (pp. 55–108). Washington, DC: American Psychological Association.

Freud, A., & Burlingham, D. (1943). *War and children*. New York: Medical War Books.

Galante, R., & Foa, D. (1986). An epidemiological study of psychic trauma and treatment effectiveness for children after a natural disaster. *Journal of the American Academy of Child Psychiatry, 25*, 357–363.

Gillis, H. (1991). Assessment and treatment of post-traumatic stress disorder in childhood. In P. A. Keller & S. R. Heyman (Eds.), *Innovations in clinical practice: A source book*. Sarasota, FL: Professional Resource Exchange.

Gillis, H., Armstrong, M., Busher, P., Landman, P., & Ruggles, J. (1990). *Severe psychological trauma in childhood: Approaches to intervention after a school sniper attack*. Presented at the annual meeting, California Psychological Association, San Francisco.

Gislason, I. L., & Call, J. D. (1982). Dog bite in infancy: Trauma and personality development. *Journal of the American Academy of Child Psychiatry, 21*, 203–207.

James, B. (1989). *Treating traumatized children*. Lexington: MA: Lexington Books.

Johnson, K. (1989). *Trauma in the lives of children*. Claremont, CA: Hunter House.

Klingman, A. (1987). A school-based emergency crisis intervention in a mass school disaster. *Professional Psychology: Research and Practice, 18*, 604–612.

Levy, D. (1939). Release therapy. *American Journal or Orthopsychiatry, 9*, 713–736.

Lyons, J. A. (1987). Posttraumatic stress disorder in children and adolescents: A review of the literature. *Journal of Developmental and Behavioral Pediatrics, 8*(6), 349–356.

Lystad, M. (1985). Innovative mental health services for child disaster victims. *Children Today, 12*, 13–17.

MacLean, G. (1977). Psychic trauma and traumatic neurosis: Play therapy with a four-year-old boy. *Journal of the Canadian Psychiatric Association, 22*, 71–76.

Mitchell, J. (1983). When disaster strikes: The critical incident stress debriefing process. *Journal of Emergency Medical Services, 8*, 36–39.

Peterson, K. C., Prout, M. F., & Schwarz, R. A. (1991). *Posttraumatic stress disorder: A clinician's guide*. New York: Plenum Press.

Pynoos, R. S. (1990). Post-traumatic stress disorder in children and adolescents. In B. D.

Garfinkel, G. A. Carlson, & E. B. Weller (Eds.), *Psychiatric disorder in children and adolescents* (pp. 48–63). Philadelphia: W. B. Saunders.

Pynoos R. S., & Eth, S. (1986). Witness to violence: The child interview. *Journal of the American Academy of Child Psychiatry, 25*(3), 306–318.

Pynoos, R. S., & Nader, K. (1988). Psychological first aid and treatment approach to children exposed to community violence: Research implications. *Journal of Traumatic Stress, 1,* 445–473.

Raphael, B. (1986). *When disaster strikes.* New York: Basic Books.

Saigh, P. A. (1986). *In vitro* flooding of a 6-year-old boy's posttraumatic stress disorder. *Behaviour Research and Therapy, 24,* 685–689.

Saigh, P. A. (1987a). *In vitro* flooding of a childhood posttraumatic stress disorder. *School Psychology Review, 16,* 203–211.

Saigh, P. A. (1987b). *In vitro* flooding of an adolescent's posttraumatic stress disorder. *Journal of Clinical Child Psychology, 16,* 147–150.

Saigh, P. A. (1987c). *In vitro* flooding of childhood posttraumatic stress disorders: A systematic replication. *Professional School Psychology, 2,* 133–145.

Saigh, P. A. (1989). The use of *in vitro* flooding in the treatment of traumatized adolescents. *Journal of Behavioral and Developmental Pediatrics, 10,* 17–21.

Saylor, C. F., Swenson, C. C., & Powell, P. (1992). Hurricane Hugo blows down the broccoli: Preschoolers' post-disaster play and adjustment. *Child Psychiatry and Human Development, 22*(3), 139–149.

Scurfield, R. M. (1985). Post-traumatic stress assessment and treatment: Overview and formulations. In C. Figley (Ed.), *Trauma and its wake* (pp. 219–256). New York: Brunner/Mazel.

Shapiro, S. H. (1973). Preventive analysis following a trauma: A 4½ year old girl witnesses a stillbirth. In R. Eissler, A. Freud, M. Kris, A. Solnit (Eds.), *The psychoanalytic study of the child* (Vol. 28, pp. 249–285). New Haven: Yale University Press.

Sugar, M. (1989). Children in a disaster: An overview. *Child Psychiatry and Human Development, 19,* 163–179.

Terr, L. C. (1981). Forbidden games: Post-traumatic child's play. *Journal of the American Academy of Child Psychiatry, 20,* 741–760.

Terr, L. C. (1983). Play therapy and psychic trauma: A preliminary report. In C. E. Schaefer & K. J. O'Connor (Eds.), *Handbook of play therapy* (pp. 308–319). New York: Wiley.

Terr, L. C. (1987). Treatment of psychic trauma in children. In J. Noshpitz (Ed.), *Basic handbook of child psychiatry* (Vol. 5, pp. 414–421). New York: Basic Books.

Terr, L. (1989). Treating psychic trauma in children: A preliminary discussion. *Journal of Traumatic Stress, 2,* 2–20.

Terr, L. (1990). *Too scared to cry.* New York: Harper & Row.

Terr, L. (1991). Childhood traumas: An outline and overview. *American Journal of Psychiatry, 148,* 10–20.

Weinberg, R. B. (1990). Serving large numbers of adolescent victim-survivors: Group interventions following trauma at school. *Professional psychology: Research and Practice, 21,* 271–278.

Yule, W., & Williams, R. M. (1990). Post-traumatic stress reactions in children. *Journal of Traumatic Stress, 3,* 279–295.

Zimmerman, I. (1983). *Adaptation to terrorism and political violence.* Presented at the Los Angeles Group Psychotherapy Society annual meeting, Los Angeles, California, June.

Ziv, S., & Israeli, R. (1973). Effects of bombardment on the manifest anxiety level of children living in kibbutzim. *Journal of Consulting and Clinical Psychology, 40,* 287–291.

10

School-Based Intervention Following a Disaster

AVIGDOR KLINGMAN

Disaster events involving schoolchildren and necessitating school-based intervention take many forms: major school-bus collisions (Klingman, 1987; Tuckman, 1973); a school bus kidnapping (Terr, 1979); lighting strike (Dollinger, 1985); tornadoes (e.g., Perry & Perry, 1959); earthquakes (e.g., Blaufarb & Levine, 1972); murder and community terror (e.g., Klingman & Ben Eli, 1981; Landgarten, 1981; Pynoos, Nader, Fredrick, Gonda, & Stuber, 1987); a skywalk accident (Blom, 1986); the homicide of a teacher (Danto, 1978); the death or suicide of a classmate (e.g., Coder, Nelson, & Aylward, 1991; Mauk & Weber, 1991); industrial (e.g., nuclear) accidents (e.g., Collins, Baum, & Singer, 1983; Frederick, 1985); war (Milgram, 1982; Raviv & Klingman, 1983); war-related traumas (e.g., Sack, Angel, Kinzie, & Rath, 1986); and sexual assault (Ruch & Chandler, 1982; Underwood & Fiedler, 1983). The emphasis in crisis intervention has been placed almost exclusively on the recovery of the primary victims, the disaster survivors. Significant others in conjoint relationship with the victim or victims, however, comprise a high-risk group also in need of attention; often, they must be helped to become aware of their own recovery process.

Situational and social support for the survivors is based, in part, on the activation of potential supporters. Thus, the social support system

AVIGDOR KLINGMAN • Chair, Department of Counseling, School of Education, University of Haifa, Mt. Carmel, Haifa 31905, Israel.
Children and Disasters, edited by Conway F. Saylor. Plenum Press, New York, 1993.

plays an important role in the recovery of both the primary victims and those in conjoint relationships with them. In the impact stage of a disaster, the resources of the entire support system and of each individual within it may be taxed to the limit, and the consequences of depleting these resources may thus affect more than the survivors: they may impinge on all components of the system both collectively (e.g., the school population and the school administration) and individually (e.g., a very close friend, a classmate, or a teacher). In this chapter, the focus is primarily on school-based intervention used by a mental health team to enhance the school as a social support system, so that it may better adjust to the taxing demands of the disaster. Specifically, the theoretical framework, procedures, and major techniques of first-order crisis intervention are presented and discussed.

THEORETICAL FRAMEWORK

Since the early 1960s, mental health professionals have developed crisis intervention services aimed at the prevention or minimization of maladaptive reactions to traumatic stress crises suffered by disaster-affected populations. Nelson and Slaikeu (1984) stated that the most significant theoretical treatise on crisis intervention for children is that of Gerald Caplan (1964; Caplan & Grunebaum, 1972), who defined a crisis as a period when one is in a state of temporary psychological disequilibrium, and who defined crisis intervention as the efforts designed to restore equilibrium by (1) offering new alternatives for dealing both with the troubling situation and with the stresses it creates and (2) modifying communitywide practices (e.g., ensuring that schools properly reorganize to provide situation-specific help during a crisis). The underlying assumption of preventive intervention following a disaster is that, if stress can be kept within manageable or tolerable bounds, the crisis will prove less intense and there will be a better chance of adaptive responding.

Levels of Prevention

Caplan's conceptual model (1964) entails three levels of preventive intervention following a disaster. *Primary prevention*, carried out when an observable stressful situation exists, is directed at the general population (e.g., a school population) that has not yet experienced maladjustment; the intervention aim is to counteract potentially harmful effects. *Secondary prevention* emphasizes a quick response to minimize the chance of long-lasting effects, that is, preventing incipient cases of maladjustment from deteriorating by identifying and resolving the crisis at its earliest stage of development. *Tertiary prevention* is applied after the crisis has eased, and it is meant to minimize residual effects and to prevent relapses by stabilizing those who experienced difficulties, received treatment, and are returning to regular activities.

Disaster intervention is defined in this chapter as a mental-health-oriented preventive intervention that proactively seeks to restore the capacity of individuals (e.g., pupils, teachers, and parents) and community institutions (e.g., schools) to cope with a traumatic stress crisis. All three preventive levels of intervention modeled by Caplan are used to reduce the community rate of posttraumatic stress disorder (PTSD) and its effects. In contrast to the traditional medical approach, in which therapists alone are responsible for their individual patients, the preventive approach involves other caregiving professions (e.g., nurses, clergy, and teachers), who proactively deal with the mental health aspects of the disaster; that is, they proactively enhance community situational and social support networks.

The School as Social Support System

Social support is commonly depicted as providing absent resources and/or as reinforcing existing resources (Hobfoll, 1988; Hobfoll, Spielberger, Breznitz, Figley, Folkman, Lepper-Green, Meichenbaum, Milgram, Sandler, Sarason, & van der Kolk, 1991). For children who have experienced disaster, the most natural support system beyond the family is the school. The school provides a unique setting for several reasons: (1) schools are public institutions sanctioned by society to have daily interaction with children; (2) pupils usually spend as much time with their teachers and classmates as with their own families; (3) school personnel have ample opportunity to systematically observe a child in crisis; (4) teachers are relatively well equipped to serve as non-mental-health professionals (i.e., caregivers attending to the mental health implications of a crisis); (5) many of the recommended preventive intervention tools and materials (e.g., class discussions and art and crafts) are readily available as an integral part of school curricula; (6) the school-based professional mental-health consulting or support staff (e.g., guidance counselors, psychologists, and social workers) is already familiar and in regular contact with the school system (and the particular school and its administrators, staff, and children); (7) teachers already have experience in relating to children in their classes who have gone through situational and developmental crises; and (8) a response through psychoeducational, pedagogical, and social activities, by the people most associated with the school, prevents the "psychiatrization" of the situation.

The Generic and the Individual Approaches

Schools are best suited for the implementation of the generic approach to crisis intervention. Essentially, the generic approach accepts the existence of identified patterns of behavior in a crisis so that large-scale intervention can focus on the characteristic course of the crisis rather than on the psychodynamics of each individual involved. The intervention is thus designed for a group (Aguilera & Messick, 1978), and all employees in the school hierarchy can play a role. The individual approach, by contrast, assesses the interpersonal and intrapsychic processes of those in crisis intervention, meeting their unique needs in the particular circumstances. In the school setting, the individual approach may thus be premature or undesirable because it can (1) stigmatize the victim and (2) make an issue of a problem that may disappear by itself or through generic intervention. The individual approach may thus be used when there is no response to the generic approach; then, too, each child's response to generic measures (e.g., stress reactions that remain acute and are identified as a posttraumatic disorder) may serve as a basis for referral for individual intervention.

The individual approach, if it is used in the school setting, differs from that in community clinics, in that school-based mental health professionals have the advantage of daily contact with the victim's educators. This apprises them of how the child is coping and of how far teachers are cooperating in conducting classroom activities to help the child through the crisis (Nelson & Slaikeu, 1984), thereby augmenting their or others' single-case intervention.

Organizational-Typological Model

Disasters that strike school populations usually create a school-related organizational crisis. Emergency reorganization that makes possible an immediate, large-scale response is crucial. To this end, a preliminary theoretical-typological model for disaster intervention in schools was developed (Klingman, 1987) by reconceptualizing Caplan's three-level preventive-intervention model as a five-level intervention model. The new model meets the specific needs of the school organization in a disaster situation by (1) introducing anticipatory intervention at the preimpact stage; (2) introducing separate reorganizational steps at the very beginning of the disaster-impact stage; (3) proactively initiating primary and early secondary measures concurrently; (4) focusing on the individual approach to crisis intervention at the recoil stage; and (5) highlighting certain components of tertiary prevention measures (e.g., facilitating the reintegration of convalescing pupils and preventing relapse).

Anticipatory intervention is the preplanning in good time of an emergency response to the impact of a disaster. Preplanning is especially important, as the professionals often cannot dissociate themselves from the predicament during the impact stage. Even those who can detach themselves are frequently exposed to many of the threats and emotions affecting their target populations, so that their work is sometimes carried out under an immediate risk to their own safety.

The impact stage of a disaster calls for *simultaneous* primary and early secondary (generic) measures. *Primary preventive interventions* consist of any activity having the minimal goal of providing relief from immediate tension, disseminating information, aiding in identifying and consolidating a support system, and enhancing existing learned resourcefulness. This intervention is generic in that it focuses on the characteristic course of the crisis. Simultaneously, *early secondary prevention* measures are taken; namely, the systematic screening of the school population (pupils, teachers, and administrators) to identify acute cases showing early signs of behavioral and emotional adjustment problems (i.e., persons not responding to the generic primary-prevention measures). Other early secondary preventive measures may include opening an in-school *ad hoc* walk-in clinic; setting up a crisis telephone hotline; searching for pupils absent from school; and screening and coordinating volunteer professionals, paraprofessionals and nonprofessionals. Also, some assessment procedures may be used through simple self-report questionnaires (e.g., Klingman, 1992a; Milgram, Toubiana, Klingman, Raviv, & Goldstein, 1988; Pynoos & Nader, 1988).

Once the immediate needs of the population have been met, the individual approach to crisis intervention becomes important. Treatment-based *secondary prevention*, which emphasizes interpersonal and intrapsychic processes, aims at meeting the unique needs of individuals to remove their present specific symptoms and to restore themselves to precrisis level of functioning. *Tertiary intervention* is directed at staff and pupils who have undergone treatment in a protected environment and are resuming an active role in the school's academic and social life. Its goals may range from the recovery of previously held academic and social competencies, to the acquisition of new skills needed for successful readjustment under specific circumstances, to the modification of environmental characteristics that have been shown to impede reintegration while relapse prevention measures are in use.

Triage and Risk Screening

There are two primary classifications of triage and risk screening: (1) exposure (i.e., intensity and proximity) and (2) other risk factors when the individual's response is out of proportion to the degree of exposure

(Pynoos & Nader, 1988; Raphael, 1986; Wright, Ursano, Bartone, & Ingraham, 1990).

Five major screening by-exposure categories can be identified: (1) "direct-exposure victims," who have been directly hit, are highly exposed, and suffer maximally; (2) "on-site victims," who went through the event but were not directly hit; (3) "contact victims," such as grieving classmates; (4) "vicariously involved victims," for example, classmates who would have been primary victims themselves had the situation been otherwise; and (5) "peripheral victims," who have strong ties to the primary victim but are not classmates or even schoolmates of the primary victims, the ties being through a sports club or youth organization or the like. School staff and the pupils' parents can be screened according to these five categories. However, rescue and recovery personnel and support providers constitute an additional category. These latter groups, though indirectly exposed, are significantly involved with the victims' group as a result of activities, roles, and relationships developed in the aftermath of the event. This category tends to be overlooked as being potentially at risk, but it should be a target of risk screening as well.

A second type of risk screening involves non-exposure-related factors that identify an individual's response by the interaction of a number of elements, such as previous trauma or loss (especially in the past year), worry about the safety of a significant other, family response, family psychopathology, and individual psychopathology.

Principles of Intervention

Because of its special nature, emergency crisis intervention involves certain principles (i.e., a general strategy) used in the community or school immediately following a disaster. This is first-order crisis intervention (Slaikeu, 1984), that is, intervention aimed at restoring a person's or an institution's immediate coping at the time and place of the disaster. The intervention is similar to that administered to soldiers suffering from combat stress reactions (Milgram & Hobfoll, 1986; Omer, 1991; Salmon, 1919) in that optimal intervention (1) takes place as soon as possible after the appearance of the symptoms (immediacy); (2) is given as close as possible to the scene of the disaster, in the natural setting (proximity); (3) includes all those similarly affected in a group setting (psychological sense of community); (4) creates a sense of being able to recover soon and resume one's duties (expectancy); and (5) ensures that steps will be taken to preserve and restore a person's or an organization's functional, historical, and interpersonal continuities while actual or potential breaches caused by the disruptive events are being repaired (principle of continuity).

SCHOOL-BASED INTERVENTION PROCEDURES

The first step in a school-based first-order crisis intervention is the immediate convening of a mental health emergency team. The team is put together according to the scope of the disaster or crisis. It may be set up as an *inside team*, to include only staff who regularly work in and with the school (e.g., the school's counselors and psychologists), or (for a large-scale disaster) as a *combined team*, using outside professionals who do not regularly work with the school (usually from the community mental health services) as well as the inside team. (For an example and further discussion, see Klingman, 1987; Rauf & Harris, 1988.)

The flowchart in Figure 1 shows a step-by-step, large-scale, school-based crisis intervention plan, defined as three intervention networks simultaneously implemented by the combined crisis team. The right of the chart displays the professional interventions directly performed by mental health personnel. The center focuses on in-school activities, including guidance and consultation by the crisis team. The left presents the responsibilities of the mental health professionals who coordinate the combined emergency-team work. (See Klingman, 1978, 1988, and Nelson & Slaikeu, 1984, for additional aspects of school- and community-based interventions outlined by flowcharts.)

What follows is an attempt to target the most common procedures of school-based interventions. A comprehensive intervention should aim at several populations: pupils in their classes, pupils in group counseling, pupils in individual counseling, educational staff, parents, school administration, and, in large-scale disasters, community agencies, volunteers, and the media. The most pronounced characteristics of the school system following a disaster are the intense emotional "disequilibrium" experienced by both staff and pupils, organizational confusion in adapting to the specific event, and the reduced defensiveness and increased openness of the system to involve mental health professionals. For the response to be effective, proactive as well as reactive services must be provided immediately. Proactive interventions represent the mental health professionals reaching out to manipulate (e.g., through decision making or planning the course of specific actions) circumstances and events that will have a later impact. Most involvement immediately following a disaster is proactive—crisis management—but some of the professional's actions will include both proactive and reactive intervention.

The proactive intervention focuses on the indirect approach (e.g., consulting with school administrators and teachers). Attention is directed toward defusing potential hazards (e.g., discouraging undue dependence), quickly mobilizing the appropriate physical and interpersonal

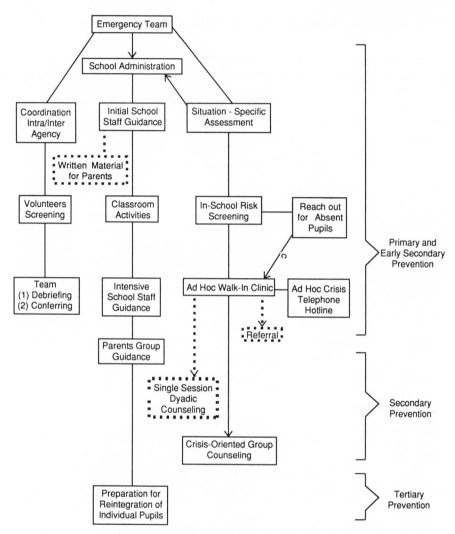

Figure 1. School-based crisis intervention steps.

resources, fostering social support, providing accurate information to the members of the school body, disseminating age-appropriate information to the pupils, and "translating" the normality of the reactions. These efforts are made on a groupwide basis; however, efforts are concurrently made to identify individuals who (1) are already in crisis; (2) do not respond well to group guidance; and/or (3) are identifiable as high risk.

Only when time and expertise allow does the mental health professional exceed liaison and consulting efforts to engage in more extensive (second-order) crisis counseling, such as group or individual counseling.

Consultation for the Benefit of the Administration

Access to the school by the mental health professional must be made through the school administration. It is important to review with the principal what happened, share concerns, note the most obvious mental health aspects, suggest initial concrete steps to be taken, and ensure the availability of professionals as on-site consultants. Steps should be taken to support the administration in reasserting itself as the guiding and steadying influence in the school, to help restore the organizational function (when and if needed) of the school while it adapts to the new demands, and to indicate the mental health aspects of administrative decisions. Such consultation has several aims. One is to augment the sensitivity of the decision makers to the pupils' needs. Another aim is to respond to the specific work difficulties and to burnout, and thereby to enhance the administrators' capacity to master problems. A third is to remedy difficulties that may interfere with decision making on the organizational level. This proactive intervention may have to be extended to the clerical staff, especially if they are overwhelmed by both administrative demands and a flood of outside events (see Klingman, 1987).

Information Dissemination

It is imperative that an authoritative figure disseminate information and that both staff and pupils have ongoing, up-to-date information. Teachers should receive guidance in telling pupils about the disaster. Pupils should be informed directly, as early as possible, by age-appropriate means, and simultaneously in all classrooms to minimize rumors. A memo or a newspaper may be read to all pupils and then discussed in detail (Klingman, 1987). Also, a fact sheet or news bulletin may be sent home to the parents (periodically when necessary) to convey, share, and update information.

Teachers' Guidance

The emphasis in the initial guidance sessions is placed on conveying information about posttraumatic reactions so as to desensitize teachers to the expected overt symptoms and thereby avert the indiscriminate referral of pupils to mental health personnel. Directive-prescriptive guidance is then provided to aid in handling the class, relating to the pupils (for an example, see Klingman, 1989), and addressing practical questions.

When more intensive intervention is called for, teachers should be encouraged first to discuss their own responses and worries and then to link these observations with those that their pupils are probably experiencing. If the teachers find this difficult, then relating the responses of their own children who may not have been directly involved in the crisis may enhance discussion. Identifying and reinforcing positive performances reported by the teachers has proved very helpful in developing their mastery, and such performances may serve as models. Teachers are to be encouraged to share their own feelings with the pupils but should not impose their burdens on the youngsters. Consultation and referral procedures should be explained, and teachers should be assured that the mental health team will be readily available. The team's overall intervention plan should be presented and discussed toward the end of the session. Supportive guidance should be assured because of the tremendous psychological responsibility thrust on the teachers, who often need continued encouragement to sustain their pupils' emotional response as long as the pupils need to express it. In teachers' guidance, the preferred role of the professional is indirect, encouraging and supporting the teachers rather than displacing them; the emphasis is on a consultive role, not hands-on intervention.

Classroom Intervention Formats

The daily teaching assignments should be put aside, so that all energy may be directed to dealing with the effects of the event on the pupils. It is strongly recommended that, if possible, the administration or the teachers not dismiss the class, at least not before information dissemination and some debriefing. School and classroom operation should be quickly resumed, with a gradual reestablishment of normal patterns. In any case, the teachers should be aware that their classroom interventions are not a substitute for individual, group, or family interventions when needed (Pynoos & Nader, 1993).

The immediate goal of classroom intervention is to defuse the emotions within appropriate limits and thus to provide means of acknowledging these feelings so that anxiety may be kept to a tolerable level. These means include reliving the traumatic event via narration interchange and/ or nonverbal expression. The intervention should match the pupils' developmental level (Eth & Pynoos, 1985; Monaco & Gaier, 1987). When necessary, encouraging affective discharge by legitimizing it may be initiated, and the process of experiencing a trauma may be described to the pupils (e.g., via metaphor; see Weinberg, 1990). Discretion, however, should be provided with regard to abreaction (see the later discussion of debriefing).

It should be noted at this point that individuals within a class should be allowed latitude in choosing how they will cope with a stressful event, as there are no "correct" stages of stress and coping (Hobfoll *et al.*, 1991). Generally, emotion-focused coping should be very effective at first and should then give way to problem-focused coping. Later on, emotion-focused coping can be suggested from time to time to allow a step back to renew strength or as a beneficial instrument in situations that the individual can do nothing about. Also, knowledge of developmental differences and of the social and sociocultural world of the pupils is paramount in successful first-order intervention. Younger children are less likely than older children and adults to speak directly about their problems or even to know they have them; they have less prior experience in coping with stressful events and may either ignore or exaggerate difficulties or situations. (For an extended discussion, see Eth & Pynoos, 1985.)

Rumors and myths about the disaster can then be addressed to allay pupils' fears about themselves ("Could this happen to me?") and their loved ones. Attempts to convey an understanding of the causes of the disaster may put it in perspective and thus alleviate some of the feelings of guilt and anger. These attempts may later be supplemented by integrating disaster-related issues into the regular curriculum. For example, social studies and history classes can lead historical perspectives (e.g., regarding war), or a natural disaster phenomenon may be thoroughly studied as part of a geography lesson. Breaking down the complex problem following a disaster into more age-appropriate, comprehensible, and manageable subcomponents by disentangling the intertwined aspects of the event can constitute the next step.

A discussion of healthy coping may follow, and any adaptive coping behaviors that pupils mention should be strongly reinforced and elaborated. Cognitive coping may be enhanced by further correcting of rumors, incomplete information, cognitive distortions, and age-appropriate misunderstandings (Pynoos & Nader, 1988). Clarifying the disaster-related terminology used by the media is especially important for younger pupils.

In the case of a suicide, the emphasis is on exploring the various ways of seeking help or giving information about available school and community support resources, and on the deromanticization of the act (see, e.g., Klingman, 1989). Death can be discussed in age-appropriate themes that give both concrete and symbolic representation of its finality. The subject can be reinforced through group drawing or storytelling the physical reality of death in a way that acknowledges sadness or anger over the loss and the unfairness of the ultimely event (Pynoos & Nader, 1988). Language and art teachers are in a very strong position to further cognitive coping and provide support by using such methods as free writing, bibliotherapy, and arts and crafts (described later). A librarian may be an excellent source of information; literature on stress, coping, and mastery could be highlighted in a media display (Johnson & Maile, 1987; Mauk & Weber, 1991). Physical education teachers are able to offer direct intervention with stress reduction exercises.

Pupils can be further helped to feel a sense of control and mastery by their being asked to take some action. Instrumental tasks include writing letters and drawing pictures to be sent to hospitalized classmates, memorializing the dead (e.g., preparing a scrapbook), helping to assess damages, and putting together a volunteer baby-sitting network through which older pupils will sit for families who cannot care for their children.

The restoration of hope and optimism is a necessary component in adjusting to a stressful event. Because of children's limited experience, it is vital that they be given positive expectations (Hobfoll *et al.*, 1991); an optimistic outlook encourages continued efforts at coping. Classroom discussions should thus end by indicating that, no matter how traumatic a situation or how hopeless it may seem, healthy solutions are always possible.

The next stage is the gradual return to classroom routine, important in providing a feeling of structure, continuity, and self-efficacy. Setting accomplishable tasks and rewarding small achievements will help pupils to avoid the victim role and enter the mastery role.

Small-Group Crisis Intervention

Some pupils will be more agitated than others and thus need closer attention than can be provided in the classroom. The program makes arrangements for first-order crisis groups of up to 12 pupils. The small-group format allows for a more careful scrutiny of pupils displaying acute posttraumatic reaction who may be at greater risk for serious long-term effects. In the case of classmates of suicide victims, it is important that the group be homogeneous. Procedures and content for conducting crisis groups are described elsewhere (e.g., Ayalon, 1983; Klingman, 1987; Pynoos & Nader, 1993; Weinberg, 1990). Generally, debriefing is the preferred group procedure for first-order intervention.

Debriefing aims at ventilating the most acute emotions through pupils' telling what happened and how it affected them. In this way they gain reassurance about the normality of their intense emotions: all expressions are granted full legitimization and are explained to the group as being normal for this stage of the crisis. Still other aims of the debriefing are enhancement of peer social support; reduction of misconceptions and correction of misinformation; reinforcement and encouragement of active coping; and assurance about the availability of professionals to assist further at any time. The prevailing view is that the expression of feelings is necessary for those who have been exposed to intense stress such as the loss of loved ones or involvement in a life-threatening event. There exist, however, wide individual differences in the willingness to abreact, in the intensity of the abreaction, and in its necessity. This is especially true in classroom (vs. small-group) intervention. It is suggested, therefore, that an opportunity for the ventilation of feelings be provided but not insisted on (Toubiana & Milgram, 1988).

The objectives of the small groups are similar to those of the classroom, except that more emphasis is placed on the group's composition, the promotion of mutual support, and each participant's concerns and difficulties, such as guilt examination, aggression channeling, cognitive reappraisal of the experience, and mapping alternatives. The small number of participants allows more time to be spent in addressing individual concerns (Weinberg, 1990).

Basic Crisis Counseling

Most dyadic crisis counseling is clinic-based and thus beyond the scope of school-based interventions. Single-session therapeutic encounters (Talmon, 1990) can be adapted for an in-school walk-in counseling center (if one is opened). The reader is referred to Aguilera and Messick (1978), Slaikeu (1984), Pynoos and Nader (1993), and Toubiana and Milgram (1988) for a description of crisis intervention methods with individual students.

Parents' Guidance

In view of the importance of the family as a natural support system, guidance for parents becomes an integral part of a school-based intervention. Parental anxiety is usually due to subjective concerns, including confusion about how to cope with the child's response to the event, loss of familial spontaneity, and the child's manipulative advantage taking at home. Moreover, children's reactions often mirror the reactions of their parents; the family's exposure to the traumatic event may create different, overtaxing psychological demands on each family member so that the child's special (or even regular) needs may be overlooked. In some cases, it is critical that parents recognize that seeking help for themselves is the best therapy for their troubled child (Hobfoll *et al.*, 1991). Thus, guidance by the mental health team aims at restoring the child's sense of security through the parents' clear understanding of the parental role. It enhances parents' awareness of the various symptoms so as to validate and legitimize the proper situation-specific symptoms. It also encourages open communication with the child, thereby helping to set situation-specific realistic goals and expectations about the course of recovery. This guidance, furthermore, is intended to offer practical suggestions about supervising the child, to promote spontaneous (commonsense) family decision making, and to assist in minimizing secondary stresses and adversities.

The goals of a small parents' group meeting with the emergency team are, in general, to give information about what happened and the psychological reactions to crisis; to allow direct sharing of the parents' own feelings, experiences, concerns, and problems; to inform the parents of and elaborate on the preventive school-based interventions; and to respond to concerns raised by the parents, such as overprotection, avoidance behavior, grief and mourning, participation in funerals, detection of suicidal intent, and their own difficulties in discussing such issues as death and suicide with their children (e.g., Blaufarb, 1972; Blom, 1986, Klingman, 1987, 1989).

Sometimes, a large parents' group is assembled. In such cases, both personal and professional experiences with disasters can be presented, including some findings from psychological studies of disaster and a survey of crisis theory. Following this formal frontal presentation, the large audience can then be divided into smaller discussion groups (Blom, 1986).

Crisis Hotline

A crisis telephone hotline is considered an effective way of reaching out to a large number of parents within a short time. Parents also find this an acceptable way of asking for help, as the hotline is easily accessible and provides a noncommital, optionally anonymous service that does not necessitate leaving home.

Such a school-based hotline was operated following a school bus disaster in Israel (Klingman, 1987). In the 48 calls monitored during the first five hours of operation, 6 callers were advised to come in immediately for diadic counseling and 9 to contact a specific resource person; 31 callers were given advice on the phone about handling their child's particular problem; and in 2 cases, a psychiatrist visited the caller's home. In another disaster, a hotline service was offered to check out rumors and "stories" (Blom, 1986).

During the 1991 Gulf War, an open line was operated by the Israeli Ministry of Education in order to relate to pupils' functioning. Two-thirds of the hundreds of calls received daily were from children. The advantage over other (clinic-based) hotlines was the ministry's open intent to respond to children's everyday functioning and thereby to prevent the attachment of the unhealthy stigma that often occurs with other hotlines. It was easier and more natural for pupils in trouble to turn to the school system's hotline (for an extended discussion, see Raviv, in press).

Volunteer Helpers and Professional Strangers

A large-scale school disaster mobilizes many professionals and lay-people to volunteer. On the positive side, they constitute a backup reserve. Outside professionals may have better disaster intervention training. In cases in which prior anticipatory planning and training have not been conducted, it is sometimes necessary, especially in large-scale disasters, for an outside expert to take charge of, coordinate, and guide the mental-health-related intervention. On the negative side, the invasion of the school by professionals with the best intentions may produce several adverse effects. Toubiana, Milgram, Strich, and Edelstein (1988) reported instances of overtreatment and suggested that some pupils asked for individual sessions because of the eagerness of mental health professionals to offer this service. They also reported teachers' complaints that well-meaning outsiders were intrusive in the corridors and classrooms and usurped the teachers' authority, thereby undermining the self-confidence of the school's primary caregivers. Outsiders' involvement, it seems, offers a mixed blessing. (For an extended discussion of the various options and the advantages and disadvantages of outside teams, see Rauf & Harris, 1988.) It is Caplan's view (1976) that the proper role of professional strangers in crisis intervention is indirect and behind the scenes, to bolster rather than displace natural support systems.

SELECTED SCHOOL-BASED TECHNIQUES AND EXERCISES

A variety of school-based techniques and exercises have been used in interventions following a disaster. These techniques require (1) a safe environment, where children feel physically safe and emotionally cared for; (2) a supportive figure (e.g., a teacher), who has proper knowledge and preparation; and (3) ongoing consultation and support by a mental health professional (e.g., a school counselor or a school psychologist).

Drawing and Playing

Few young children are able to talk directly about their emotions or to explore the roots of the difficulties they experience in a crisis. Playing and drawing are considered very good ways for young children to create and express their own interpretations. Play and art activities (e.g., with paints, clay, and dolls) are natural modes of communication in schools and thus sidestep the stigma associated with receiving psychological treatment. These activities can be initiated by caring adults (including parent volunteers and older pupils) able to project themselves into the child's situation and to see the world through the youngster's eyes. These activities can be used as a shared group experience (e.g., joint drawing and sociodramatic play). They may be structured and/or unstructured.

At the simplest general level, allowing children to create their own pictures of what happened, including their feelings about the disaster, enhances intrapsychic processes. It may also be useful in large-scale screening for high-risk pupils and may eventually assist mental health professionals in diagnosis and counseling. The literature reveals limited research in this area in the context of school-based first-order crisis intervention. Galante and Foa (1986) reported the use of school-based drawing and play activity with first- to fourth-grade pupil groups following a devastating earthquake. Children who were drawing while listening to stories became involved in a large joint drawing of the locality as well as in free drawing. They were also furnished with small toys to stimulate their "acting out" the earthquake, and they role-played parents teaching children to survive in emergency situations. The authors concluded that such an intervention can be handled by locally trained personnel and does not necessarily require specially trained professionals.

Landgarten (1981) discussed a classroom art therapy intervention with third-graders in a public school following a shootout between law enforcement officers and terrorists in the neighborhood. The obvious themes depicted were loss and the fear of separation, the use of denial as a defense mechanism, sadness, kidnapping fears, and identification with the victim. In the author's opinion, the single art therapy experience provided the pupils with an opportunity to explore their thoughts and emotions concerning the threatening event; pupils with stronger egos used the device as a way of working through the trauma.

Schwarcz (1982) analyzed the positive effect of an art program that explicitly encouraged children living in an area struck by rockets during a war to draw war-related themes. Three hundred drawings and paintings were collected, together with some artwork from before and after the war. It was concluded that these works expressed conscious disquiet associated with identifiable objects more frequently than they did unconscious associations or repressed or defensive maneuvers, and that this activity clearly led to interaction with peers who had undergone the crisis and who viewed and commented on the art productions.

Art used as a first-order preventive measure with a large group of seventh-graders has been reported with regard to a school bus disaster (Klingman, Koenigsfeld, & Markman, 1987). Of the 94 works collected for the phenomenological study, 40 attempted a graphic portrayal of the accident, 41 contained written words, 36 included name lists of the dead pupils, 6 illustrated graves and gravestones, 6 portrayed a friend who was killed, and 3 included various scattered body parts. Case analyses demonstrated that painting, drawing, and collage works facilitated affective and cognitive aspects of the recuperative process, provided a temporary "protected environment," and did not require excessive time of mental health professionals.

The foregoing observations strongly suggest that art activity can be used effectively with large groups of nonpatient populations in mass first-order crisis intervention.

Drama, role playing, and puppet activity can also be used in the classroom. Sociodramatic enactment and role playing promote the expression of feelings, allow symptom relief, and enhance personal coping. They permit the pupils to step back from the turmoil of their own situation and examine the situation and conflicts within a shared, structured, controlled, supportive, and constructive "safe space." New perceptions and alternative behavior can be "discovered" and examined, and mastery (vs. helplessness) promoted; the group learns to interact cooperatively and to empathize directly with one another's situation by actually becoming part of it through role taking (Dallas, 1978; Farrelly & Joseph, 1991).

Puppets are another kind of play activity suited for the classroom. Puppets are readily available and easy to use (e.g., hand and stick puppets; any doll can be hand-held and used as a puppet; and children can make their own puppets out of papier-mâché, plasticine, socks, etc.); children easily relate to puppet play. Puppets can stimulate interaction among classmates and provide the emotional distance needed to allow the verbalization of feelings (James, 1989).

Biblioguidance and Bibliotherapy

Biblioguidance includes the distribution of written material, such as guideline pamphlets for parents and practical manuals for teachers. Excerpts from articles and books as well as an annotated bibliography were distributed to teachers several times, both before and during stress points, in the course of the week following a mass school bus disaster (Klingman, 1987). For example, preparation for the pupils' participation in the funerals included written material concerning funerary and mourning customs, grief reactions in cultural contexts, and so on. Biblioguidance, in this respect, provided the means for a gradual exposure to the different aspects of the funeral and of grief processes.

Lystad (1985) presented other examples of outreach materials for victims of disaster. These materials include descriptions of common feelings and reactions (during, immediately following, and as time goes on); suggestions of what can be done; information on support networks (e.g., home visits and support groups); common behaviors (e.g., school avoidance); how parents can help the child; and "tips" for teachers (e.g., age-appropriate reactions of children, when to refer to mental health professionals, and age-appropriate classroom activities).

A bibliotherapy-related approach used in schools in the aftermath of a disaster was described by Koubovi (1982) as therapeutic teaching. Basically it involved carefully chosen literary texts that presented disaster-related concerns, as well as classroom discussions on the texts and related topics. Such an approach, using the supportive group setting of the classroom, serves as a middle course between uncontrolled or unstructured ventilation of feelings and deniallike or defensive avoidance of disturbing events. When uncontrolled ventilation predominates, the pupils can be directed to the topics of the texts, and intellectualization can be promoted to interpose a requisite distance from upsetting issues. This method proved very helpful, too, in preventing extreme reactions by teachers, helping them to find a middle way between the two extremes of ventilation and denial of their own emotional reactions.

Another medium that lends itself to biblioguidance is the coloring books especially developed to help young children express their feelings, to learn about a specific disaster (i.e., by a simple explanation of what occurred), to observe how people cope, and to learn safety measures. Some pages may be left blank for children to add their own drawings and/or comments. For example, one page might define a tornado by showing rain and cold and hot air coming together; a house may be pictured with instructions for youngsters to go to a safe area and listen for warning signals (e.g., Earberow & Gordon, 1981; Frederick, 1985, p. 90); an earthquake's lateral shift and "the move that makes sounds" can be graphically outlined; children helping at home, outside helpers, and the rebuilding process may be illustrated by other pictures (e.g., Lystad, 1985, pp. 123–160). The Persian Gulf War necessitated the creation of coloring booklets to prepare young children to cope with the threat of chemical warfare; an example is a story-and-coloring booklet designed to help children deal with the anxiety and noncompliance associated with gas masks, and it focused on coping statements (the story in this case specifically related to a child's teddy bear, for which the child makes a gas mask) (Klingman, 1992, 1992b).

Free Writing

Free writing, a group-administered paper-and-pencil intervention tool, serves to elicit a direct expression of feelings and thoughts. Based on principles similar to those of projective measures (e.g., association and completion techniques), the free writing technique introduces utterances that are essentially a raw, relatively uncalculated, and spontaneous verbalized rendition of personal experience. If guided (vs. self-initiated), free writing is a method of eliciting expression by either verbal or nonverbal stimuli. For example, *in vitro* exposures, such as ambiguous pictures and photographs that trigger free writing, can be used (Ayalon, 1983). For pupils under stress, writing is a socially accepted medium of expression in the classroom. The result of a preliminary study (Klingman, 1985) suggests the feasibility of using free writing following a crisis.

Self-Calming

Self-calming techniques (e.g., modified yoga, visualization, and deep breathing) may be used in school settings. Children can benefit from relaxation exercises through a reduction in the tension they experience and learning that they have some control over their body tension, which in turn gives them a sense of mastery. Deep breathing is considered the easiest self-calming method to teach children in crisis. (For basic patterns of breathing and various exercises, see Everly, 1989; James, 1989.)

Simulations

Simulations are mainly used within a program of anticipatory preparation (e.g., Klingman, 1982, 1987), but they can be developed for the recovery stages after a disaster. For example, an experiment carried out with Israeli elementary-school children following a terrorist attack (Ophir, 1980) found that a simulation game resembling the game "battle ships" significantly reduced their state anxiety. The participants took an active part in creating the structure of the game and then playing it. The game, consisting of two separate board games, included role taking and the participants' assessment of the probability of terrorists' reaching their neighborhood, school, classroom, and home.

Field Trips

In our context, a field trip is any reasonable outing that provides for desensitization. For example, Klingman and Ben Eli (1981) found that following a terrorist attack from the sea, children avoided approaching the beach, which had usually been a very popular gathering place for them. Therefore, groups of children were taken to visit the site of the incident. After the visit (i.e., gradual *in vivo* exposure), they were provided an in-class opportunity to express and share emotionally charged contents. Dallas (1978) reported encouraging temporary "peer car pools" to desensitize pupils to the location of a murder tragedy.

CONCLUDING REMARKS

In this chapter, I have attempted to present a school-based prevention model that has already been field-tested. This model makes use of a didactic exposition of studies of stress, posttraumatic symptoms, descriptive studies of proactive psychoeducational measures, and recommendations stemming from both personal experience and the literature. Currently, there are no well-controlled empirical data to support the full effectiveness of the proposed model. It should be noted that, because implementation of the model is meant for a natural school setting, restrictions are imposed on experimental design as well as on measurement. Moreover, there are difficulties in and limitations on research during the impact stage of a disaster because of the overinvolvement of the professionals themselves and the pressure to attend professionally to the population's mental health needs.

As yet, there have been few attempts to investigate the effectiveness of some components of school-based interventions. Such studies have investigated the effectiveness of specific tools, for example, the use of free writing as a palliative tool (Klingman, 1985) and of art activity as a coping process (Klingman *et al.*, 1987; Schwarcz, 1982). Much needed is an assessment of children's self-generated coping strategies (e.g., Weisenberg, Schwarzwald, Waysman, Solomon & Klingman, in press), the data for which are of a self-report, retrospective nature; thus, they are subject to the errors of memory, distortion, and social desirability. With all the limitations imposed, however, this appears to be the most desirable approach. By building interventions based on the coping skills of children who function optimally under stressful conditions, it may be possible to develop more effective intervention programs that consider the preferred age-related, coping modes. Also needed are face validity studies that investigate whether pupils and teachers actually understand and/or recall the information, instructions, and exercises provided.

Some organizational issues, such as coordinating interagency intervention plans and volunteer helpers (Rauf & Harris, 1988; Toubiana *et al.*,

1988) and responding to media intrusion, were not covered in this chapter; they deserve separate study. Indeed, it is impossible to deal with all the aspects of intervention in a single chapter. What I have attempted to delineate are the major assumptions and some components of the implementation of these assumptions. Similarly, I have made an explicit attempt to integrate theory, research findings, and practice in school-based first-order crisis intervention.

REFERENCES

Aguilera, D. C., & Messick, J. M. (1978). *Crisis intervention: Theory and methodology.* St. Louis: C. V. Mosby.

Ayalon, O. (1983). Coping with terrorism: The Israeli case. In D. Meichenbaum & M. Jaremko (Eds.), *Stress reduction and prevention* (pp. 293–339). New York: Plenum Press.

Blaufarb, H., & Levine, J. (1972). Crisis intervention in an earthquake. *Social Work, 17,* 16–19.

Blom, G. E. (1986). A school disaster—Intervention and research aspects. *Journal of the American Academy of Child Psychiatry, 25,* 336–345.

Caplan, G. (1964). *Principles of preventive psychiatry.* New York: Basic Books.

Caplan, G., & Grunebaum, H. (1972). Perspectives on primary prevention: A review. In H. Gottesfield (Ed.), *The critical issues of community mental health* (pp. 127–159). New York: Behavioral Publications.

Coder, T. L., Nelson, R. E., & Aylward, L. K. (1991). Suicide among secondary students. *The School Counselor, 38,* 358–361.

Collins, D. L., Baum, A., & Singer, J. E. (1983). Coping with chronic stress at Three Mile Island: Psychological and biochemical evidence. *Health Psychology, 2,* 149–166.

Dallas, D. (1978). Savagery, show and tell. *American Psychologist, 33,* 388–390.

Danto, B. L. (1978). Crisis intervention in a classroom regarding the homicide of a teacher. *The School Counselor, 26,* 69–89.

Dollinger, S. J. (1985). Lightning-strike disaster among children. *British Journal of Medical Psychology, 58,* 375–383.

Earberow, N. L., & Gordon, N. S. (1981). *Manual for child health workers in major disasters.* Rockville, MD: National Institute of Mental Health (DHHS Pub. No. ADM 81-1070).

Eth, S., & Pynoos, R. S. (1985). Developmental perspective on psychic trauma in childhood. In C. R. Figley (Ed.), *Trauma and its wake* (pp. 36–52). New York: Brunner/Mazel.

Everly, G. S. (1989). *A clinical guide to the treatment of the human stress response.* New York: Plenum Press.

Farrelly, J., & Joseph, A. (1991). Expressive therapies in a crisis intervention service. *The Arts in Psychotherapy, 18,* 131–137.

Frederick, C. J. (1985). Children traumatized by catastrophic situations. In S. Eth & R. S. Pynoos (Eds.), *Post-traumatic stress disasters in children* (pp. 73–99). Washington, DC: American Psychiatric Press.

Galante, R., & Foa, D. (1986). An epidemiological study of psychic trauma and treatment effectiveness for children after a natural disaster. *Journal of the American Academy of Child Psychiatry, 25,* 357–363.

Hobfoll, S. E. (1988). *The ecology of stress.* New York: Hemisphere.

Hobfoll, S. E., Spielberger, C. D., Breznitz, S., Figley, C., Folkman, S., Lepper-Green, B., Meichenbaum, D., Milgram, N., Sandler, I., Sarason, I., & van der Kolk, B. A. (1991).

War-related stress: Addressing the stress of war and other traumatic events. *American Psychologist, 46,* 848–855.

James, B. (1989). *Treating traumatized children: New insights and creative intervention.* Lexington, MA: Lexington Books.

Johnson, S., & Maile, L. J. (1987). *Suicide and the schools: A handbook for prevention, intervention, and rehabilitation.* Springfield, IL: Thomas.

Klingman, A. (1978). Children in stress: Anticipatory guidance in the framework of the educational systems. *Personnel and Guidance Journal, 57,* 22–26.

Klingman, A. (1982). Persuasive communication in avoidance behavior: Using role simulation as a strategy. *Simulation and Games, 13,* 37–50.

Klingman, A. (1985). Free writing: Evaluation of preventive programs with elementary school children. *Journal of School Psychology, 23,* 167–175.

Klingman, A. (1987). A school-based emergency crisis intervention in a mass school disaster. *Professional Psychology: Research and Practice, 18,* 604–612.

Klingman, A. (1988). School community in disaster: Planning for intervention. *Journal of Community Psychology, 16,* 205–216.

Klingman, A. (1989). School-based emergency intervention following an adolescent's suicide. *Death Studies, 13,* 263–274.

Klingman, A. (1992a). Stress reactions of Israeli youth during the Gulf War: A quantitative study. *Professional Psychology: Research and Practice, 23,* 521–527.

Klingman, A. (1992b). School psychology services: Community-based first-order crisis intervention during the Gulf War. *Psychology in the Schools, 29,* 376–384.

Klingman, A. (1992c). The effects of parent-implemented crisis intervention: A real life emergency involving a child refusal to use a gas-mask. *Journal of Clinical Child Psychology, 21,* 70–75.

Klingman, A., & Ben Eli, A. (1981). A school community in disaster: Primary and secondary prevention in situational crisis. *Professional Psychology: Research and Practice, 12,* 523–532.

Klingman, A., Koenigsfeld, E., & Markman, D. (1987). Art activity with children following disaster: A preventive oriented crisis intervention modality. *The Arts in Psychotherapy, 14,* 153–166.

Koubovi, D. (1982). Therapeutic teaching of literature during the war and its aftermath. In C. D. Spielberger, I. G. Sarason, & N. A. Milgram (Eds.), *Stress and anxiety* (Vol. 8, pp. 345–349). Washington, DC: Hemisphere.

Landgarten, H. B. (1981). *Clinical art therapy: A comprehensive guide.* New York: Brunner/Mazel.

Lystad, M. (Ed.). (1985). *Innovations in mental health services to disaster victims.* Washington, DC: National Institute of Mental Health (Pub. No. ADM 86-1390).

Mauk, G. W., & Weber, C. (1991). Peer survivors of adolescent suicide: Perspectives on grieving and postvention. *Journal of Adolescent Research, 6,* 113–131.

Milgram, N. A. (1982). War-related stress in Israeli children and youth. In L. Goldberg & S. Breznitz (Eds.), *Handbook of stress: Theoretical and clinical aspects* (pp. 656–676). New York: Free Press.

Milgram, N. A., & Hobfoll, S. E. (1986). Generalization from theory and practice in war-related stress. In N. A. Milgram (Ed.), *Stress and coping in time of war: Generalization from the Israeli experience* (pp. 316–352). New York: Brunnel/Mazel.

Milgram, N. A., Toubiana, H., Klingman, A., Raviv, A., & Goldstein, I. (1988). Situational exposure and personal loss in children's acute and chronic stress reactions to school disasters. *Journal of Traumatic Stress, 1,* 339–352.

Monaco, N. M., & Gaier, E. L. (1987). Developmental level and children's responses to the explosion of the space shuttle Challenger. *Early Childhood Research Quarterly, 2,* 83–95.

Nelson, E. A., & Slaikeu, K. A. (1984). Crisis intervention in the schools. In K. A. Slaikeu,

Crisis intervention: A handbook for practice and research (pp. 247–262). Boston: Allyn & Bacon.

Omer, H. (1991). Massive trauma: The role of emergency team. *Sihot Dialogue: Israel Journal of Psychotherapy, 3,* 157–170 (in Hebrew).

Ophir, M. (1980). Simulation game as an intervention to reduce state anxiety. In A. Raviv, A. Klingman, & M. Horowitz (Eds.), *Children under stress and in crisis* (pp. 274–279). Tel-Aviv: Otzar Hamoreh (in Hebrew).

Perry, H. S., & Perry, S. E. (1959). *The schoolhouse disaster: Family and community as determinants of the child's response to disaster.* Disaster Study No. 11. Washington, DC: National Academy of Science.

Pynoos, R. S., & Nader, K. (1988). Psychological first aid and treatment approach to children exposed to community violence: Research and implications. *Journal of Traumatic Stress, 1,* 445–473.

Pynoos, R. S., & Nader, K. (1993). Issues in the treatment of posttraumatic stress in children and adolescents. In J. Wilson & B. Raphael (Eds.), *The international handbook of traumatic stress syndromes.* New York: Plenum Press.

Pynoos, R. S., Nader, K., Fredrick, C., Gonda, L., & Stuber, M. (1987). Grief reactions in school age children following a sniper attack in school. *Israeli Journal of Psychiatry and Related Sciences, 24,* 53–63.

Raphael, B. (1986). *When disaster strikes.* New York: Basic Books.

Rauf, S., & Harris, J. (1988). How to select, train and supervise a crisis team. *Communique, 17*(4), 19.

Raviv, A. (in press). The use of hotline and media interventions in Israel during the Gulf War. In L. A. Leavitt & N. A. Fox (Eds.), *Psychological effects of war and violence on children.* New York: Lawrence Erlbaum.

Raviv, A., & Klingman, A. (1983). Children under stress. In S. Breznitz (Ed.), *Stress in Israel* (pp. 138–162). New York: Van Nostrand Reinhold.

Ruch, L. O., & Chandler, S. M. (1982). The crisis impact of sexual assault on three victim groups: Adult rape victims, child rape victims, and incest victims. *Journal of Social Service Research, 5,* 83–100.

Sack, W. H., Angel, R. H., Kinzie, J. D. & Rath, B. (1986). The psychiatric effects of massive trauma on Cambodian children: The family, the home, and the school. *Journal of the American Academy of Child Psychiatry, 25,* 377–383.

Salmon, T. (1919). The war neuroses and their lessons. *New York State Journal of Medicine, 109,* 933–944.

Schwarcz, J. H. (1982). Guiding children's creative expression in the stress of war. In C. D. Spielberger, I. G. Sarason, & N. A. Milgram (Eds.), *Stress and anxiety,* (Vol. 8, pp. 351–354). Washington, DC: Hemisphere.

Slaikeu, K. A. (1984). *Crisis intervention: A handbook for practice and research.* Boston: Allyn & Bacon.

Talmon, M. (1990). *Single-session therapy.* San Francisco: Jossey-Bass.

Terr, L. (1979). Children of Chowchilla: Study of psychic trauma. *Psychoanalytic Study of the Child, 34,* 547–623.

Toubiana, Y. H., Milgram, N. A., Strich, Y., & Edelstein, A. (1988). Crisis intervention in a school community disaster: Principles and practices. *Journal of Community Psychology, 16,* 228–240.

Tuckman, A. J. (1973). Disaster and mental health intervention. *Community Mental Health Journal, 9,* 151–157.

Underwood, M. M., & Fiedler, N. (1983). The crisis of rape: A community response. *Community Mental Health Journal, 19,* 227–230.

Weinberg, R.B. (1990). Serving large number of adolescent victim survivors: Group interventions following trauma at school. *Professional Psychology: Research and Practice, 21*, 271–278.

Weisenberg, M., Schwarzwald, J., Waysman, M., Solomon, Z., & Klingman, A. (in press). Coping of school-age children in the school room during Scud missile bombardment and postwar stress reactions. *Journal of Consulting and Clinical Psychology*, Department of Mental Health, Medical Corps, Israel Defense Forces.

Wright, K. M., Ursano, R. J., Bartone, P. T., & Ingraham, L. H. (1990). The shared experience of catastrophe: An expended classification of the disaster community. *American Journal of Orthopsychiatry, 60*, 35–42.

11

Community-Level Intervention after a Disaster

CATHY DODDS JOYNER and CYNTHIA CUPIT SWENSON

Many disaster victims require intervention at the level of the individual, the family, a small group, or the school, as described in earlier chapters in this book. However, certain disasters are so enormous in scope that they require communitywide intervention. Federally funded agencies such as the Federal Emergency Management Agency (FEMA) and the National Guard, as well as nonprofit relief groups such as the Red Cross and the Salvation Army, have been trained in disaster preparedness, particularly in recognition of the physical and financial need to reach hundreds, even thousands, of families after a large-scale disaster.

In addition to its physical and financial consequences, a natural disaster potentially carries with it tremendous social and emotional consequences for individuals and communities. Although not all disaster victims experience severe psychological difficulties after the disaster, research in the disaster area has documented adverse psychological consequences for some victims following disaster exposure. In a review of disaster research, Rubonis and Bickman (1991) reported psychopathology in disaster victims at a rate of 17%. Pathology among disaster victims may not surface for up to three months, when between 15% and 25% will need more specialized assistance (Brom & Kleber, 1989; Roberts, 1990). The

CATHY DODDS JOYNER and CYNTHIA CUPIT SWENSON • Charleston–Dorchester Community Mental Health Center—Division of Children, Adolescents and Families, 4 Carriage Lane, Suite 40S, Charleston, South Carolina 29407.
Children and Disasters, edited by Conway F. Saylor. Plenum Press, New York, 1993.

negative psychological consequences of natural disaster are not unique to adults; they are found among children as well (Bloom, 1986; Dollinger, 1985; Dollinger, O'Donnell, & Staley, 1984; Galante & Foa, 1986; Swenson, Powell, Foster, & Saylor, 1991).

The specific negative effects of disaster are inconsistent because disaster is experienced differently by different communities and individuals. Several researchers have looked at the mediating factors that affect one's experience with disaster. Gibbs (1989) reported large individual differences in disaster reactions; for example, higher education and higher income level were related to less psychological distress after disasters. Further, an internal locus of control has been related to fewer emotional effects of disaster.

In regard to situation-specific factors, Rubonis and Bickman (1991) emphasized that psychopathology is greater among disaster victims if there are many casualties and if the cause of the disaster is natural. Baum (1987), on the other hand, reported that long-term psychological consequences are more often associated with disasters of human design than with natural disasters. Quarantelli and Dynes (1985) indicated that the negative emotional consequences of disaster are due to the perception of failed community cohesion. Freedy, Shaw, Jarrell, and Masters (1992) found a positive relationship between psychological distress and resource loss. Resource loss includes four categories: (1) object resources, such as the home or household items; (2) condition resources, such as marriage or employment; (3) personal characteristic resources, such as a sense of optimism or a sense of purpose; and (4) energy resources, such as time. Freedy *et al.* argued that because resource loss may be a risk factor in the development of psychological distress, addressing the loss of the various resources should be an important postdisaster intervention.

Given the data indicating negative psychological consequences following disasters and the importance of individual and community factors in postdisaster adjustment, it is surprising that the incorporation of a mental health component after a disaster is relatively recent. One example of a mental-health-focused disaster plan is the Disaster Response Project developed as a collaborative effort on the part of the American Psychological Association (APA) and the American Red Cross in 1991. This project includes a countrywide network of psychologists trained by the Red Cross to provide *pro bono* emergency mental health services to disaster victims (American Psychological Association, 1991). Although psychological intervention has been indicated as needed in disasters, and important work such as the APA–Red Cross project addressing psychological needs in disaster has begun, a paucity of data exists about particular models for community intervention. Children in particular tend to be underrepresented.

In this chapter, we present one of the first major federally funded community-mental-health outreach programs set in motion following a disaster, the Hugo Outreach Support Project. In addition to discussing the existing literature on postdisaster intervention strategies, we use the Hugo Outreach Support Project as a vehicle for commenting on the issues in developing and implementing such a program. First, we briefly discuss the development of crisis intervention as a postdisaster strategy. Second, we present specific information on the Hugo Outreach Support Project. Third, we examine the outreach approach as a special kind of crisis intervention. Fourth, we address special issues in outreach intervention. Fifth, we discuss specific intervention techniques that may be included in an outreach program. And finally, we consider "hard-to-reach" populations.

COMMUNITY-LEVEL CRISIS INTERVENTION

Development of Crisis Intervention

Crisis intervention programs were initially developed to address issues such as suicide prevention in the late 1940s. In the 1960s and 1970s, they were valued because they were short term and cost-effective (Slaikeu, 1990). The focus of crisis intervention is the prevention of later psychopathology. There are three types of prevention: Primary prevention is implemented to prevent crises from occurring; secondary prevention focuses on minimizing the harmful effects of a crisis after it has occurred; and tertiary prevention aims to repair damage long after is has occurred (Caplan, 1964).

Federal funding for postdisaster crisis intervention first became available in 1974 with the enactment of Public Law 93-288, the Disaster Relief Act and Amendment. The National Institute of Mental Health (NIMH) was mandated to provide crisis counseling assistance and training for individuals with mental health problems (Farberow & Frederick, 1978).

Recently, the Red Cross outlined a disaster mental-health-service plan that includes crisis intervention for Red Cross staff and disaster victims. The crisis intervention plan includes two sessions and two follow-up sessions for an individual or a family (American Red Cross, 1991). For individuals requiring counseling beyond this service, referrals are made. Fraser and Spicka (1981) discussed a disaster plan that was a collaboration of the Red Cross and Mental Health in Dayton, Ohio. They recommended a crisis intervention model in which mental health therapists and Red Cross volunteers are deployed to the site of the disaster. In addition to this program, several manuals have been developed that outline actions to be taken to assist with the victims' psychological functioning after a disaster (Farberow & Gordon, 1986; Tierney & Baisden, 1983).

Crisis intervention models have also been used in other situations involving trauma. Pynoos and Nader (1988) proposed an early intervention program for children who experience violence. Although such an incident is smaller in scope than a natural disaster, some of the same interventions are applicable. This program included restoring the school community via intra- and intergroup sharing, maintaining normal school functions, and increasing communication among parents, teachers, and other school staff. After the school community is restored, the plan involved providing help to individuals and groups. Tuckman (1973) described an intervention program used by mental health professionals following a school bus–train accident. This intervention included participation in meetings with school personnel and parents and making rounds at the hospital to support individual children.

Project Hugo: A Recent Example of Community-Level Crisis Intervention

One of the first major federally funded community-outreach programs was developed and implemented in a southeastern Atlantic Coast state following a major hurricane. At midnight on September 21, 1989, hurricane Hugo, a Category 4 storm, slammed into the South Carolina coast with sustained winds of 135 miles per hour at the center and a tidal surge of almost 20 feet. In its wake, 26 South Carolinians were dead, 5,000 homes had been destroyed, and 18,000 homes had been damaged severely (Brinson, 1989). Governor Carroll Campbell requested that President Bush declare 24 South Carolina counties federal disaster areas. This declaration, coupled with a needs assessment provided by the South Carolina Department of Mental Health (SCDMH), set in motion a 60-day immediate-services grant funded by FEMA through the NIMH to provide crisis counseling services.

The SCDMH had already activated its emergency response plan, which brought in mental health professionals from unaffected centers to provide service to Hugo victims. Under the emergency grant, crisis counselors were hired to replace emergency workers, and by November 2, 1989, Hugo Outreach Support Teams (HOSTs) were operational in the affected areas. Nine teams were located strategically throughout the 24 affected counties. A second NIMH grant of $1.5 million to the SCDMH supported Project Hugo through March 15, 1991, almost 18 months after hurricane Hugo had struck.

Each of the nine teams worked independently to provide services that fit the needs as well as the values and norms of their areas. Monthly statewide meetings were held for training and for sharing information on processes and strategies. A public information specialist was hired to coordinate media events statewide. The project administrator and his staff were centrally located in the state's capital. Although complete statistics are not available at this time, figures indicate that in the period from December 1, 1988, to March 15, 1991, HOST counselors had contacted 4,062 clients individually and had seen over 30,000 Hugo victims in the 1,149 groups that were held. This number does not include the thousands of contacts made through the media or through educational materials that were distributed.

The Charleston–Dorchester HOST employed 12 counselors. All had worked in human services, and 2 had graduate degrees in counseling. The area served was ethnically diverse, including white, African-American, Hispanic, and native American populations. The victims were from all socioeconomic strata. Their communities were both cosmopolitan and rural. The HOST mandate was to provide outreach crisis-counseling services to all segments of the population, and to help affected individuals and communities deal with Hugo-related stress, with the goal of minimizing long-term posttrauma consequences. The duration of the grant allowed the counselors to identify and provide services to those victims unable to progress through the stages of recovery by using their existing coping mechanisms. Project Hugo went beyond a typical crisis-counseling program and was established as a community-level outreach counseling service designed to meet the needs of Hugo victims in their homes and communities.

A Closer Look at Community-Level Outreach

In a natural disaster, mental health clinics typically serve a secondary-prevention function. It is assumed that the disaster is unavoidable, and the focus is to help people to increase their problem solving and coping via a short-term therapeutic process and to resolve the crisis. Resolving the crisis may take many forms, such as expressing feelings, and is typically directed by a trained professional such as a counselor. Secondary crisis intervention typically takes place in a private room, and the counselor and the individual or family participate in a session (Slaikeu, 1990).

In the event of a disaster, mental health professionals are generally in short supply and may be overtaxed by the stress of having been victims of the disaster themselves. To meet the needs of a community as a whole, professionals with training in areas other than mental health and nonprofessionals are often involved. First-order crisis intervention, which may be restricted to one session and offers immediate assistance, is often used. This form of intervention is aimed at providing support and helping to connect individuals with other resources, and it may be conducted by individuals such as volunteers, physicians, or attorneys. First-order crisis intervention may take place wherever it is needed (e.g., in a bus station or over the telephone) (Slaikeu, 1990). Outreach programs combine features of second-order and first-order crisis intervention.

According to Frederick (1977), in crisis interventions after a disaster, the strategies used should be appropriate to the needs of the community and the nature of the crisis. In addition, Frederick indicated that outreach programs are more effective than programs in a single location.

For several reasons, outreach crisis intervention is thought to be more appropriate than traditional mental health services following a disaster. First, most victims do not develop a serious mental illness as a result of the disaster and instead require short-term therapeutic assistance. Second, following a disaster, many individuals are reluctant to seek out therapy services; thus, what is needed is an open, flexible, pragmatic approach of providing services where the victim is located (Fraser & Spicka, 1981; Tierney & Baisden, 1983).

Proximity has been cited as critical to developing and implementing an effective program (Slaikeu, 1990). Recovery must begin even before community activity normalizes. In the initial postdisaster phase of hurricane Hugo, HOST counselors met each morning to develop assignments. A list of all major locations providing assistance to disaster victims was developed. These included FEMA Disaster Assistance Centers (DACs), Red Cross centers, shelters, and community food banks and soup kitchens. Counselors visited these centers daily and provided services to staff and victims. Contact was made several times daily by phone with a team coordinator who provided counselors with new referrals and assignments. The coordinator also tracked down items needed by the workers in the field. At the end of the day, an assessment of the day's work provided the framework for the following day's activities.

The most basic task confronting the disaster victim is survival (Slaikeu, 1990). Only after survival needs are met can victims begin to confront the emotional consequences of the disaster. HOST realized early the importance of helping victims at the survival level. Counselors daily gathered information on and networked with the emerging caregiving system. Days were often spent tracking down and transporting water, rice, diapers, or blankets, or working in soup kitchens, cooking, cleaning, and sometimes eating meals with victims. Counselors hauled debris, swept Hugo mud, and advocated with insurance companies and FEMA. These helping activities were consistent with the needs of the disaster victims (Brom & Kleber, 1989) and established the outreach counselor as a non-threatening presence in the affected communities when emotional consequences began to surface and denial became stronger (Seroka, Knapp, Knight, Siemon & Starbuck, 1986).

After a disaster, systems that normally provide support are often disrupted. Communication and services are limited. The pattern of neighborhoods may change. Those who generally provide support—neighbors, family, and friends—are involved in their own recovery and may be emotionally unavailable. In both natural and human-made disasters affecting large geographical areas, the loss of this social matrix makes coping more difficult. The disruption of disaster robs victims of their normal support system and provides a daily reminder of victimization (Fraser & Spicka, 1981; Lystad, 1985). The outreach counselor may temporarily replace the victim's support system and may help establish a new support network through referrals to appropriate agencies.

Victims of disaster are not often aware of the services available and may not have access to them or time to use them. In addition to providing support, presenting practical information on services is an important step in restoring equilibrium for the disaster victim (Brom & Kleber, 1989). The outreach worker's presence makes the use of services more likely.

Crisis intervention requires counselors to be action-oriented and flexible. They must be able to assess the lethality of a situation as opposed to the normal problems in living experienced by most disaster victims. They must be able to enter the victim's personal space, often without being asked (Roberts, 1990; Slaikeu, 1990). The effective use of paraprofessionals in crisis intervention has been documented and may be preferable to the use of mental health professionals because of the uniqueness of their crisis intervention orientation (Aquilera & Messick, 1986; Cohen, Claiborn, & Specter, 1983; Farberow & Frederick, 1978). The personality of the crisis counselors, their ability to cope effectively with their own disaster experience, their knowledge of the community, and their ability to assimilate and use the information offered in training relate directly to their effectiveness.

Networking: The Focal Point of Effective Crisis Intervention

Interagency Liaison. Initial postdisaster activity revolves around meeting survival needs. Therefore, a first step for crisis counselors is developing a network of resources and a trusting relationship with the agencies that offer assistance to disaster victims (Golan, 1978; Pynoos & Nader, 1988; Roberts, 1990; Tierney & Baisden, 1983). If no such link exists before the disaster, a great deal of time during the initial postdisaster phase should be given to developing lists of referrals for the needed goods and services as well as to establishing working relationships with other providers. For those relationships to be established, a clear understanding of the roles and responsibilities of the various individuals and agencies must be achieved (American Red Cross, 1991). Each agency should work from the same base of information, including the community's history of disasters, the previous services provided during disasters, the response to the previous services, the demographics of the population that may affect mental health service delivery, the need for training in disaster mental-health issues among service providers, the willingness of the media to broadcast mental health information, and plans to meet the needs of at-risk groups such as children and the elderly (American Red Cross, 1991).

Networking with local agencies such as social services and federal agencies such as FEMA may prove difficult. Agencies generally have established methods of operation and procedure and may have difficulty recognizing the need to incorporate crisis counseling into their own services. In attempts to access these systems, identifying a key contact and working through that person are useful. During hurricane Hugo, HOST counselors often remarked that they felt like salespersons. Not only did crisis counselors "sell" their services in the face of denial and resistance, but they also had to "sell" themselves to community agencies as individuals worthy of trust if they were to network effectively for their clients. Crisis counselors must be willing to consistently prove their usefulness if they are to be effective throughout the recovery process.

Persistence and respect are keys to effective networking, which is at the center of an effective outreach crisis-counseling program. Once a level of trust is established, agencies more readily accept crisis counselors' referrals and are also more willing to refer their clients for counseling.

Networking with Caregivers.   Regardless of the important formal agency-to-agency contacts made with groups such as the Red Cross, the development of on-site working relationships with caregivers is necessary. When working with these caregivers, one must keep in mind that local caregivers are also victims, and that caregivers from outside the area may quickly become entrenched in a parallel process with the disaster victim.

Outreach counselors may minimize caregiver stress by assessing the situation and filling in the gaps when providing services at assistance centers. The counselors' presence must not create stress for the caregiver. In project Hugo, the teams spent time at disaster assistance centers distributing juice, fruit, or cookies; walking the lines; calming people and offering them support; and listening to Hugo stories. At some locations, play centers were set up and supervised for children who came with their parents. Individuals who had more immediate psychiatric and emotional needs were immediately assessed. The HOST teams were also called on to help out-of-town service providers in understanding the more colloquial speech of the area's rural population.

In addition to providing professional assistance, another aspect of networking is providing support at a personal level to caregivers. This is done primarily on an informal basis as the caregivers' pace is often frantic, and they may perceive themselves as strong people who should not need counseling. These feelings and constraints must be respected if caregiver intervention is to be effective. A skilled crisis counselor can use downtime as an opportunity for caregiver ventilation and debriefing, always showing respect for the caregiver's work and an understanding of the immensely stressful nature of that work.

Cultural Considerations in Disaster Outreach

Outreach provides an important opportunity to understand the cultures of the diverse populations affected by the crisis. Understanding values, norms, and belief systems is essential to developing and implementing effective programs for emotional recovery (Roberts, 1990; Tierney & Baisden, 1983). Cultural beliefs also influence how the victims view themselves and how the victims who seek out psychological help are viewed (Lindy, Grace, & Green, 1981). Populations served by HOST were both urban and rural and from diverse socioeconomic backgrounds. The manner of approaching these populations, the language used, and the printed material offered had to be consistent with the culture of the population. The coping mechanisms of each community had to be respected, and the programs had to be developed to fit the community (NIMH, 1986; Tierney & Baisden, 1983). For example, in one area, printed information was provided through a town festival. In a more rural area, verbal information was provided by HOST members joining in on a church social. Overall, HOST found that it was important to spend time in communities observing the manner of interaction among community members and community leaders and the level of general trust in the community. Through observations, individuals who were effective leaders were noted, and then a decision was made regarding whom to involve in HOST work. For example, in some communities, involving the minister was vital, whereas in other communities, involving the elected officials was more effective. Interventions were then created based on understanding the community through observation. It is unlikely that the levels of sensitivity to community values could be accomplished by a program that did not venture into the community.

Ethical Issues in Disaster Outreach

Although using a community-outreach counseling service after a disaster allows for great flexibility in a constantly fluid process, this flexibility, coupled with the dynamics of recovery, may present certain drawbacks. When dealing with the vastness of postdisaster needs, counselors may lose sight of the goal of enabling the victim to regain control and mastery over the disaster experience. Counselors may find it easier to "do" for clients rather than to have clients assume responsibility for their own recovery. Because recovery begins with regaining control over aspects of one's life, denying the victim the opportunity to participate may slow down the recovery process.

Outreach counselors are frequently victims as well. This dual role may be difficult to maintain. Blending of these roles may diminish the counselor's effectiveness (Golan, 1978). After Hugo, HOST met in weekly staff meetings to discuss client needs as well as personal recovery experiences. Debriefing was periodically conducted in staff meetings with both a confrontational and supportive tone.

The dual role of victim and counselor may lead to disclosure by the crisis counselors of their own disaster experience and recovery. Some disclosure may be useful to clients who are in denial. The key to the measure of disclosure is that it not be a catharsis for the counselor, but a tool that facilitates the therapeutic process. HOST staff found working in teams a useful way to minimize the possibility of disclosure's being used inappropriately.

Maintaining confidentiality with the outreach client is as critical as maintaining confidentiality in any therapeutic environment. It often proves more difficult in the chaotic aftermath of natural disaster, when the counselor is involved with many clients within the same community and with multiple agencies. The outreach setting may often be so informal and the need so pressing that it leads to laxity in confidentiality (Cohen et al., 1983; NIMH, 1986). An effective crisis counselor realizes that maintaining confidentiality is tantamount to maintaining trust and must be guarded. When information must be communicated by one agency to another, a written release may be necessary. In the initial aftermath of a disaster, it may not be possible to get a release. However, a verbal agreement must be obtained from the client, and the client should be made aware of the avenues the counselor is planning to pursue.

SPECIFIC INTERVENTION TECHNIQUES

Reaching Children via Widespread Outreach to Adults

Interventions with children may be conducted directly with a child or through the parents. Interventions may be aimed at helping children vent their feelings and develop effective coping mechanisms, or they may be aimed at providing parents with the information and skills necessary to help their children. Providing parents and caregivers services that reduce their personal stress may also indirectly diminish stress for children, who are likely to mirror the stress of their caregivers (Boyd-Webb, 1991; Farberow & Gordon, 1986; Seroka et al., 1986).

Disaster-Specific Fliers for Adults. Following a disaster, educational literature is often an invaluable tool for reaching large portions of the population. Literature provides a nonthreatening way to educate and normalize (Lindy et al., 1981). It can be left sitting on a tabletop until the victim needs it. The victim is put in control of when or if the material will be read and counseling services will be sought. This element of control is especially important for disaster victims who have experienced a loss of control in many areas of their lives.

Many people can effectively use existing coping skills to deal with the consequences of trauma if they are made aware of the normal and predictable responses they can expect to experience as recovery progresses (Brom & Kleber, 1989; Slaikeu, 1990). In addition, self-help materials assist individuals through self-monitoring, guided coping-skills practice, and positive self-reinforcement (Savage, 1990). Because communities process recovery at different rates, depending on the degree of devastation and on how quickly their expectations of recovery are met, literature must be tailored to fit a community's needs. The educational level of the reader and the values and norms of the community must also be considered.

Following hurricane Hugo, HOST developed several fliers that addressed posthurricane recovery. One flier presented the process of recovery and the normal and predictable responses to trauma. Another flier gave hints to parents on helping their children cope with stress. HOST phone numbers for assistance appeared on all fliers, which were distributed to the FEMA Disaster Assistance Centers, the Red Cross disaster-relief centers, soup kitchens, grocery and drugstores, libraries, doctors' offices, and service stations and were also placed in church bulletins. HOST teams consistently reassessed the needs and the dominant emotional theme expressed within communities and updated the literature aimed at coping with these feelings. Half-page newspaper ads, television commercials, and mass mailers inserted in local newspapers were other methods used to reach potential clients during the hurricane season of 1990 and to educate the public about ways to cope with storm anxiety.

Booklets. HOST developed a booklet entitled *Dealing with Stress— Normal and Post-Traumatic* (Charleston–Dorchester HOST, 1989). This booklet explained the concept of loss and the difference between normal and traumatic stress; identified the stages of recovery and the dominant emotions experienced during these stages; and offered suggestions for coping with stress. The booklets were left with clients to use between sessions. As recovery progressed, more specialized brochures were developed on diet, exercise, anger management, assertiveness, meditation, and progressive muscle relaxation, and on managing the cognitive component of stress.

During the school year, over 40,000 FEMA booklets entitled *Coping with Children's Reactions to Hurricanes and Other Natural Disasters* were distributed to parents of children in Charleston and Dorchester County schools (FEMA, 1989). These booklets normalized children's responses and offered tips for parents to use in helping their children cope. The HOST phone number was included for referrals.

Crisis Hotline Service. Crisis hotlines have been recognized as valuable intervention tools during disasters. Hotlines reach a large number of people, and individuals may remain anonymous, so that they are more likely to use the hotline. A school-based hotline was operated in Israel following a school bus disaster. Forty-eight calls were answered during the first five hours alone (Klingman, 1987). During the Gulf War, a crisis hotline was operated in Israel to meet children's needs. Hundreds of calls were received and two thirds of those calls were from children (Raviv, in press).

Following hurricane Hugo, an 800 number was established to provide counseling by phone or to link victims with counselors in various parts of the state. Counselors answered specific questions regarding the hurricane, disseminated psychological information, and provided assistance with parents' concerns about their children's behavior and with anxiety reduction. In one 40-day period, from late August 1990 to early October 1990, almost 200 calls were received over this line.

A two-hour television special on SCETV, "Windswept Heart," was aired live in July 1990. HOST clients from various parts of the state were interviewed, as were HOST counselors and other experts on disaster and recovery. During the program, HOST counselors were available to provide counseling on toll-free lines set up at the SCETV station in the state capital. Over 100 calls were taken, and many callers requested further counseling services.

Support Groups.   The issue of whether support buffers against stress continues to be hazy because of the many different definitions of support (Thoits, 1982). However, research indicates that support functions as a coping resource that helps with the immediate recovery from psychological effects (Cook & Bickman, 1990). Support comes in many forms, and one format is a structured support group. After Hugo, support groups were established in three of the most severely affected areas. Although attendance at these groups was often sporadic, HOST chose to be available at the designated meeting time to display a commitment to recovery and to provide structure and support. If a group member did not attend for several weeks, this member knew that he or she could return and a counselor would be available.

Church Activities.   Churches provide another avenue for reaching entire families and communities. After Hugo, churches sponsored educational presentations and group debriefings, disseminated literature, and provided facilities for individual and group counseling. These components served all segments of the population and were aimed at minimizing stress and aiding recovery. Outreach efforts were particularly effective through churches in areas where the church was the center of social life as well as a reflection of the values of the community. Working with ministers and church officials who were respected within the community added credibility to the outreach program and promoted access to clients.

Direct Intervention with Children

Direct intervention with children following a disaster can be implemented by community agencies and parents but is often implemented by a child's own community, the school system. In Chapter 10, Klingman presents a thorough account of school intervention during a disaster. Following are more examples that have been suggested in the literature and that were found helpful by HOST following hurricane Hugo.

Books and Songs.   A four-part program was developed around the book *Kelly Bear Feelings* (Davies, 1989). Quantities of these books were donated by a civic organization. The Kelly Bear Program was designed to (1) help children identify and vent their feelings; (2) identify existing coping mechanisms and their effectiveness; and (3) introduce new coping skills.

The "Weather Song," written by a member of the team, was a component of a program that reinforced positive aspects of rain and thunder storms and looked at ways children can experience these phenomena without anxiety. This program was designed for grades K–3.

For older children, one team member wrote the "Hugo Rap," which identified the problems families were experiencing and reinforced the need to find someone to talk to about problems. The rap was used to educate individuals and groups and as a coping tool when children felt anxious. Via HOST, the rap was produced and played as a public service on radio stations popular with teens. A puppet show was also written and presented. This show addressed normalizing children's storm anxiety and helping children identify coping mechanisms.

Play. Play and the expression of feelings have been shown to be an important strategy for adjustment following trauma (Rigamer, 1986; Sullivan, Saylor, & Foster, 1991). Following hurricane Hugo, children were often debriefed in play centers through play, art, or storytelling. The SCDMH distributed a coloring book, "Hurricane Hugo," which helped children normalize their experiences and place the event in time.

School Programs. At a more formal level, children can be reached effectively through the school system or through organizations and community activities oriented toward children. Working in conjunction with programs established to meet Hugo-related problems, HOST reached children through the local county school system. In areas where no disaster response programs were in place, meeting with area superintendents and sending letters to principals and guidance counselors initiated student contact. Both short- and long-term interventions were offered. Educational presentations, time-limited experiential programs, and individual and group counseling, as well as in-service training for teachers and guidance counselors, were used at the discretion of the school administration and guidance personnel.

"Hurricane Blues," a movie produced by Project Hugo, was shown over the state educational network in all South Carolina schools. Information on follow-up activities for children and on signs of stress in children was supplied to classroom teachers as an adjunct to the film. The film was also shown for family viewing in the evenings over SCETV.

Reaching children in the summer months was more difficult but was crucial, as hurricane season creates the potential for a recurrence of disaster. HOST developed a children's hurricane preparation booklet that was distributed in the most heavily affected schools before dismissal for the summer. This booklet provided the child with things to do to help the family prepare in the event of another hurricane, and it included instructions on visualization, deep-breathing techniques, and progressive muscle relaxation. This booklet was designed to give the child some control and role in beginning recovery through preparation.

ACCESSING HARD-TO-REACH POPULATIONS

Rural Families

Rural families are one particularly difficult population to reach because of a lack of transportation or communication resources. Following hurricane Hugo, many poor rural families were reached with the help of FEMA. The agency provided lists of those who had received grants. These were generally people who lacked significant resources for recovery. Letters offering services were sent to each of these families. A flier on posttrauma responses and phases of recovery was included in the mailing. Home visits were made at the request of the grant recipient.

To further assist in reaching rural families, HOST initiated "sweeps" in designated communities. The entire team would walk through the community chatting and leaving literature. HOST often became involved in physical recovery, helping to remove debris or putting down a pump. These sweeps proved to be wonderful opportunities to meet families and begin the process of counseling. Gradually, team members became an accepted and trusted presence. This method was especially useful in sparsely populated areas, where access to information and institutions was limited and mistrust of the "system" strong.

Children on a Reservation

Various cultures within communities may not align themselves with the general community because of cultural and religious differences. Because of their separation from the general community and lack of trust of the government and agencies within the community, these populations do not readily accept outside intervention.

After Hugo, the children of the native American reservation in a local county were a second target population. After months of trying to gain access to these families, the persistence of two counselors was rewarded. With the help of a key community contact, HOST counselors participated in a field day for the reservation children. Some of the events focused on learning to normalize and cope with Hugo's consequences. The highlight of the afternoon was the hurricane relay race.

Children of Migrant Workers

Like the children of native American reservations, the children of Hispanic migrant workers share a cultural and ethnic diversity. This population is difficult to reach because of that diversity. Most of the migrant workers' children who experienced Hugo spoke Spanish. HOST chose to have some literature translated into Spanish and to work to provide services through the religious organization and migrant Head Start that normally served this population.

Children in Housing Projects

Individuals living in inner-city housing projects generally lack sufficient resources for recovery. This population may exhibit a distrust of government and outside agencies and thus may find accepting services difficult. After Hugo, outside the school system, specific populations of children were targeted for services. Children in inner-city housing projects were reached through networking with the city housing authority. By assisting in an authority Hugo survey, counselors were able to meet families living in the housing projects. In cooperation with the tenants' association of several housing projects, HOST offered educational programs and debriefings to the residents and provided services to children at housing-project centers.

Whenever children were identified as being in significant distress, an effort was made to contact and work with the family. The child's behavior was generally a barometer of the family's functioning. When intervening with these parents, it was important not to threaten the individuals' feeling of competency as parents but to frame what was happening with the child in the context of disaster response and recovery (Boyd-Webb, 1991; Farberow & Gordon, 1986).

FACTORS AFFECTING SERVICE USE AND IMPLEMENTATION

Ethnicity

Ethnicity and the value systems specific to different ethnic groups have a bearing on the way individuals view themselves in relation to the world. This perception affects victims' ability to recover from disaster and their decision to seek outside assistance (Lindy et al., 1981).

Ethnic groups that function outside the mainstream may be suspicious of outsiders and may reject offers of assistance. This reaction can be minimized by early presence in communities and by showing respect for the norms and values of the community at the outset. If outreach counselors continue to meet with rejection, they must work through existing religious and community agencies to provide assistance (NIMH, 1986; Tierney & Baisden, 1983).

Faith played a strong role in the lives of the ethnically divergent populations that HOST served. The belief that Hugo was God's will, that God had sent this storm to teach a valuable lesson, and that their lives were in God's capable hands was strongly held. The crisis counselor had to respect this belief system and to use it in helping the victims integrate the disaster experience.

Problems in dealing with diverse ethnic and socioeconomic groups can result from insensitivity to the values of these groups. HOST cases were staffed as they came in based on client need and on the caseload of the counselor. If a counselor, after meeting a client, found it difficult to develop rapport, the case was transferred. Group presentations were staffed on the basis of availability and the fit of the counselor to topic. HOST found it important to emphasize to counselors that providing crisis-counseling services at the client's level of need was the goal to keep in mind, rather than changing the values and opinions of the client or the community.

Disaster Victim Mistrust

Being consistent in presence and in helping victims at their basic level of need helps somewhat to overcome the mistrust that begins to develop soon after victims realize that recovery will not proceed as quickly as they had hoped (Cohen *et al.*, 1983). After disaster, many agencies and private individuals come into an area to offer assistance. It soon becomes apparent that agencies must function within guidelines and cannot meet all needs. A secondary victimization may occur as the victims find themselves dealing with unscrupulous individuals who have supposedly come to the disaster area to be helpful. HOST counselors were able to deal with the mistrust engendered by Hugo victims by their consistent presence, helpfulness, and patience, and by never promising what they could not deliver. Being in the community makes the outreach worker sensitive to the emotional climate of the community.

Resistance to Services

In the initial aftermath of a disaster, there is a strong need to care for one's own and a level of denial that is initially useful in surviving trauma (Roberts, 1990). As the existing coping mechanisms begin to fail, victims experience normal and predictable responses to an extraordinary event (Bergmann & Barnett-Queen, 1989). Crisis counselors must be prepared to deal with normal and predictable responses to trauma as well as with resistance to mental health services. Traditionally, these services have been equated with mental illness. Many disaster victims fear being labeled as "crazy" if they seek counseling (NIMH, 1986). Others, who have survived with little tangible loss, may feel that they do not deserve or should not need counseling. They may not realize that disaster extends to intangible loss (Fraser & Spicka, 1981) or that past traumas often surface at the time of a disaster (Slaikeu, 1990).

HOST counselors sought to minimize resistance in several ways. First, their manner of dress—primarily jeans, tennis shoes, and t-shirts—was inconsistent with the public perception of a mental health professional. They did not use the language and terminology that are commonly equated with mental health services (Cohen *et al.*, 1983; Roberts, 1990; Tierney & Baisden, 1983). The name, HOST, implied an offer of help and support. As an outreach agency, HOST could provide services at locations where clients felt comfortable. It was common to meet a client at a fast-food restaurant or to counsel her or him sitting on a park bench. As services were also provided in the client's home, the stress of finding child care or transportation to a mental health center was eliminated. Providing service in the client's home also made the process of debriefing more powerful, as client and counselor relived the event at the location of the trauma. The counselor could also get a more realistic picture of the "fit" between the client's actual loss and his or her perception of loss.

CONCLUSION

Each disaster presents a unique set of circumstances to each individual and community that experiences that disaster. Because of these unique circumstances, no one program or intervention will prove effective in all disasters or for all individuals. Intervention strategies must fit the specific needs of each disaster experience.

Outreach provides the opportunity to understand more fully the dynamics of individual communities and to use intervention strategies based on that understanding. From work following hurricane Hugo's aftermath, seven important factors in helping disaster victims through outreach came to light.

First, the presence of outreach counselors in the community as early after the disaster as possible is important in establishing acceptance by and rapport with the community.

Second, all services must be based on an understanding of the recovery process and must also be uniquely designed to address specific community needs based on an individual rate of recovery and on ethnic and cultural considerations.

Third, the development of positive interagency relationships increases the chances of efficient and effective delivery of services after a disaster.

Fourth, shortly after a disaster, specific populations may be targeted as being in special need of services, such as children or elderly persons. A reassessment should be made periodically to see if these needs are being met and if additional populations should be targeted.

Fifth, disasters are often so broad in scope that not all victims can be reached one-to-one. Literature provides an important tool for normalizing the disaster experience and for helping victims obtain services.

Sixth, consideration must be given to the special needs of the caregivers who provide services for disaster victims. These people are generally reluctant to address their own emotional needs because of the monumental needs of the population they serve. Outreach should provide support and should be available to provide informal therapeutic interventions.

Seventh, outreach counselors who are also disaster victims must be able to recognize that they process recovery at two levels, both as victim and as caregiver. They must recognize their personal limitations as well as the physical limitations of providing services after a large-scale natural disaster.

Given all these factors, an outreach program can be accomplished only through the commitment of a well-trained outreach counseling team whose flexibility and boundless energy carry the project through to completion.

ACKNOWLEDGMENTS. We would like to give special thanks to the Charleston–Dorchester HUGO outreach team who worked diligently, often under adverse circumstances and their commitment never wavered. They are: Gilbert King, Chris Wells, Ramona Gethers, Veronique Aniel, Eric Hutchison, Tiannia Wall, Gina Hardwick, Debbie Pearson, Nita Jung, Linda Lane, Magdalene Maclin, April Conover, Mary Lutrario, and Tom Chicora.

REFERENCES

American Psychological Association (1991, October). *APA–CPA Disaster Response Project: Interim Project Report*, Sacramento, CA.

American Red Cross (1991) *Disaster services regulations and procedures.*

Aquilera, D., & Messick, J. (1986). *Crisis intervention: Theory and methodology.* St. Louis: C.V. Mosby.

Baum, A. (1987). Toxins, technology, and natural disasters. In G. R. VandenBos & B. K. Bryant (Eds.), *Cataclysms, crises, and catastrophes; Psychology in action* (pp. 9–53). Washington, DC: American Psychological Association.

Bergmann, L., & Barnett-Queen, T. (1989). *Facilitating post trauma recovery.* Unpublished manuscript, Counseling and Readjustment Services, Columbia, SC.

Bloom, G. E. (1986). A school disaster—Intervention and research aspects. *Journal of the American Academy of Child Psychiatry, 25,* 336–345.

Boyd-Webb, N. (Ed.). (1991). *Play therapy with children in crisis.* New York: Guilford Press.

Brinson, C. S. (1989). *The State.* Columbia, S.C.: State Printing Company.

Brom, D., & Kleber, R. J. (1989). Prevention of post traumatic stress disorders. *Journal of Traumatic Stress, 2,* 335–351.

Caplan, G. (1964). *Principles of preventive psychiatry.* New York: Basic Books.

Charleston–Dorchester HOST. (1989). *Dealing with stress—normal and post-traumatic.* Unpublished pamphlet.

Cohen, L. H., Claiborn, W. L., & Specter, G. A. (Eds.). (1983). *Crisis intervention.* New York: Human Services Press.

Cook, J. D., & Bickman, L. (1990). Social support and psychological symptomatology following a natural disaster. *Journal of Traumatic Stress, 3,* 541–556.

Davies, L. (1989). *Kelly Bear feelings.* Lafayette, AL: Kelly Bear Books.

Dollinger, S. J. (1985). Lightning-strike disaster among children. *British Journal of Medical Psychology, 58,* 375–383.

Dollinger, S. J., O'Donnell, J. P., & Staley, A. A. (1984). Lightning-strike disaster: Effects on children's fears and worries. *Journal of Consulting and Clinical Psychology, 52,* 1028–1038.

Farberow, N. L., & Frederick, C. J. (1978). *Training manual for human service workers in major disasters.* Rockville, MD: National Institute of Mental Health.

Farberow, N. L. & Gordon, N. S. (1986). *Manual for child health workers in major disasters.* Rockville, MD: National Institute of Mental Health.

Federal Emergency Management Administration (1989). *Coping with children's reactions to hurricanes and other natural disasters.* Pamphlet developed by the San Fernando Valley Child Guidance Clinic.

Fraser, R. P., & Spicka, D. A. (1981). Handling the emotional response to disaster: The case of the American Red Cross/Community Mental Health collaboration. *Community Mental Health Journal, 17,* 255–264.

Frederick, C. J. (1977). Psychological first aid: Emergency mental health and disaster assistance. *The Psychotherapy Bulletin, 10,* 15–20.

Freedy, J. R., Shaw, D. L., Jarrell, M. P. & Masters, C. R. (1992). Towards an understanding of the psychological impact of natural disasters: An application of the conservation resources stress model. *Journal of Traumatic Stress, 5,* 441–454.

Galante, R., & Foa, E. (1986). An epidemiological study of psychic trauma and treatment effectiveness in children after a natural disaster. *Journal of the American Academy of Child Psychiatry, 25,* 357–363.

Gibbs, M. S. (1989). Factors in the victim that mediate between disaster and psychopathology: A review. *Journal of Traumatic Stress, 2,* 489–514.

Golan, N. (1978). *Treatment in crisis situations.* New York: Free Press.

Klingman, A. (1987). A school based emergency crisis intervention in a mass school disaster. *Professional Psychology, 18,* 604–612.

Lindy, J. D., Grace, M. C., Green, B. L. (1981). Survivors: Outreach to a reluctant population. *American Journal of Orthopsychiatry, 51*(3), 468–478.

Lystad, M. (1985). Human response to mass emergencies: A review of mental health research. *Emotional First Aid, 2*(1), 5–18.

National Institute of Mental Health (1986). *Training manual for human service workers in major disasters.* Rockville, MD: National Institute of Mental Health.

Pynoos, R. S., & Nader, K. (1988). Psychological first aid and treatment approach to children exposed to community violence: Research implications. *Journal of Traumatic Stress, 1,* 445–473.

Quarantelli, E. L., & Dynes, R. A. (1985). Community responses to disaster. In B. J. Sowder (Ed.). *Disaster and mental health: Selected contemporary perspectives,* National Institute of Mental Health, Rockville, MD: 158–168.

Raviv, A. (in press). The use of hotline and media intervention in Israel during the Gulf War. In L. A. Leavitt & N. A. Fox (Eds.). *Psychological Effects of War and Violence on Children.* New York: Erlbaum.

Rigamer, E. F. (1986). Psychological management of children in a national crisis. *Journal of the American Academy of Child Psychiatry, 25,* 364–369.

Roberts, A. R. (1990). *Crisis intervention handbook: Assessment, intervention and research.* Belmont, CA.: Wadsworth.

Rubonis, A. V., & Bickman, L. (1991). Psychological impairment in the wake of disaster: The disaster-psychopathology relationship. *Psychological Bulletin, 109,* 384–399.

Savage, S. A. (1990). Self-help manuals for problem drinking: The relative affects of their educational and therapeutic components. *British Journal of Clinical Psychology, 29,* 273–382.

Seroka, C. M., Knapp, C., Knight, S., Siemon, C. R., Starbuck, S. (1986, Jan.). A comprehensive program for post disaster counseling. *Social Caseworker: The Journal of Contemporary Social Work,* 37–44.

Slaikeu, K. A. (1990). *Crisis intervention: A handbook for practice and research* (2nd ed.). Boston: Allyn & Bacon.

Sullivan, M. A., Saylor, C. F., & Foster, K. Y. (1991). Post-hurricane adjustment of preschoolers and their families. *Advances in Behavior Research and Therapy, 13,* 163–171.

Swenson, C. C., Powell, M. P., Foster, K. Y., & Saylor, C. F. (1991, Aug.). *Long-term reactions of young children to natural disaster.* Paper presented at the annual meeting of the American Psychological Association, San Francisco.

Thoits, P. A. (1982). Conceptual, methodological, and theoretical problems in studying social support as a buffer against life stress. *Journal of Health and Social Behavior, 23,* 145–159.

Tierney, K. J., & Baisden, B. (1983). *Crisis intervention programs for the disaster victim: A sourcebook and manual for smaller communities.* Rockville, MD, National Institute of Mental Health.

Tuckman, A. J. (1973). Disaster and mental health intervention. *Community Mental Health Journal, 9,* 151–157.

Index

233